International Perspectives on Democratization and Peace

International Perspectives on Democratization and Peace

EDITED BY

N. GANESAN

Hiroshima Peace Institute

Hiroshima City University

emerald PUBLISHING

United Kingdom – North America – Japan – India – Malaysia – China

Emerald Publishing Limited
Howard House, Wagon Lane, Bingley BD16 1WA, UK

First edition 2020

British Library Cataloguing in Publication Data
A catalogue record for this book is available from the British Library

ISBN: 978-1-80043-068-6 (Print)
ISBN: 978-1-80043-067-9 (Online)
ISBN: 978-1-80043-069-3 (Epub)

Printed and bound by CPI Group (UK) Ltd, Croydon, CR0 4YY

ISOQAR certified Management System, awarded to Emerald for adherence to Environmental standard ISO 14001:2004.

ISOQAR REGISTERED
Certificate Number 1985
ISO 14001

INVESTOR IN PEOPLE

Contents

List of Figure

List of Tables

Notes on Contributors

Margarita Cuervo Iglesias is currently a PhD Student at the Bundeswehr Universität München where she researches the relation between civil-military relations and security sector reform. She is a Member of the doctoral program for Security and Development of the Konrad Adenauer Foundation – KAS – where she has worked as Research Assistant in the Department for Latin America, and Project Manager for Colombia. She holds an MA in Development Studies from Los Andes University, Colombia. Her research focuses on Peacebuilding, Security and Conflict Resolution.

Mónica Dias is the Head of the PhD Program at the Instituto de Estudos Políticos of the Universidade Católica Portuguesa (UCP) where she teaches since 1992. She holds a PhD in Political Science and International Relations from the IEP-UCP (on Woodrow Wilson's concept of peace) and works currently in the field of Democracy Studies, Peace Studies and International Conflict as a Professor and a Senior Researcher. In her MA thesis, developed in the field of Cultural Studies at the Humanities Faculty, University of Lisbon, she discussed the concept of utopianism in Western political thought. Besides her academic experience, which includes lecturing at the University of Cologne, Germany, and participating in the Summer Institute sponsored by the United States Information Agency (FLAD), she translated several books and was a lecturer at international youth seminars on multi-cultural Education, Leadership and Conflict Management organised by the European Commission. From 1996 to 2000, she worked at the Portuguese Parliament as consultant for the Committee on Education, Science and Culture at the IEP.

Raquel Duque, PhD, is an Assistant Lecturer at the Institute for Political Studies (Catholic University of Portugal, IEP-UCP) and at the Institute of Police Sciences and Internal Security. She holds a PhD in Political Science and International Relations – Security and Defence (IEP-UCP), MA in International Security and Terrorism (University of Nottingham), and a BA in Political Science and International Relations (Nova University of Lisbon). She was a Visiting Graduate Student at St Antony's College, University of Oxford. She is a Researcher at ICPOL, CIEP, and CAPP. She is also an Auditor on both National Defence and Civil Management of Crises. She has been an adviser to the Portuguese Minister of Foreign Affairs since February 2019 to the present.

N. Ganesan is Professor of Southeast Asian politics at the Hiroshima Peace Institute in Japan where he has been since 2004. Prior to his current appointment, he served as a Senior Lecturer in political science and Southeast Asian Studies at the National University of Singapore. His teaching, research, and publication interests are in sources of interstate and intrastate tensions and conflict in Southeast Asia. Major recent edited works include *State Violence in East Asia* (with Sung Chull Kim, 2013), *Conjunctures and Continuities in Southeast Asian Politics* (2013) and *Bilateral Legacies in East and Southeast Asia* (2015).

Robert Jacobs is a Historian of nuclear technologies and radiation technopolitics. He is a Professor at the Hiroshima Peace Institute and Graduate School of Peace Studies of Hiroshima City University. He has published widely, his books include: *The Dragon's Tail: Americans Face the Atomic Age* (2010), *Filling the Hole in the Nuclear Future: Art and Popular Culture Respond to the Bomb* (2010), *Images of Rupture in Civilization Between East and West: The Iconography of Auschwitz and Hiroshima in Eastern European Arts and Media* (2016), and *Reimagining Hiroshima and Nagasaki: Nuclear Humanities in the Post-Cold War* (2017). He has conducted extensive fieldwork on the human and social impacts of nuclear technologies and radiation exposures.

Gen Kikkawa, PhD, is a Professor at the Hiroshima Peace Institute where he has been since 2013. Prior to his current appointment, he served as a Professor at Sophia University in Tokyo, and the Graduate Law School at Kobe University in Kobe, Japan. His research interests are in international security issues and peace studies. He has been working on CSCE/OSCE and its idea of a security community. He is currently working on East Asian international relations and the security architecture of East Asia. He has published widely and his books include: *The Collapse of the Soviet Bloc* (in Japanese,1992), *CSCE: Internationalization of Human Rights and Development of Democratic Assistance* (in Japanese, 1994), *After Self-determination: The Development of International Security Thesis over National Minority* (in Japanese, 2009), *What Is International Peace?* (in Japanese, 2015).

António L. Fontes Ramos, retired Lieutenant-General, is a Guest Professor at the Political Studies Institute of the Portuguese Catholic University (Domestic Conflicts Chair) and at the Faculty of Social and Political Sciences of the Mozambique Catholic University (Conflict Resolution Chair). He is the Vice-President of Eurodefense Portugal and a Member of the Military Sciences Section of the Geography Society of Lisbon. His operational and crises management experiences involve activities in Mozambique (1968/1970), Timor-Dili (1974/1975), and Angola (1991/1992) where he was the Chief of Staff of the Portuguese Mission to implement the Bicesse Peace Agreements and an Adviser for the formation of the integrated Armed Forces of Angola. He was the Portuguese Military Representative at the NATO and the EU Military Committees (1999/2003) where he took part in the collective management of the 11th of September, Bosnia-Herzegovina, Macedonia and Iraqi crises.

José Carlos Sanabria Arias is the Coordinator of the Socio-political Research Department of the Research and Social Studies Association (ASIES). He has an MA in Management and Public Policy (Universidad de Chile) and a University Degree in Political Science (Rafael Landívar University). He was a Fulbright Scholar of the Organization of American States (OAS) and has held Professorships in many universities in Guatemala. He is a regular columnist and researcher on issues related to elections, democracy, political participation, peace, and public policy.

Makiko Takemoto is an Associate Professor at Hiroshima Peace Institute of Hiroshima City University. She studied history and politics at Senshu University in Japan and Carl von Ossietzky University at Oldenburg, in Germany. She specializes in the history of peace movements and pacifism in the twentieth century. Her recent publications includes *Doitsu no heiwa shugi to heiwa undo – waimar kyowakokuki kara 1980 nendai made* [German Pacifism and Peace Movements: From the Weimar Republic to 1980s], Kyoto: Horitsu Bunka Sha, 2017.

Raul Tati, Angolan citizen, has a PhD in Moral Theology from the Alfonsianum Academy in Rome. He was a Visiting Lecturer at the Catholic University of Angola (2000–2003). He also teaches African History at ISCED (Instituto Superior de Ciências de Educação) and Internacional Relations at Lusiada Institute of Cabinda (Angola). He recently obtained a PhD in Political Science and International Relations at IEP (Instituto de Estudos Políticos) in Lisbon and is a Deputy Member of the Angolan Parliament. He has published the following books: (1) *Crise Africana e Processo de Democratização em África* (1999); (2) *Cabinda - Percurso Histórico de uma Igreja entre Deus e César* (2014); (3) (Co-author) *Corrupção, Democracia e Desenvolvimento Sustentável em Angola* (2014); (4) *Cabinda- Órfã da Descolonização do Ultramar Português* (2017); (5) A Construção do Estado Pós-colonial em África e o Desafio do Renascimento Africano, in *Estratégia*, Vol. XXVII, 2018.

Acknowledgments

The collection of chapters contained in this book draw from an international workshop on Democratization and Peace held at the Catholic University of Portugal in Lisbon in December 2018. While not all the papers presented are included in this volume, some effort has been made to ensure that the entire project coheres theoretically and in terms of geographical representation. The fundamental puzzle addressed in this volume is what is the impact of the process of democratization on civil conflicts?

The workshop and the chapters presented drew on the efforts of academics from the Hiroshima Peace Institute in Japan and the Institute for Political Studies at the Catholic University. The workshop was facilitated by Professor Joao Carlos Espada, the founding Director of the Institute and a distinguished scholar in his own right. The workshop also benefitted from the assistance provided by Monica Dias who attended to the paper writers from Lisbon. On the Japanese side, the team was financially supported by a peace project research grant provided by the Institute and the Hiroshima City University. Makiko Takemoto was the project leader and chapter contributor on Cambodia in this book.

At the broader level, the workshop was supported by a generous grant from the German Konrad Adenauer Stiftung and its Madrid office manager Dr Wilhelm Hofmeister. The Stiftung has been a generous supporter of projects that address important political issues, and we are deeply thankful for this and other support that has been forthcoming for more than two decades in various parts of Asia and Europe now.

Lastly, we would like to thank the administrative and support staff at the Institute for Political Studies in Lisbon as well as the assistance provided by Nick Wolterman from the Emerald Publishing Group. The Hiroshima Peace Institute has an ongoing Memorandum of Understanding with the Institute for Political Studies that hosted the meeting. We are especially thankful to Nick Wolterman for his early and sustained interest in the chapters and providing us the opportunity to publicize the work to a broader audience.

Introduction

N. Ganesan

This edited volume examines two important concepts in political science and their interrelatedness in turn. The first of these, peace, is a state of being that minimizes social conflicts and seeks to allow individuals and groups to live harmoniously with each other. Traditionally, it was defined *via negatio* as a condition that precludes conflict. However, this definition has since been revised to identify peace in more positive ways that enhance human fulfillment rather than just a situation where no overt conflict obtains. Additionally, as Mónica Dias notes in the first chapter it is to be regarded as a process that involves non-violent means in the resolution of potential conflicts that abound in human interactions.

The second concept democratization harkens to the notion of sovereignty residing in the citizens of a country. This idea traces itself to the Enlightenment and Rosseau in particular who wrote on contractual government that exercised powers in the public domain on the basis of the explicit agreement of citizens. In other words, since state sovereignty resided in citizens, their explicit consent had to be obtained in order for them to be governed. And the transfer of this power was done through a competitive election that is free and fair in terms of participation as well as contestation. Broad-based participation that is typically extended to all adults is often referred to as universal suffrage. This inclusion also undergirds the important recognition of the equality of all citizens. Contestation, on the other hand, is a reference to the existence of a plural party system that offers choice and precludes a monopoly on the exercise of power. States also invariably impose term limits on elected governments so that their exercise of power is subjected to constant and regular approval by citizens. American political scientists have also long claimed that the presence of a sizeable middle class tends to guarantee that democratic norms obtain. This segment of the population is also valued for the stability of society and in turn the state as well.

There are other norms that are typically associated with a democracy. Such norms often include certain freedoms that are regarded as fundamental to human existence. These are the freedom of speech, thought, action, and association. Naturally, such liberties only obtain on the basis of the proviso that others may exact an equivalent portion of such liberties and these do not infringe on the like rights of others. Liberal democracies that are popular in the West also include

International Perspectives on Democratization and Peace, 1–9

doi:10.1108/978-1-80043-067-920200014

constitutional safeguards for the exercise of such rights so that even an elected government has to observe them as constitutive rules of the game.

Given the popularity of democracies and the political legitimacy that is thought to accrue from them, this regime type has been the favorite of countries that regard themselves to be politically developed and transparent in terms of governance. Consequently, it is a goal that developing countries often aspire toward and is certainly strongly supported internationally. During the Cold War, this regime type was associated with Western countries and in particular the United States and Europe, while the Soviet Union championed socialism and communism that theoretically at least privileged the importance of the community over the individual. Given the ideological conflicts associated with this period, it was unsurprising that both types of government were heavily politicized then.

The end of the Cold War and the collapse of communism in the late 1980s brought renewed interest in liberal democracy and the United States in particular celebrated what it regarded as the triumph of its political model over all others. Liberal democracy had seemingly emerged victorious in the battle of ideologies and there was much interest and enthusiasm in the Third Wave of democracy as proposed by Samuel Huntington. The conclusion of the Cold War also decoupled many civil conflicts from their external linkages as countries sought to bring about a peaceful end to internal strife. And democracy and democratization were viewed as ways to bring about such reconciliation and development. Democracy was seen as a way to mediate conflicts by channeling them into legitimate and peaceful forms of political contestation. Additionally, it was also hypothesized that democracies had a much lesser propensity to become involved in conflicts and in particular into conflict among themselves. United Nation's Secretary General Boutros Boutros Ghali's call for a peace agenda in 1992 provided further impetus to solving internal conflicts and the UN became deeply involved in peacekeeping operations in order to actualize this agenda.

These are the theoretical and structural considerations that have informed the authors of this book. Chapter writers were specifically tasked to work on how democracy and democratization had impacted on civil conflicts and whether the introduction of it had indeed yielded a peace dividend. They were specifically asked to address how the conflicts were linked to great powers outside and many of the authors indicate how the civil conflicts were artefacts of the Cold War. Additionally, they were also asked to detail the historical roots of the conflict and previous attempts at mediating them. Then they were tasked to look at the impact of democratization on the conflict and importantly how the introduction of democracy had transformed the conflict. In other words, did democracy yield the peace dividend that is often attributed to its adoption?

Arising from this core consideration were related methodological issues that had to be resolved in order for an edited volume to cohere. As a result of such considerations, it was decided that the book would be divided into three parts. The first part that anchors the entire enterprise begins with a theoretical exploration on the two concepts of democracy and peace and how and why they can be interrelated. Accordingly, Mónica Dias's chapter in the first section addresses this core question and also helps to undergird the case studies that appear in the second section. She emphasizes the importance of removing the possibility of indirect violence in order to achieve the goal of human fulfillment within a free and just environment that is conducive to human development in general. The argument also regards such development as premised in turn on political empowerment and participation. Such a situation should involve the rule of law and only allow the state and its agencies the legitimate use of force. It should also obtain social justice and encourage and sustain pluralism as a virtue that promotes the conflict transformation into peaceful outcomes.

The second chapter in the first section is devoted to looking at how colonization has had a deleterious impact on democratization and peace. Robert Jacobs who writes about the horrendous experiences of the Pacific Islands that were subjected to nuclear weapons testing during the Cold War provides a worst-case scenario on how bad things could get. The Marshall Islands and French Polynesia were trust territories and colonies where the United States and France, respectively, tested large numbers of the most destructive nuclear weapons that made these atolls uninhabitable. The inhabitants' weak political situation and the callous disregard of the colonial countries are described as major reasons for their fate. There was no moral responsibility accepted for the wanton violence inflicted on entire territories and little by way of compensation and remedy of the situation afterward. While the countries chosen for the case studies themselves have not undergone such dramatic negative impacts on their peoples, this chapter informs readers on the impact of decisions made in remote places on the lives of colonized peoples. And it is noteworthy how many of the writers who examine the country case studies directly link the colonial process to some of the problems that obtain there today. The case of Myanmar and Sri Lanka in Asia and Angola and Mozambique in Africa in particular stand out in terms of the negative impact of the process and its impact on democratization in turn. This issue will be further discussed in the conclusion at the end of the book.

The second section comprises a total of seven case studies that are drawn from three different continents. Three of the case studies are drawn from Asia and they are Cambodia, Myanmar, and Sri Lanka. Then, there are two chapters that examine the Latin American countries of Guatemala and Colombia. The latter case is one of the most recent and celebrated cases of the end of civil conflict. And in fact it may be remembered how this region was a source of intensive research on democratization in the 1970s given its proliferation of military authoritarian regimes many of which were also artefacts of the Cold War. Finally, there are two case studies from Africa as well and they are Angola and Mozambique. The intention of such broad representation and number of cases was again driven by methodological considerations. The first of these was the representativeness of the volume in examining case studies from all over the world. The second was the tradeoff between specificity and generalizability. The literature on comparative studies regards these two qualities as somewhat mutually exclusive and often inversely correlated. We wanted to have a list of generalizable propositions drawn from the large number of case studies and importantly the cases would also be drawn from different geographical regions for content and context validity.

All of the countries chosen were in a state of civil conflict and democracy had an impact on the conflict. Cambodia had a dramatic UN-supervised intervention that sought an end to a political situation that had led to the loss of approximately 1.5 million lives. It is regarded as the worst case of state sponsored violence in Southeast Asia. The chapter writer, Makiko Takemoto, draws on the Western and Japanese literature to examine the nature of the intervention and how democracy had impacted on the civil conflict. The first obstacle was the Khmer Rouge that refused to go into cantonment and disarm. Fortunately though, the group relocated to peripheral areas in the country and over time was partly defeated and partly absorbed into the national army.

She goes on to conclude that while the initial impact was positive in the installation of co-Prime Ministers as part of a government of national reconciliation in 1993, that situation collapsed shortly afterwards in 1997 with renewed factional fighting. While international mediation again brought that conflict to an end, the democratic peace that had previously obtained did not have an enduring quality. And she attributes this development to the authoritarian tendencies of Prime Minister Hun Sen who sought to consolidate his own power to the detriment of the political opposition. This development appears to be seemingly aided by China, the country's external sponsor that does not impose conditionalities on aid and assistance unlike Japan and the European Union that were the two major earlier sponsors of the peace process. She ends the chapter by wondering whether Asian cultures and political systems have tendencies that may not support democracies.

The chapter on Myanmar by N. Ganesan looks at the country's ethnic peace process following the onset of democratization in 2010. This conflict has some of its roots in British colonization of the country and its uneven development as well as the failure of territorial and political unification prior to the country's political independence in 1948. A long-lasting military authoritarian regime and the reification of ethnicity all fed into minority disenchantment and insurgency. While the first government of President Thein Sein was only nominally civilian, it undertook to bring the large number of ethnic armed groups in the country into a process of sustained engagement that subsequently led 8 of the 16 groups to sign on to a Nationwide Ceasefire Agreement (NCA) in October 2015. Although the NCA was unable to include all the groups, the number of groups that signed it have grown to 10 under the government led by Aung San Suu Kyi that came into power in 2016. While democratization has had a transformative impact on the civil conflict in Myanmar, levels of political violence have continued to remain high. This is especially true in Kachin and the northern Shan states. Fighting has continued between signatories and non-signatories and the military as well as among the ethnic groups themselves. Such fighting is often over control of territory and resources. This is one of the case studies that is not embedded within Cold War dynamics since the country adopted an isolationist foreign policy after the military coup of 1962. However, there are external linkages since geographically proximate countries like China, India, and Thailand are involved in the conflict. The European Union and Norway in particular have been very supportive of the peace process, and China has recently stepped up its role to try and broker the peace between the Northern Alliance that brings seven groups together and the Myanmar government.

Raquel Duque's chapter on the conflict in Sri Lanka between the Liberation Tigers of Tamil Eelam and the Sri Lankan government is the third Asian case study. This case is a little different from the others in that a democratically elected government chose to wage war to end the conflict leading to very high levels of political violence and a large number of casualties. The recently elected government appears to be more moderate in its approach and sought to include the minority Tamil community structurally and electorally. Again, in this case, the grievances are deep rooted and trace themselves back to the colonial period when the Tamils had an advantage politically and socio-economically. In terms of external linkages, India which is the regional power in South Asia intervened directly in the conflict taking different sides at different times. The reconciliation process is described as ongoing although there are international concerns over the large number of missing persons associated with the conflict. In fact, the government announced in January 2020 that the some 20,000 missing Tamils should be presumed to be dead. There has also been recent turbulence in the political process in terms of disagreements between the President and the Prime Minister in 2019 with the former attempting to subvert the electoral process. Fortunately though, the threat of political instability which is always a harbinger of violence has been put to rest, at least for now.

The case studies from Latin America are complicated and in the case of Colombia were only recently solved. Margarita Cuervo Iglesias's chapter on Colombia is an extremely important case study of a very recent successfully engineered end to five decades of violence in Colombia, an achievement that won President Juan Manuel Santos the Nobel Peace Prize in 2016. She traces the roots of the conflict and points to deeply embedded structural causes of violence with multiple actors. The situation was exaggerated by center-periphery tensions that made governance of the country an issue. A long history of violence that included paramilitary organizations and drug trafficking networks is described as having contributed to the violence. Regional and social exclusion resulting from an unfair land tenure system and the state's poor response to social transformations that occurred in the 1960s and 1970s are also viewed as important contributing factors to the situation. The ensuing vicious cycle of violence is described as being exaggerated by the use of paramilitary groups even by the state. The resulting instability in the country is also described as having had a spillover effect on the neighboring countries of Ecuador and Venezuela that were used by some of the armed groups to wage rearguard action. Important external sponsors to the national peace process included Norway and Germany in the 1990s although early efforts bore little success. Consequently, the peace process was long drawn out and staggered. Additionally, democratization did not initially advance the peace process since political violence was regularly employed competitively and democracy brought administrative decentralization that in turn empowered regional elites who were often part of the cycle of violence. It was only after 51 rounds of negotiations that an agreement was finally reached and even then a plebiscite handed the peace deal a narrow defeat on account of issues related to justice and political participation.

Fortunately, negotiations with disgruntled political and social groups eventually produced an agreement that was subsequently ratified by the Senate. In this regard, it may be noted that the country's political executive were involved in some rather ingenious and tactical maneuvers that eventually yielded an acceptable peace agreement. Notwithstanding the agreement, Iglesias describes the ongoing challenges to operationalize the agreements and how local and regional elections in 2019 will offer more glimpses of how the new situation will affect politics at the ground level. However, she does acknowledge significantly lower levels of violence since 2016.

José Carlos Sanabria Arias's chapter on Guatemala harkens to many of the same reasons that accounted for the political violence in Colombia. Sanabria flags the unfair land distribution system inherited from Spanish colonization as one of the root structural causes of the civil conflict in Guatemala. However, in this case, the situation was exaggerated by the direct involvement of the United States in support of the United Fruit Company as part of its involvement in the Cold War. The subsequent overthrow of the Arbenz government in 1954 that included major reversal of previous land reforms in turn sparked an insurgency. The American involvement in the country and its support of the military in dealing with the insurgency further exaggerated the scale and scope of the violence. It was the dynamics associated with the end of the Cold War and the establishment of the *Grupo Contadora* led by regional countries aimed at promoting democracy in Central America that yielded substantive results toward peace in Guatemala. Sanabria alerts us to a drawn out decade long negotiation process spread over four governments that began in Madrid in 1987 and culminated in the 1996 peace agreement. Again, just like in the case of Myanmar, Sri Lanka and Colombia, Norway was involved in brokering the dispute and hosting the peace talks. Key to resolving the conflict is structural and institutional reforms that promote human development in an integrated manner. Strengthening democracy and its related institutions and processes was also identified as a key priority to move the reconciliation process forward. The ongoing political changes since 2015 are identified as part of an important and ongoing process in the entrenchment of democratic norms that are meant to ensure long term political stability. The strengthening of the plural political party system and constitutional reforms are an integral part of this process. Similarly, the justice system and the rule of law are also identified as important issues that require attention. Sanabria concludes by noting how the peace process and democratization are deeply intertwined and that there is no prospect for peace without substantive democratization. He goes on to argue that those involved in the peace process are deeply aware of this coupling and the ability of the democratic process to positively transform the country's civil conflicts.

Two African case studies conclude the second section of the book on case studies. The first of these is Angola that achieved its independence from Portugal rather late in 1975 and was faced with three movements that were involved in the struggle for independence. Not unlike many of the other case studies Angola also became embroiled in the dynamics of the Cold War and had a number of external powers including the United States and the Soviet Union involved in the proxy civil war. Consequently, the settlement of the conflict was also linked to the Cold

War and began in New York in December 1988 and it was formalized with the Bicesse Agreements of May 1991. In the Angolan case democracy and a multiparty system was introduced in order to transform the conflict into a legitimate political process involving electoral contestation. However, the introduction of democracy only unleashed political violence that lasted for a decade until 2002 and came to an end when one of the insurgent leaders was killed. Raul Tati argues that Africa in general is plagued with tribalism and related militias and therefore countries that democratize tend in the direction of authoritarianism in order to consolidate state control in the first instance. Consequently, political violence was rife, a situation compounded by the greed associated with the extraction of natural resources. As a result, he argues that democracy in the African context did not carry the positive connotative values and structural norms associated with the Western variant but rather served as a convenient façade for authoritarian appropriation of power and resources. In other words, the landscape of political contestation was always configured in zero sum terms and extremely prone to political violence as a result. Political independence from Portugal therefore only resulted in internal factional fighting for power and control that was exacerbated by the involvement of external powers. He argues that in Angola violence always existed alongside peace talks as all parties sought to strengthen their bargaining position through military means. Hence, the troika of Portugal, the Soviet Union and the United States together with the United Nations simply handed the transition process to the warring factions. And as a result of trying to hurry the process through without proper supervision Tati argues that the process of democratization benefitted one of the insurgent groups that then drew up the rules for the democratic transition strongly skewed in its favor. He concludes by noting that the transformation of the conflict was deeply flawed in the Angolan case and that national interests should have taken greater priority through a slow and mediated reconciliation process fair to all parties. In this regard, he views democracy as having had a deleterious effect on the country in terms of the appropriation of power and spoils arising from it.

António L. Fontes Ramos's chapter on Mozambique begins by looking at the competing Western colonial interests in Africa between Portugal, England, Germany, and Holland. He notes how Mozambique's location close to other resource-rich African countries has led in turn to a skewed horizontal development in the country's communication grid and how this development in turn affected the country's political landscape in terms of poor linkages between the north and south. This situation is exaggerated by strongly rooted mutually exclusive ethnic identities that work against an inclusive national identity. The country was home to a number of anti-colonial movements in the 1960s, and these movements were often based in neighboring countries and drew support from them. Frelimo, the major insurgent group was plagued by ethnic tensions but remained the paramount organization and strongly benefitted from the situation when Portugal transferred power to it in 1975.

Notwithstanding the presence of many other groups that contested political power, Frelimo was able to ruthlessly suppress them and consolidate its own political power. The evolution of a left-leaning autocratic state then worked toward the consolidation of its own power and sought the creation of a new model citizen. Forced communalization of farmers and economic mismanagement of the country by the new government created new enemies and organizations that often operated from neighboring countries. Consequently, a new organization called Renamo was able to challenge Frelimo and force the latter into peace talks that were held in Rome in 1990. Frelimo however hurried through a new Constitution that privileged it and an election was called two years later with little time for political reconciliation and rehabilitation. A United Nations peacekeeping mission was established during the political transition, but it was too short-lived to ensure national reconciliation. Hence, although the country went through democratization, the voter turnouts became lesser over time and Renamo became disenchanted with Frelimo's structural control of the country. The latter then sought its own political consolidation in provinces where it previously had military strength. Eventually both parties agreed to make changes to the Constitution in 2016 to make it more democratic and representative through political and administrative decentralization. The process of national reconciliation is still fluid and ongoing.

The third section of the book that follows on from the seven case studies has two chapters. The first of these, authored by Gen Kikkawa is a return to broad considerations regarding conceptions of state and human security and possible reasons why non-Western countries do not have the same consensus as the European countries with regard to political structures and procedural norms. His basic argument is that there was a political consensus in the Euro-Atlantic region with regard to the virtues of democracy and peace undergirded by liberal norms. Arising from this fundamental agreement is the region's ability to fashion norms and structures that reflected this pervasive belief. Derivatives of this convergence were multilateral security institutions that promoted shared values and common goals. On the other hand, Kikkawa argues that no such strategic convergence of vision and values obtained in the Asia-Pacific region. Additionally, the Cold War also had a deleterious impact on the region in the competition between the United States and the Soviet Union that led to greater regional tensions and conflict. And the superpowers further worsened the situation by often supporting autocratic clientelist regimes that had little regard for democratization and human rights. Following the collapse of the Cold War, Western and UN-inspired interventions also did not build sufficient state capacity to make liberal democratic values cohere. Rather, these were fleeting attempts to bring a modicum of fast paced peace without structures to deeply embed social rehabilitation to create mutual trust and social capital. Other factors worsening the situation are the US continued reliance on its hub and spokes security strategy derived from the Cold War to maintain peace and stability in the Asia-Pacific. This strategic posture negated in turn the ability of regional states to fashion a collective and comprehensive approach to security and peaceful coexistence. Equally challenging is the rise of China and its willingness to ignore domestic political arrangements and grievances to further its own agenda. A convergence of all these developments has shortchanged the region from evolving into an enduring security community with shared norms and values. In fact, Kikkawa's sentiments are echoed in many of the case studies where the Cold War had made democratization and the achievement of domestic political peace and order difficult as external powers sought their own leverage and gains. The Latin American and African case studies certainly make this observation abundantly clear.

The final chapter of the book is a comparative conclusion that seeks to bring the key research questions back into focus and assess the value of the case studies and how these in turn inform us about the impact of democratization on civil conflicts. Especially important questions addressed include the impact of the Cold War on democratization and peace. Equally important are questions regarding the pervasiveness of Westphalian norms with regard to territorial control and the legitimate use of force by the state in the countries examined. Suffice it to say for now that many of the countries outside Western Europe and North America do not have consolidated states that are able to monopolize the legitimate use of coercive power. In fact, that is part of the problem and the reason why many such countries are in a state of civil conflict. And when the state is not sufficiently consolidated, it is unable to bring its will to bear on the inhabitants of the state. Consequently, the all-important rule of law proviso that is required for peaceful coexistence does not obtain, and without this important feature, might becomes right.

Regional disparities, ethno-religious differences, and weak national identities are some additional problems that have compounded the situation in the countries examined in this book. These create center-periphery tensions that become a part of the political landscape over time inhibiting state building and democratization. Another important observation is the linkage between state security and regime security. Political elite who rise to positions of power often seek to manipulate the very institutions that placed them there in order that their own narrow interests are served. And in many of the country case studies, there is a clear deterioration of democratic norms over time when external supervision or guarantees cease to exist. It is for this reason that many of the authors deplore the brevity of the reconciliation and reconstruction process that did not lead to long term and sustainable structural changes that would have entrenched democratic norms. Hence, even as writers applaud the triumph of liberal democracy and the virtues of democratization and push for an international order borne out of the peaceful coexistence of peoples within and between countries the realities on the ground indicate that there is much more work to be done.

Chapter 1

Open Roads to Peace and Democratization

Mónica Dias

> Since wars begin in the minds of men, it is in the minds of men that the defenses of peace must be constructed. (United Nations Educational, Scientific and Cultural Organization (UNESCO), 1945)

Human nature has a propensity for conflict as well as a need for peace. As Immanuel Kant suggested, we are characterized by an "unsociable sociability" (1998)[1] that urges us to compete aggressively as we fight to become taller and stronger and to cooperate and conciliate in order to guarantee our development in a prosperous environment. Both faculties (necessity/passion and reason/morality) determine our physical and mental survival whether we think of ourselves as individuals or as a community.

Here, we should take into account that "conflict" does not necessarily mean aggression nor war, but that it represents, in general, inner and outer tensions or confrontations that can be dealt with in multiple ways – open and direct aggression or even war being only the most extreme and violent forms of conflictual response. Curiously, conflict transformation through negotiation and non-violent means, in fact, much more common in human relationships than war,[2] but as we are so focused on violence, peace is often either invisible or taken for granted. If we look closer, we realize that conflict transformation can be observed in all cultures and societies, and in small or big, simple or complex communities alike, although it might obtain in very different ways.

---

[1]Immanuel Kant in the essay Idea for a Universal History with a Cosmopolitan Purpose, originally published in 1784.

[2]The arguments we present here rely mainly on the definitions of "conflict" worked out by Lewis Coser (1956), Johan Galtung (1967), Dieter Senghaas (1996), Kalyvas et al. (2008) and Ramsbotham et al. (2011) whose theoretical approach in the field of peace studies we share.

International Perspectives on Democratization and Peace, 11–25

doi:10.1108/978-1-80043-067-920200001

If peace can be defined as conflict transformation, we should analyze, firstly, what this means and how it can be achieved, and secondly, if there are (political and social) core rules that facilitate this process. Although there are undeniably many roads that lead to this concept of peace (among many other possible conceptions), it seems to us that the political principles of modern liberal democracies are the most fruitful ones to build a path for sustainable peace, because they develop, in themselves, from a process of individual and collective conflict transformation as the touchstone of a political learning of self-governance.

Peace as Conflict Transformation

In order to explain these connections, it is important to emphasize from the beginning that we do not understand peace outside the conflict paradigm that characterizes human existence, but rather as the competence to find ways to attenuate the intensity or the expression of conflict and to engage in permanent negotiation and imagination toward reconciliation. Peace conceived as the end of all conflict would, indeed, be more similar to a cemetery, as ironically suggested by Kant in his seminal essay "Perpetual Peace."[3] By trying to find a solution for war, the German philosopher "invented" in 1795 a system of internal and external cooperation (the *foedus pacificum*, a man-made device founded on the constitution and the laws of modern Republics), that broke the millenary tradition of a God-given and therefore apolitical conceptions of peace and introduced an idea of peace as a man-made device and collective political task. In both classical and medieval understanding, peace had generally been defined in a negative way as the absence of war (or a period between wars) or at its best as a state of "iustitia, securitas, tranquilitas, caritas,"[4] but in either cases as a momentum of order and harmony without any perception of conflict or difference. The "pax romana" is a good example for such an understanding of peace as order – but also of submission to an imperial power from above. In his groundbreaking work *Paix e Guerre entre les Nations* (1962), Raymond Aron distinguishes this model of peace (the peace achieved by the imposition of an empire) from the attempts to reach peace through law (either by balance of power or cooperation) and it is precisely in this sense that Immanuel Kant can be regarded as an inventor of a modern and political concept of peace (Howard, 2002).

Fully aware of the "crooked timber"[5] of mankind, of human passions and evil, Kant introduced a notion of peace as a continuous political process, that derived from reason and morality and depended on the capacity of humans to

---

[3]Kant's essay Zum Ewigen Frieden was originally published in 1795. In the English translations of this work, we find commonly as title "Perpetual Peace," that is not entirely accurate, misleading the reader by eliminating the idea of movement/process implied in the word "zum" (best reflected in the expression "towards").

[4]As for example in Saint Thomas Aquinas or Saint Augustin.

[5]Again, this is an expression Kant uses in the essay Idea for a Universal History with a Cosmopolitan Purpose, originally published in 1784.

introduce transparent laws and rules, to keep them and to debate and negotiate, to cooperate and to reach for consensus through conflict and, eventually, to trust and carry on, again and again.

Accordingly, we must ground our debate on the path toward peaceful communities on an understanding of peace that is adjusted to our human nature (characterized as we have seen by passion and by reason and morality alike, as well as by conflict and the capacity to create political devices to overcome it), in other words, on a "worldly" and possible peace and not on an ideal of absolute peace, a heavenly peace for angels alone – or a vain illusion for dreamers and fools.[6]

In his referential book *Politics and Peace* (1986), the political scientist Dolf Sternberger calls our attention to the fundamental distinction between these two concepts of peace. For him, the idea of a status without any conflict (or a full elimination of our potential for violence) would suggest a radical change of human nature. And this brings up an ontological problem: When "the wolf shall dwell with the lamb," as announced in the vision of Jesaia's Book (Isaiah 11:6), then, we could argue, wolves wouldn't be wolves anymore. This means that the heavenly vision of peace cannot be conceived as a paradigm for peace on earth, because the idea of a unitarian and timeless "community peace' does not correspond to our human (and social, political and cultural) quest for peace, as elaborated by Sternberger:

> Humanity, whether biologically of one species and morally compelled to solidarity, does not exist as unity on a political level, but as multiplicity, not in a unique conviction and is not unitarian [...] but lives in plurality, in competition, in contrasts and conflicts, as well as in confrontations. [...] No, the point of departure for all efforts toward an earthly peace is the pluralty of the "political" humanity. (Sternberger, 1995, pp. 100–101)[7]

In order to elucidate this idea of peace as "conflict management" in plurality, the understanding of Lewis Cosner (1957) regarding "conflict" seems to be very helpful. For Cosner, conflict is natural (and even healthy) for communities, because it permits gradual change "*within* the system" when approached

[6]Curiously, James Madison presents a similar idea when he claims in "Federalist 51" that government would not be necessary, if men were angels (Federalist Papers). In fact, the institution of government as form of power management (and politics) is precisely needed because we are no angels, nor governed by angels.

[7]Free translation of the following quotation from the essay "Über die verschiedene Begriffe des Friedens": "Die Menschheit, wiewohl biologisch von einer Art, moralisch auf Solidarität angewiesen und verpflichtet, existiert politisch nicht als eine Einheit, sondern als eine Vielheit, nicht in einerlei Gesinnung, und nicht einmütig (...) sondern in Pluralität, in Konkurrenzen, Kontrasten und Konflikten, auch Konfrontationen. (...) Nein, die Ausgangslage aller Bemühungen um irdischen Frieden ist die Pluralität der politischen »Menschheit«." (1995, pp. 100–101)

in a peaceful manner (through debate and reform) – instead of a revolutionary (and violent) clash that would lead to the change "*of* the system." Going back to George Sorel, he stresses that "conflict [...] prevents ossification of the social system by exerting pressure for innovation and creativity" (Cosner, 1957, p. 197). In a broader sense, conflict competence is suggested as an important tool for permanent adjustment (or conciliation) not only regarding plurality within, but also threats and challenges that derive from outside of a community.

The idea of peace as a *process* rather than a final *state* draws from a very similar understanding of conflict as source of permanent dialog that leads to a capacity to adjust through negotiation opening paths of understanding and compromise toward conciliation. Within this productive conflict model (of gradual processes of adjustment), peace is understood as intelligent "conflict management" that can be learned.

The problem is that in violent environments and in so called post-conflict situations the ability for dialog and peaceful conflict management is much more difficult to achieve and must be, in fact, learned (again). And this is a complex task. First of all, because there is no true or "ideal" post-conflict "*state*," no "*Stunde Null*"[8] for peace. As evidence in the field of Peace Studies has shown, there is no "post-conflict" state, but only a permanent process of conflict resolution through non-violent means, a manifold process that implies a continuous learning in negotiation and consensus building (mostly by trial and error), and hard work. Although we will use the "post-conflict" concept in order to characterize moments of truce after a period of war or conflict escalation involving violent confrontation or terror, this is rather a conceptual simplification trying to define a still unstable state because, in most cases, post-war societies continue as violent and dangerous as during the war, sometimes even more so. The major conflict potential after a war that has ended has to do with the violent remains of the clash, such as individual and collective shock and trauma, extreme poverty and destruction, displacement and dispossession, family separation, constant fear of retaliation and discrimination, sexual violence, torture and, in a larger sense, loss of any future perspectives (Jarstad & Sisk, 2008).

In this context, we must also consider the massive emergence of a new pattern of war since the 1990s, blurring the lines that distinguished interstate and intrastate wars, as well as civil and ethnic wars and unleashing unbounded violence. There are more and more wars without any "war code" (whether as understood in a post-Westphalian tradition or as defined by Clausewitz) fought for many and interwoven reasons, involving a plurality of actors, waged at a "low intensity" but progressive level (van Creveld, 2009), with complex economic ties and targeting especially civilians. In fact, most of these "new wars" (Kaldor, 1999; Münkler, 2005) are intrastate (and not between states) and more than 80% of the victims

[8]The expression "Stunde Null" (hour zero) was used to describe post-war Germany in 1945, but became very controversial, as it suggested the possibility to rebuild a society from the scratch, without considerations of guilt / truth considering the past, and to "cut" History in pieces.

have been civilians so that the prospects for a just and enduring peace process become very difficult to sustain.[9]

An Agenda for Peace

It was precisely for this reason that former Secretary-General of the United Nations Organization Boutros Boutros-Ghali, presented in 1992 the groundbreaking report "An Agenda for Peace."[10] Drawing attention of the Security Council to the "changing context" of our world order, where the conventional peace efforts that characterized UN peace missions since the Second World War would not work anymore, he appealed to the urgency of "post-conflict peacebuilding" strategies in order to break the chain of ongoing causes and effects of violence during wars and to allow the development of peace building processes.

More than 25 years after Boutros-Ghali's appeal, does the Agenda for Peace still obtain? In our view, Boutros-Ghali's legacy is still stimulating new ways of conflict resolution. One of the reasons for its enduring strength is the innovative conception of "Post-conflict Peace Building," a major development in the field of peace research with concrete effects on the ground. Firstly, because it made clear that traditional means of ending wars would not fit in today's conflict configuration. As witnessed in the old saying that "more important than winning a war is winning peace," the *Agenda* focuses not merely on the effort of keeping up a peace treaty, but even more on building fair and just conditions for peace to grow. Beyond this idea we can find a new paradigm of peace: peace as a comprehensive task that cannot be "made" but must develop out of a fertile soil involving the entire society affected by conflict. Accordingly, the *Agenda* conceives an arrangement of peace work that does not only aim at a political truce, including security and reformation of political institutions, but specially on the reconstruction of infrastructures and the development of economic, social and cultural capacities and institutions that empower people, stimulate civil society, foster cooperation within the community and the whole region and eliminate the seeds of extreme poverty, fear, oppression, hate and resentment.

Secondly, *An Agenda for Peace* reminded both the Security Council and the members of the General Assembly that conventional UN Peace Missions, although gradually expanded in almost half a century of outstanding experiences, could not answer the new threats to peace anymore and had to adjust to contemporary forms and means of conflict. This implied a stronger engagement not only during a violent conflict, but particularly before the possible escalation

[9]In comparison, in the wars in the post-Westphalian tradition, 90% of the direct victims were soldiers. For a more detailed debate on the concept of "new wars," see the seminal works by Mary Kaldor (1999) or Martin van Crefeldt (1991), that shape our interpretation, and are of major relevance.

[10]Information retrieved from http://www.un-documents.net/a47-277.htm on 2018, December 3.

of violence – and also after escalation, when basic relief and reconstruction must be integrated into a sustainable common roadmap to peace.

Two major guidelines could be traced here, one regarding the concept of peace itself, the other regarding the practice of peace missions, but both interwoven and concerned with peace as a *possible goal* that could be attained as a medium-term strategy.

On the one hand, peace is understood as *compound* or *comprehensive* value in Boutros-Ghali's statement: Relying on the foundational studies of critical peace research developed by experts such as Johan Galtung (1969) or Dieter Senghaas (1971), peace is not only conceived as the absence of direct violence or war, but moreover as the possibility of life without indirect violence (such as, for example, political and social repression) and with full participation in free and just institutions (including forms of education) that generate civil capacities for tolerance, consensus building through pluralistic debate and competition and conflict resolution.[11] Peace building is looking far beyond truce and onto a whole environment where people can live freely, with means not only to survive, but to live with dignity, including the pursuit of hope.

On the other hand, post-conflict peace building is supposed to widen and deepen traditional peacekeeping on the ground. It is not conceived as a replacement or upgrade to peacekeeping missions, but as a natural complement that might provide a stronger outreach to the more and more complex work (and network) of the UN.

Thanks to the impact of *An Agenda for Peace* that anticipated many trends in the international political arena, peacekeeping missions have expanded a lot since 1992. A simple analysis of the number and the nature of missions, but also of the resources involved (including funding, materials, structures and manpower) enhances its growing force. This is particularly true when we consider the ability of the UN to involve NGOs in peace operations and to foster the cooperation of military, paramilitary and civil peacemakers on the ground. So, since its beginning in 1948 there have been 72 UN Peacekeeping Missions (of which 15 are active today), evolving more than 103.000 people (uniformed personnel, international civilian personnel and volunteers) from more than 124 countries and operating all across the world[12] – but the greatest impact was felt in the 1990s, after the implementation of Boutros-Ghali's post-conflict peace building strategy.

Although the strategies for peace were always based on the idea that it would be possible to capacitate any community for peace, every peace operation is different, depending on the conditions before and after the conflict, the intensity of the conflict and the parts involved, the remaining resources and infrastructures at the end of the escalation of violence and the political organization before, but even if we follow the very solid insights of Michael Doyle and Nicholas Sambanis (2006) in their attempt to evaluate United Nations Peace Operations – and also their critical but nonetheless constructive concerns – the overall findings are encouraging (Michael Doyle and Nicholas Sambanis, 2006). In spite of its many

[11]Senghaas' approach will be analyzed more closely in the sequence of our arguments.
[12]Information retrieved on January 14, 2018 from UNO's website.

imperfections, it would be accurate to suggest that the positive results achieved in a time span of just one generation, affecting millions of lives and peoples, reveal these operations as a worldwide stronghold for hope. In this sense, we could conclude that, more than answering the request of the Security Council to make recommendations in order to strengthen peacemaking and peacekeeping in the post-Cold War era, *An Agenda for Peace* revitalized the whole of UN peace efforts bringing peace operations to a more wide-ranging and also rewarding level.

But underneath this general assessment, the fundamental contribution of the *Agenda* was precisely the idea of peace building as a political and participatory process. The more the affected communities were integrated in the mechanisms of political participation and the more the individual people (especially women) were encouraged to participate and take responsibilities in public causes, the greater the chances for the process to succeed. In this sense, peacebuilding translated in many cases as empowerment for self-government. Political empowerment can be considered as a way of making peace processes visible. There was, however, still another and deeper impact expected in Boutros-Ghali's roadmap for peace, namely, the gradual transformation of a culture of hate and revenge into a culture of trust creating in due course an environment and a whole disposition for non-violent conflict management.

One last, but not least feature recognizable in the legacy of the *Agenda* today: Within the many and diverse experiences in conflict resolution made by the UN since the 1990s, peacebuilding is not only understood as inclusive and comprehensive (regarding actors and scope), as we have seen, but it also enlarged the understanding of "peace" in itself, conceived more and more as an ongoing and *open* or *plural* process. This means that it is not seen as a finished construction or state, but as a continuous effort with many possible expressions and outcomes, depending on each community where it is supposed to grow. This is a seminal feature of peace: it cannot be made, it must grow. It cannot be designed from top down, nor institutionalized by decree, but it must be worked out day by day, step by step, from grassroots level up and in many different colors.

But how can we build an environment for peace to grow as an open and plural process? How can we foster the learning of non-violent conflict resolution? How can we replace a culture of war for a culture of trust? Or in a nutshell, as wisely postulated in the Constitution of UNESCO, how is it possible to build the defenses of peace in the minds of men?

One possible answer is, in our view, as already suggested earlier, the institution of social and political rules that allow full and free political participation within a framework of division of power and competition and cooperation, based on freedom from want and from fear and generating habits of self-government and "civilization" understood as praxis of conflict transformation. Liberal democracy might have many flaws, but more than any other political system, it seems to fit into this demanding list of pre-conditions toward sustainable peace.

Peace and Democracy

Peace and democracy are connected in many ways. First of all, they have a similar nature. As previously described, in our understanding, they are both dynamic and reveal themselves as vibrant ongoing processes, rather than as a final destination. Both are based on conflict and consensus finding through non-violent means and mutual trust. Both cannot be "made" but must grow. And both are political through and through, depending on plural participation and a consolidated experience of self-governance. This is also the reason why they are both so fragile and difficult to attain. Too many are the challenges in modern complex societies. But their potential to be transformed and to regenerate should not be underestimated.

Many authors in the field of Democracy Studies enhance the impact of Democracy and Democratization processes on (social or political) peace, especially in moments of change. For example, according to Philippe C. Schmitter and Terry Lynn Karl (1991), democratization is particularly valuable in fostering political institutions that can peacefully compete to form governments, channel social and economic conflicts through regular procedures, and that have sufficient linkages to civil society. Unlike authoritarian regimes, they claim, democracies can modify their rules and institutions consensually in response to changing circumstances.

If we look at the most relevant features of liberal democracy, we will recognize that they represent essential (though not exclusive) elements for peacebuilding – among other possible elements – in the sense that they open the way for conflict transformation. Consider for example the contribution of the liberal principle of *rule of law*, as guarantee for a permanent and transparent framework, based on a common code (and not on the will of a person or a group of persons), or the *limitation of power*, sealed not only in the separation of the executive, legislative and judicial branches of power but also in many and diverse mechanisms of checks and balances, on different *institutions* and on *regular* and *free elections* aiming at a fair representation of the people. Within the rule of the majority, think of the respect for the minorities and for *human rights* based on the plurality of individual dignity. Take particularly into account the *freedom of speech* and, in consequence, the freedom of the press as an important indicator of *open and plural societies*. Finally, reflect upon the key role of *civil society* both as political "watchdog" and social "glue" expressing necessary conflict and cohesion, as well as the capacity to respond to specific social needs in an autonomous and plural way, and by doing so simultaneously relieving and reinforcing the State. Here, we agree with Larry Diamond (1999) who claims that civil society is a decisive factor for the vitality of democracies, for it represents, maybe, the highest form of self-government, balancing conflict and consensus within the established system.[13]

The elements identified here are relevant on the roadmap to peace because they all imply the ability for conflict transformation, in the sense that they represent the capacity to submit the own (individual or group) interest to general rules (and to trust that this system will consider this) as well as to express this difference in a non-violent manner based on commonly agreed mechanisms.

[13]In his Essay "Towards Democratic Consolidation," Larry Diamond defines Civil Society as "the realm of organized social life that is voluntary, self-generating (largely), self-supporting, autonomous from the State and bound by a legal order or set of rules" (1999, p. 221).

This process is very similar to Dieter Senghaas' idea of peace as a process of "civilization" of conflicts. A closer look at the model of the "civilizational hexagon" (Senghaas, 1971), used by the author to elucidate this concept of peace, will reveal many affinities with the working praxis of consolidated democracies:

Inspired by Kantian suppositions, the expression "civilization" represents a cultural process in which individuals (and, as an extension, communities) learn to respond to conflicts in a non-violent way, by "taming" their natural impulses and exchanging aggression for negotiation, based on rules agreed on in a hypothetical "social contract". In this sense, peace is a continuous process of "becoming" (more "civilized" or moralized, from a Kantian understanding). This individual faculty of "conflict transformation" is then projected on a social arena (within a community or state) and, eventually, onto an international level. In Sengaas' view, peace begins within a community, where however private and public, and individual and social performances are interwoven. In order to reach for peace, the permanent interaction of six different political/social key factors must be given. This "network" can be represented in a hexagon, which we will explain by looking briefly at all interdependent and non-hierarchical factors:

The first factor to foster peace is the *legitimate monopoly of violence* by the state. According to Senghaas, the disarming of the population and the general prohibition of armed groups (outside the scope of the state) would permit a *discursive* management of conflict in the public realm. This aims at a gradual elimination of force as a pattern of conflict resolution and furthermore as a stimulus for alternative forms of dispute, such as debate, persuasion or voting. The second factor focuses on the *rule of law* as an imperative institutional framework for peaceful political life, as well as for trust-building. The third factor calls our attention to the *control of passions* understood as the capacity, as we have already seen, to exchange violent response for tolerance, and radicalism (in speech and actions) for an attitude of political moderation. Curiously, this means that, for Senghaas, the possibility of peace does not depend merely on institutional, social or political arrangements alone, but transcends these, and calls upon *individual* capacities of self-control and moderation, as well. Accordingly, we could say that peace depends on every member of the community. This is probably why the fourth factor focuses on *democratic participation*. In Senghaas' view, this does not mean only political participation (in general), but a critical commitment with the system including the faculty to discuss, to accept and to follow rules, to make questions and compromises, to disagree and agree and to search for common solutions and to cooperate.

Social justice constitutes the fifth factor of this model that visualizes a roadmap to peace. Departing from different examples in which violent clashes occurred, Senghaas strikes the importance of social justice as guarantee for equality of opportunities and solidarity. At the same time, social justice is believed to raise hope regarding the state, as well as trust – values that suggest a sort of institutional "fair-play" and create a disposition to cooperate and to respond to conflicts with both confidence and moderation. As final factor, Dieter Senghaas brings in the competence for *constructive conflict management*. As we have seen before, the ability to work out differences in a non-violent manner and to decide freely for peaceful forms of conflict response suggests a whole culture of conflict transformation that is already the result of previous experiences and conditions. It presumes long learned habits and good practices, as well as certain social "virtues" (for instance, tolerance, moderation, empathy, responsibility, trustfulness and respectfulness as well as the ability to make compromises and keep them) that facilitate the pacific involvement and association in plural and multicultural open societies. This factor hints immediately at the synergy of all factors that constitute the hexagon, opening a road for a culture of peace conceived therefore as a process of moralization or "civilization." Now, it is very evident that all six factors are also defining elements in modern liberal democracies.

A similar argument is presented by Michael Doyle (1983a, 1983b) in his "Democratic Peace" thesis. Like Senghaas, Doyle goes back to Kant's conception to explain that peace in international politics is based on the inner political structure of states because the constitutional framework that is able to stimulate habits of peaceful conflict resolution within the state would foster a greater predisposition to develop politics of peace regarding other countries and, in general, to engage with peace processes abroad. As a consequence, Doyle concludes that democracies would be more "peace loving" (Doyle, 1983a, 1983b).[14] Although this thesis is very controversial and some of its presumptions have proven to be wrong, it is difficult to deny that certain liberal democratic principles work, in fact, as substantial elements for sustainable peace processes.[15] They also tend to blunt indiscreet actions by authoritarian regimes that do not require broad-based support for state actions. In this regard, there is a virtuous cycle that is attendant on democratic culture that negates aggressive and individualistic impulses that may obtain from structural norms where power is not obtained on the basis of a democratic franchise.

There are other similarities we could trace between the processes of peace and democratization. For example: there is the importance of the economic factor in both democratization and peacebuilding. As suggested by many authors, among others Steven Haggard and Robert Kaufmann (1995), Guillermo O'Donnell and Philippe Schmitter (1990) or Samuel Huntington (1991), democracy (even consolidated democracies) will not cohere without a solid economic basis and a shared idea on the distribution of justice. Another connection could be established regarding the problems of definition of either peace or democracy (as we have already seen). Furthermore, both seem not only difficult to achieve (as none is a fruit of a first generation, but take time to grow), but also to hold and to consolidate, since they contain (within) a permanent challenge of conflict and dissent. The article by Larry Diamond debating the "Three Paradoxes of Democracy" (1993) explains the intrinsic tensions of democracy clearly.[16]

---

[14]Writing in the end of the eighteenth century, Immanuel Kant would not speak of "modern Democracies," of course, but of "Republics."

[15]For a critical assessment of Doyle's thesis, see Michael Brown et al. (1996).

[16]According to Diamond, these paradoxes are the tricky tensions between (1) "consent versus effectiveness," (2) representativeness versus governability and (3) "conflict versus consensus" and that have to be worked out again and again.

In our context, the most striking similarity is however the perception that both peace and democracy have plural expressions – and embrace plurality as a defining feature. The works by UNESCO chair holder at the Innsbruck School of Peace Studies Wolfgang Dietrich focus precisely on the idea of "Many Peaces" (2012), in the sense that peace should not be regarded as a homogeneous concept nor classified as "noun in singular," but rather as intrinsically plural in meanings and expressions. So, if we recognize that there are many "Democracies" (depending on political culture and experience), we should also conceive the possibility of "*many peaces.*" And, likewise, many possible approaches to reach them. This would introduce a plurality of approaches in Peace Studies, not only on a practical level (when working in regions affected by war and violence and striving for forms of conciliation), but also on a theoretical level, including insights from different cultures and communities. The experience of "Truth and Conciliation Commissions" in peace processes or the insights obtained from concepts such as "ubuntu," as mindwork/peacework in South Africa are certainly valuable examples for us here. Last, but not the least, the notion of "many peaces" would also moderate overwhelming expectations regarding the conquest of "a perfect state of peace" and bring it back onto a humble and human path that would nonetheless be possible to endeavor.

Peace as Plurality

This brings up the complicated question of transition. If peace is manifold and there is no blueprint for peace, there cannot be any formula to "reprint" it. If we conceive peace to be *plural* (materializing in the diversity of many different cultures), we cannot presume a singular path for reaching it. This means that we cannot expect peace to develop in a conflict-ridden region in South America in the same way as, for instance, in central Europe or northern Africa. Besides, the methods and experiences of negotiation in the peace process must be *inclusive*, that is, the habits and traditions of the community affected by violent conflict must be taken into consideration – and these vary from region to region. Although some general rules might be presumed (like suggested in the well thought model of Senghaas), too many factors depend on the particularities of the affected region or culture, as well as on the nature of each conflict, as mentioned earlier. So, the success to reach out for peace depends on the perception and acceptance of these open roads to peace.

The intrinsic plurality and openness of peace processes seems to us very similar to the idea of a plural path to democratization. For that reason, it is useful for us to observe the debate in democracy studies regarding transition processes. The idea of Democratization as open process was already suggested by Schmitter and Karl (1991) who called our attention to the plural meanings of democracy, characterized as an imprecise political concept and allowing only consensus concerning a minimal set of conditions for its development. The outcome of transition processes would therefore remain uncertain.

For our reflection, the criticism of Thomas Carothers (2002) regarding the "transition paradigm" is a very useful insight. In an essay that provoked a lively debate among scholars – and within institutions fostering/funding democracy abroad – Carothers argues that transition from authoritarian regimes would not lead to democracy, but most likely into a "gray zone" of mixed regimes, as was shown by many examples from political experiences of change all over the world:

> Most of the transitional countries, however, are neither dictatorial nor clearly headed toward Democracy. They have entered a political gray zone. They have some attributes of democratic political life, including at least limited political space for opposition parties and independent civil society, as well as regular elections and democratic constitutions. Yet they suffer from serious democratic deficits, often including poor representation of citizens. interests, low levels of political participation beyond voting, frequent abuse of the law by government officials, elections of uncertain legitimacy, very low levels of public confidence in state institutions, and persistently poor institutional performance by the state. (Carothers, 2002, p. 10)

In contrast to the presumption of a general (and implicitly universal) "transition paradigm" to Democracy, as suggested by Guillermo O'Donnell and Philippe Schmitter (1990), Thomas Carothers draws attention to the complexity and irregularity of democratization processes and questioned the core assumptions presented by these authors. These were the following: (1) a country moving away from dictatorial rule is in transition toward democracy, (2) democratization unfolds in a sequence of stages, namely "opening," "breakthrough," and "consolidation," (3) elections were given determinative importance for the success of transition, (4) underlying country conditions have no influence on the transition process, and finally (5) democratic transitions are built on coherent, functioning states and state-building and democracy-building are mutually reinforcing.

As evidence of many regime change cases documented by Carothers made clear, these assumptions would simply not hold. On the contrary, in most of the cases, the outcome of democratization attempts would be uncertain, open and plural, depending on many conditions of the realities on the ground.

This is what interests us most about Carothers' declaration of an "end of the transition paradigm," for we should not count on any "transition paradigm" regarding sustainable peacebuilding, either. In fact, Carothers critique seems very fruitful when applied to peace studies.[17] Peacebuilding processes are not linear, and we should not presume that a truce or even an official and multilateral peace treaty

---

[17]An interesting exercise would be to replace the word "Democracy" with "Peace" regarding the five core assumptions of democratization mentioned above. The result would be a sort of "transitology" for peace that was, in fact, presumed for a long time. Too often peace was expected to develop gradually after the signature of a Peace Treaty. But this does not apply in most of the cases – with dramatic consequences for the population affected by war and post-war violence.

will lead naturally to a peaceful society, able to respond to conflict in a non-violent way. There is no "paradigm" regarding the processes toward sustainable and participative peace – that should be better expected as plural, inclusive and open.

The outstanding work (and experience) of John Paul Lederach in peacebuilding is another testimony to the plurality of peace processes. In his seminal *Preparing for Peace. Conflict Transformation Across Cultures* (1995), Lederach points to the diversity of ways that lead to peace always understood as an ability at conflict transformation that must be learned and become a political habit. Accordingly, peace efforts must be continuously developed anew and working models reviewed and adjusted to every particular conflict situation. But this does not mean that there is no framework for conflict transformation and that we cannot learn from mutual experiences. For him, the most important features for preparing for peace are, among others, participation and representation of the people, as well as a strong civil society. As we have seen before, these are also elementary ingredients for democracies to flourish.

Because of their innate pluralism, liberal democracies provide a solid basis for peaceful conflict transformation to develop. They are certainly not a guarantee for peace, and neither the unique political system that might lead to more peaceful societies, but at least, they are based on institutional mechanisms, power separation/sharing devices and liberties that embrace political participation allowing an important balance of majority minority relations and that are essential to conflict resolution.

However, pluralism is in danger today. And this development can overshadow liberal democracies, as well as democratization and peace processes. As Diamond, Plattner, and Walker (2016) have explained in a very clear way, liberal democracies are threatened today by a new authoritarianism that has not much concern for minorities and that despises pluralism. Although democracies are resilient and have regenerative capacities, it is important to raise awareness toward these tendencies that could spread and change the way we live and conciliate our differences and conflicts within a constitutional, political and cultural framework. This, in turn, could have consequences for peacebuilding efforts all over the world, but also on the peaceful relationship between countries in regions where war is/was hoped to be eradicated.

The challenges to democracy we are witnessing at present seem to be a strong argument for us to reconsider and renew the processes of peace and democratization, both at a national and international level. In a globalized world, we cannot stop working out new ways to reach out for and to sustain peaceful communities. But that means also to focus again on the plural devices of liberal democracies in the complex and compound exercise of conflict transformation. With these devices in mind, we will certainly understand the beautiful suggestion by John Paul Lederach (1997) that concludes our reflections – and that can be understood as an invitation to open roads to peace and democratization:

> "The delight of building peace?
> Like fishing, it is the pursuit of what is elusive but attainable.
> A perpetual series of occasions for hope."

References

Aron, R. (1962). *Paix e Guerre entre les Nations*. Paris: Calmann-Lévy.

Brown, M., Lynn-Jones, S., & Miller, S. (Eds.). (1996) *Debating the democratic peace*. Cambridge, MA: MIT Press.

Carothers, T. (2002). The end of the transition paradigm. *The Journal of Democracy*, *13*(1), 5–21.

Coser, L. (1956). *The Functions of Social Conflict*. New York: The Free Press.

Cosner, L. (1957). Social conflict and the theory of social change. *The British Journal of Sociology*, *8*(3), 197–207.

Creveld, M. (1991). *The Transformation of War*. New York, NY: Simon & Schuster.

Diamond, L. (1993). Three paradoxes of democracy. In L. Diamond & M. Plattner (Eds.), *The global resurgence of democracy* (pp. 111–123). Baltimore, MD: The Johns Hopkins University Press.

Diamond, L. (1999). *Developing democracy: Toward consolidation*. Baltimore, MD: The Johns Hopkins University Press.

Diamond, L., Plattner, M., & Walker, C. (Eds.). (2016). *Authoritarianism goes global: the challenge to democracy*. Baltimore, MD: The Johns Hopkins University Press.

Dietrich, W. (2012). *Interpretations of peace in history and culture*. London: Palgrave Macmillan.

Doyle, M. (1983a, Summer). Kant, Liberal legacies and foreign affairs Part 1. Philosophy and Public Affairs, *12*(3), 205–235.

Doyle, M. (1983b, Autumn). Kant, Liberal legacies and foreign affairs Part 2. Philosophy and Public Affairs, *12*(4), 323–353.

Doyle, M., & Sambanis, N. (2006). *Making war and building peace: United Nations Peace Operations*. Princeton, NJ: Princeton University Press.

Galtung, J. (1969). Violence, peace, and peace research. *Journal of Peace Research*, *6*(3), 167–191.

Haggard, S., & Kaufman, R. (1995). The challenges of consolidation. In L. Diamond & M. Plattner (Eds.), *Economic reform and democracy* (pp. 1–12). Baltimore, MD: The Johns Hopkins University Press.

Howard, M. (2002). *The invention of peace*. London: Profile Books.

Huntington, S. (1991). The third wave: Democratization in the late twentieth century. Norman, OK: University of Oklahoma Press.

Jarstad, A., & Sisk, T. (Eds.). (2008). *From war to democracy: Dilemmas to peacebuilding*. New York, NY: Cambridge University Press.

Kant, I. (1998). *Kants Werke*, 6 vols., edição de Wilhelm Weischedel. Darmstadt: Wissenschaftliche Buchgesellschaft.

Kaldor, M. (1999). *New and old wars: Organized Violence in a Global Era*. Stanford, CA: Stanford University Press.

Kalyvas, S. N., Shapiro, I., & Masoud, T. (Eds.). (2008). *Order, conflict and violence*. Cambridge: Cambridge University Press.

Lederach, J. P. (1995). *Preparing for peace: Conflict transformation across cultures*. Syracuse, NY: Syracuse University Press.

Lederach, J. P. (1997). *Building peace: Sustainable reconciliation in divided societies*. Washington D.C.: United States Institute of Peace.

Münkler, H. (2005). *The new wars*. Cambridge: Polity Press.

O'Donnell, G., & Schmitter, P. (1990). *Transitions from authoritarian rule: Tentative conclusions about uncertain democracies*. Baltimore, MD: The Johns Hopkins University Press.

Ramsbotham, O., Woodhouse, T., & Miall, H. (Eds.). (2011). *Contemporary conflict resolution*. Cambridge, MA: Polity Press.

Schmitter, P., & Karl, T. (1991). What Democracy is … and is not. *Journal of Democracy*, *2*(3), 75–88.
Senghaas, D. (Ed.). (1971). *Kritische Friedensforschung*. Frankfurt am Main: Suhrkamp Verlag.
Sternberger, D. (1986). *Die Politik und der Friede*. Frankfurt am Main: Suhrkamp Verlag.
Sternberger, D. (1995). Über die verschiedene Begriffe des Friedens. In D. Senghaas (Ed.), *Den Frieden Denken* (pp. 137–159). Frankfurt am Main: Suhrkamp Verlag.
United Nations Educational, Scientific and Cultural Organization (UNESCO). (1945). UNESCO Constitution. Retrieved from http://portal.unesco.org/en/ev.php-URL_ID=15244&URL_DO=DO_TOPIC&URL_SECTION=201.html
van Creveld, M. (1991). *The transformation of war*. New York, NY: Free Press.
van Creveld, M. (2009). *The transformation of war*. New York, NY: Simon & Schuster.

Chapter 2

Post-nuclear/Post-colonial Challenges to Democratization in the Pacific

Robert Jacobs

Introduction: Roots of the Conflict

The Republic of the Marshall Islands (RMI) and French Polynesia (FP) are both collections of islands and atolls in the Pacific Ocean that were formerly under the direct control of colonial or trust nations, and that now operate with either full independence (RMI) or with limited independence (FP) from their former rulers. Both nations were the locations of large-scale nuclear weapon testing sites although neither nation has ever possessed or deployed nuclear weapons (Begkvist & Ferm, 2000). In part, it was their status as a trust and a colony that led to their being used for nuclear weapon testing, and in the aftermath of those tests, this history has placed significant burdens on both in their efforts to develop fully functioning and autonomous democratic nations (Jacobs, 2013). This is, in part, because of ongoing military control being exerted by the former nuclear testing nations. Additionally, each nation also faces immense and vexing environmental challenges from the legacy waste of those tests, as well as from the widespread distribution of fallout radionuclides that contaminate large areas of both land and sea (Merlin & Gonzalez, 2010, pp. 167–202).

Pacific atolls are made up of coral reefs that had grown around undersea volcanoes, and as the volcanoes receded the remaining, roughly circular coral reefs became free-standing atolls. Typically, a Pacific atoll is very low-lying, often with an elevation no higher than several meters. Being roughly circular, they have a largely enclosed lagoon in the center and face the open ocean on the exterior (Emery, Tracey, & Ladd, 1954). They are desirable places to live in the mid-Pacific because of the utility of the lagoons. The ocean water flows freely in and out of the lagoons, and so it affords an easy place to fish in still waters very close to where atoll residents live. Additionally, it is much easier to take a traditional canoe out into the ocean by first launching into the still waters of the lagoon

International Perspectives on Democratization and Peace, 27–42

doi:10.1108/978-1-80043-067-920200002

and then transiting between atoll islands into the ocean than it is to take a canoe directly into the strong waves of the oceanside parts of the atoll. These factors, among others, have long made atolls preferred locations for community building in the open ocean (Kahn, 2011).

The RMI lies on the eastern edge of Micronesia in the Central Pacific Ocean, roughly 2,000 miles southwest of Hawai'i. As currently configured, the republic consists of 29 atolls and 5 islands. Each atoll is made up of several smaller islands. The Marshalls were a trust territory of the United States during the years of nuclear weapon testing (1946–1957). The islands were originally settled by Micronesians over the past 4,000 years. The populations operated with relative independence until the period of colonization by large ships from European countries in the early modern era. The Marshalls became a Spanish colony in 1526 and operated with relative independence during the following 300 years, only receiving occasional contact from missionaries, and as resupply stops for Spanish ships. In 1885, the islands became a German protectorate after an agreement between Spain and Germany, and then at the outset of World War I the Marshalls became a Japanese protectorate. The Japanese fought intense naval battles with the United States in the Marshall Islands during World War II, and the Americans took the islands from Japan in 1944; they then became an American protectorate. In 1947, the islands formally became a United Nations Trust Territory and continued to be administered by the United States under authorization from the UN for several decades (Kiste, 1974).

In the summer of 1946, the United States began testing nuclear weapons in the Marshall Islands, the first detonations of nuclear weapons after their use in the nuclear attacks on Hiroshima and Nagasaki at the end of World War II. The first tests were conducted on Bikini Atoll, and it was in because of these first tests that bikini bathing suits became a part of the cultural lexicon (Hendrix, 2018). The United States staged an informal meeting, filmed by American military cameramen, in which the Bikinians "agreed" to allow the Americans to test nuclear weapons on their atoll, and to be relocated by the Americans, although they had no real choice in the matter (Weisgall, 1994). Twenty-three nuclear weapons were tested on Bikini, and the Bikinians can still not return to their former homes because of long-term radiological contamination (Weisgall, 1980). Most Bikinians currently live on Majuro Atoll, the capital of the RMI, although they were moved to and from numerous other small islands by the US military, where they experienced starvation and disease, before they evacuated themselves to Majuro (Kiste, 1974). In addition to Bikini Atoll, the United States also conducted 43 nuclear tests on Enewetak Atoll between 1948 and 1958. The population of Enewetak was also forcibly evacuated by the United States and can only live for very short periods in their former homes (Wall, Jose, & Hinzel, 2018).

While the United States conducted over 900 nuclear tests in its domestic test site in Nevada, it tested all of its thermonuclear weapons (which are thousands of times more powerful than earlier fission weapons) in the Marshall Islands. While only 14% of American nuclear tests were conducted in the Marshall Islands, these tests released 80% of the force of all of the American nuclear tests (Glasstone & Dolan, 1977). As a result, the radiological contamination of the Marshall Islands was catastrophic. In 1954, the United States conducted its largest nuclear weapon test, Castle-Bravo, at Bikini Atoll. The resulting fallout cloud spread a lethal band of radiation for over 500 km across the Northern Marshall Islands (Steton, Schuert, Perkins, Shirasawa, & Chan, 1956). This cloud engulfed several downwind atolls, including Rongelap Atoll. On the day of the test, American radiation monitors arrived at Rongelap to check on radiation levels and found them so high that they panicked and left. Three days later a US naval ship arrived, and residents were told they had one hour to gather their belongings before being forcibly evacuated. Even today the Rongelapese cannot return to their homes because of radiological contamination (National Research Council, 1994). Additionally, spending three days in the fallout in the immediate wake of the Bravo fallout cloud led to all Rongelapese present at that time to have suffered from radiation sickness.

FP consists of 118 atolls and islands spread across a vast area of the South Pacific that was settled by Polynesians thousands of years ago. The main island of Tahiti became a French Protectorate in 1840 and the entire island group became a French protectorate in 1842. It has remained under various forms of French administration ever since. In 1946, it became an "overseas territory" with the right to vote in French elections. In 2003, its status changed to "overseas collectivity" (COM), and in 2004, it changed again to that of "overseas country of France." Under this current status, FP operates with relative independence, however, all issues and policies related to justice, security and defense matters remain under French control. France also controls the currency and foreign policy of the island group (Fisher, 2013).

Originally, the French tested nuclear weapons in Algeria (1960–1966). Recognizing that it would soon lose control over its African colony because of the Algerian war for independence, the French began building a second nuclear test site in FP during the Algerian testing period (Hecht, 2012). The French have never detonated a nuclear weapon inside of France. Nuclear testing in FP began in 1966 and the French tested 193 nuclear weapons there in total before ending testing in 1996 (D'Amato, 1967, pp. 66–77). The French tested all of their thermonuclear weapons in FP. The tests were conducted on two uninhabited atolls in Southeastern FP: Moruroa Atoll and Frangataufa Atoll. In 1964, the two atolls were formally ceded from the Territory of FP directly to the French state, "giving control of the test sites to the French government and military" (Maclellan & Chesneaux, 1988).

French nuclear testing in the South Pacific spread radiation across a vast area. Even though the United States, the Soviet Union and the United Kingdom had agreed by treaty to ban the testing of nuclear weapons in the atmosphere in 1963, since atmospheric testing distributed such large amounts of radioactive fallout across wide areas, the French continued to test weapons atmospherically in FP until 1974. Official French documents declassified in 2013 revealed that the French had hidden the extent of this contamination during the testing era, and that Tahiti, approximately 1000 km to the Northwest, had received levels of plutonium that were over 500 time above legal limits (Chrisafis, 2013). Plutonium particles remain dangerous for over 100,000 years once deposited into the local ecosystem.

The model that we have of health risks from nuclear weapons comes from studies done in Hiroshima and Nagasaki after the nuclear attacks on those two cities in 1945. After the war, the United States established the Atomic Bomb Casualty Commission (ABCC) with a facility in each of the two towns, to study the long-term health effects of those who were exposed to radiation. Over 100,000 hibakusha (survivors of the nuclear attacks on Hiroshima and Nagasaki) participated in these studies. The most important study to emerge from the ABCC was the Life Span Study (LSS) (Lindee, 1994).

The exposures to radiation that occurred in Hiroshima and Nagasaki were very different from the exposures that people living in nuclear test sites were to experience. In Hiroshima and Nagasaki, a nuclear weapon was detonated directly on cities and the populations living there received a very high dose of external gamma radiation (Schull, 1995). Those living near nuclear test sites were not attacked directly, weapons were detonated nearby their homes. They experienced heavy amounts of radioactive fallout which fell upon their homes and lands from the drifting mushroom clouds after the tests (Miller, 1991). They did not receive high external doses as one does nearby to a nuclear explosion. What they experienced was the deposition of large amounts of radiation in particulate form (not waves like gamma radiation). While gamma waves last only a few minutes, the radiation in fallout particles may last from weeks to millennia, depending on the specific chemical particle. As mentioned above, plutonium remains dangerous for over 100,000 years after deposition. Once this distribution of particles has occurred over a region, the individual particles enter into the ecosystems, being taken up by plants and soil, moving around with wind and water currents. So, the dangers that these particles pose are irregular and change over time, often for thousands of generations of inhabitants (Sternglass, 1981).

The LSS studied only the effects of external doses of gamma radiation on human health. The study does not consider the health effects of internalizing a radioactive particle (Shigematsu, Ito, Kamada, Akiyama, & Sasaki, 1995). Therefore, there existed no medical model to assess the health risks to people living in nuclear test site locations. This scientific compartmentalization of risk and harm from radiation allowed nuclear weapon states (NWS) to dismiss all but the most egregious health effects from testing nuclear weapons, and especially very large thermonuclear weapons, on test site populations. Because of this dynamic, NWS such as the United States and France were able to position their activities as not having posed significant harm to the populations downwind from their nuclear weapon tests, unburdening them from compensating the illnesses and early mortality that followed exposure to high levels of radioactive fallout (Nixon, 2011). It also relieved them of the burdens of full remediation of nuclear test site locations and downwind areas from the radiological contamination that resulted from the fallout (Bertell, 1985).

Previous Attempts to Remediate Contaminated Lands, and Compensate Individuals

In both the RMI and FP, ongoing protests led both the United States and France to take small steps to address the damages of their nuclear testing programs, to compensate those who had been made sick, and to remediate test site contamination. In both cases, the efforts can be said to have been reluctant and insufficient (Ruff, 2015, pp. 775–813).

The Marshall Islands negotiated their independence from the United States as part of the Compact of Free Association (the Compact), formalized in 1986, along with two additional Pacific island nations held under trust by the United States: the Federated States of Micronesia and Palau. The Compact included many agreements that both extended and attempted to resolve the points of conflict and specific damages of the nuclear testing era. While the compact included a negotiated settlement to claims made by the RMI, and by individual Marshallese, regarding damage resulting from the nuclear tests, it also extended the right of the United States to use the largest atoll in the nation, Kwajalein Atoll, as a military base: the Ronald Reagan Ballistic Missile Defense Test Site (RTS). A renegotiation of the Compact has extended the Military Use and Operating Rights (MUORA) for the base to 2066, which the United States can extend to 2086 (Johnson, 2018).

Section 177 of the Compact, known as Agreement 177, established the Nuclear Claims Tribunal. Article IV, Section 1, of Section 177 declared that the Tribunal would render final judgment on,

> claims past, present, and future of the Government, the citizens and nationals of the Republic for loss or damage to person or property which are based on, arise out of, or are in any way related to the Nuclear Testing Program. (Republic of the Marshall Islands, 1987)

The United States Congress established a $150 million trust fund to pay out the claims legally established by the Tribunal; this money was deposited into an account, and claims were to be paid partially on an annual basis from the interest, however, due to the instability of financial markets, the fund was depleted and paid out only a fraction of the claims awarded before it went bankrupt in 2011. According to Bill Graham, the Public Advocate for the fund, the average awarded claim received a payout of approximately 10%–15% of the full awarded value (Brown, 2014, pp. 40–44).

Remediation of irradiated land was even less successfully executed. After the end of testing in the Marshall Islands (the United States continued to test nuclear weapons in the Pacific island nation of Kiribati, and also domestically in Nevada), the United States attempted to remediate Bikini, Enewetak and Rongelap atolls. It did extensive sampling of soil and water, pushed topsoil into the lagoons, and built new buildings. The United States returned the evacuated residents of Rongelap to their atoll in 1957, however, it informed them that they restricted to very limited parts of the atoll, and that they could not fish from certain areas, or eat certain foods. The actual landmass on Rongelap is very limited, and residents knew that not fishing from certain locations did not keep the fish they might catch from swimming to areas that were "safe" to fish from (Eknilang, 2003, pp. 315–321). The small number of Rongelapese that did return to the remediated atoll began to suffer from illnesses and asked to again be evacuated. The United

States claimed that it had met its obligations and took no action to support the wishes of the Rongelapese. In 1996, the United States initiated a second resettlement program for Rongelap Atoll, and a small group of Rongelapese now spends a limited amount of time on the atoll each year (Johnson & Takala, 2016).

The United States attempted to remediate a small area of Enewetak Atoll in 1980 and reclaimed 3 of 40 islands in the atoll and declared them safe. A small number of residents live part of the year on Enewetak. Bikini Atoll has been deemed too radioactive for habitation, although there is a thriving dive business visiting World War II wrecks that serves the Atoll (Niedenthal, 2002).

France passed the Morin Law in 2010 that aimed to compensate those harmed by French nuclear testing in Algeria and FP. As of 2018, 1,245 claims have been made under the Morin Law, which conducts inquiries behind closed doors, and of those 147 have come from Polynesians, of which only 11 have received any award (Feldman, 2018). The majority of the claims made and awarded were to French military personnel who participated in the nuclear tests. The atolls that were subject to nuclear weapon testing remain under French military control and information about remediation is not publicly available.

External Linkages

In both the RMI and FP, the societies remain deeply linked with the states that irradiated them. In the case of the RMI, while it has achieved independence, the Marshall Islands remain deeply dependent on the United States. The currency of the Marshall Islands is still the US dollar, and the postal service is the United States Postal Service. The United States still operates a vast military base on the largest atoll in the island nation and is the primary health care provider throughout the country. While the RMI is independent, in many ways it remains a client state of the United States.

Its economy is currently built on both the US military, and on selling the rights for large-scale tuna fishing. Tuna has long been the most valuable resource for export in the Marshall Islands. Here too, we can see the legacies of colonial dynamics continue to operate. Currently, the distant water fleets that pay licensing fees to the RMI for access to tuna fishing grounds in the country, primarily from Japan, South Korea and Taiwan, pay revenues of US$4-2 million per year for those rights, while these national industries each have annual tuna sales in the billions of US dollars (Barclay & Cartwright, 2007).

The RTS has been a primary site in the multiple decade development of ballistic missile defenses by the United States (Department of the Army Historical Summary, 1990, pp. 154–158). As part of the Strategic Defense Initiative, or *Star Wars* as it was popularly known in the 1980s, missiles are launched from Vandenberg Air Force Base in California, and then anti-ballistic missiles are launched from the RTS in an attempt to shoot down the ballistic missile in mid-flight. This has led to Kwajalein being called, in American military circles, the "world's largest catcher's mitt." Dozens of tests have been conducted over multiple decades with very limited success in producing a functional outcome that could ever be effectively deployed. However, these efforts and this funding have been at the core of United States military activities in the Marshall Islands, and remains a driver of American military investment in the nation (Zorpette, 1989).

The government of FP remains largely under French control. As an "oversea country of France," France still controls access to the former nuclear test sites, controls the currency of FP, all security and defense issues, and exercises tremendous control over French Polynesian politics. French expats own most of the high value businesses in FP, and much of the land. Both Australia and New Zealand have played an active part in opposing French nuclear testing in FP. New Zealand especially has sailed military vessels nearby to the test site during tests in the 1980s and 1990s to monitor radioactive fallout as it moved toward their territories, which resulted in exposures to their own military personnel (Barrett, 2008, pp. 25–52).

French authorities actually countered New Zealand opposition to its nuclear program in FP with an overt act of terrorism in 1985. The antinuclear group Greenpeace was actively opposing the resumption of French nuclear testing in FP in the 1980s. One tactic was to sail a boat into the restricted zone around the test site to try to disrupt or delay the weapon test. The French began a program of testing 6 weapons in 1985 and 1986, beginning in September of 1985. During the summer of 1985, Greenpeace anchored a ship, the *Rainbow Warrior*, in the harbor at Auckland, New Zealand. On the night of July 10, 1985, agents of the French foreign intelligence service the *Direction générale de la sécurité extérieure*, planted two bombs on the hull of the *Rainbow Warrior*. Shortly before midnight, the two bombs were detonated. Most of the crew members scrambled off of the ship, however, one crew member, Portuguese photographer Fernando Pereira was killed. Over the subsequent weeks, New Zealand police quickly identified French agents carrying Swiss passports, as the perpetrators. Several were apprehended while several others had already fled New Zealand. The two agents that had actually planted the bomb in what the French intelligence service had labeled *Opération Satanique*, were found guilty of manslaughter, sentenced to 10 years in prison, but served only 2 and were then deported (Robie, 2015).

Tying together these two nuclear test nations, FP and the RMI, the Greenpeace ship the *Rainbow Warrior* had actually just arrived at the Port of Auckland from a mission in the Marshall Islands when it was attacked by the French intelligence agents. The Bravo test at Bikini Atoll in 1954 had resulted in the radiological contamination of downwind Rongelap Atoll, and the population of Rongelap that had been evacuated a few days after the test and then resettled there after a botched remediation attempt by the United States, as mentioned above, had been seeking to be evacuated again from Rongelap for many years. Many had self-evacuated and settled on the capital atoll Majuro in the years after the resettlement by the United States in 1957, however many others could not afford to leave. In 1995, the Greenpeace boat the *Rainbow Warrior* came to Rongelap Atoll and had evacuated all of the community members that wished to leave their contaminated homes. The *Rainbow Warrior* transported them to Majuro Atoll, which is where Rongelap City Hall is currently located (as is Bikini City Hall and Enewetak City Hall). Upon completion of that humanitarian task, the Rainbow Warrior sailed to Auckland to prepare to disrupt the upcoming French nuclear weapon testing series scheduled to begin a few months later. The evacuation of the Rongelapese was the last voyage of the *Rainbow Warrior* before it was destroyed in what New Zealand Prime Minister David Lange referred to as the state-sponsored terror attack conducted in Auckland harbor (Robie, 1987).

Democratization as Part of the Resolution Process

Democratization has taken different forms in the RMI and FP because of the distinct political forms each nation has taken in its post-colonial era. In the RMI, the Compact of Free Association was negotiated with the United States, and it became a self-governing independent nation in 1987. Elections in the RMI are fair and free, however, a deep and continued dependence on the United States has inhibited democratization.

Ongoing health and environmental costs that burden the RMI are the direct result of the nuclear testing program of the United States, however the United States does not bear that burden beyond the negotiated terms of the Compact. The US military base on Kwajalein Atoll is a primary employer of Marshallese. Approximately 1,000 US military personnel are stationed on Kwajalein, and approximately 15,000 Marshallese live on tiny Ebeye island, which is part of the atoll, to provide labor at the base and support the 1,000 Americans. Overcrowding on Ebeye, and unsanitary conditions are rampant. Ebeye is only 80 acres, yet with a population of 15,000, it is the most populous island in the nation. The Marshallese that live and work on Kwajalein each must have explicit permission to live on the atoll by the US military (Smith, 2009, pp. 51–71).

Elected governments in the RMI must operate within these boundaries. While they exercise independence in many aspects of governance,

> subsidiary agreements regarding sections 321 and 323 of the compact, the sections that deal with us military facilities and operating rights in Federated States, create a right of permanent strategy denial in the area by the United States armed forces. Such a right can hardly be reconciled with "full independence" or with the "sovereign status" that…is the goal of free association. (Firth, 1989, p. 79)

Thus, certain primary aspects of sovereignty and self-determination are structurally walled off from influence by the democratic process or the will of the citizens of the Marshall Islands.

The French Polynesians do not enjoy sovereignty over their own lands, as sovereignty is directly exercised by the French. The imperative of military operations and nuclear testing has positioned the French as antagonistic toward independent rule by French Polynesians since the testing era began in the 1960s, although that antagonism predates the nuclear testing period. At that time, opposition leaders advocating independence were routinely jailed, and the two major political parties that opposed nuclear testing and demanded a Polynesian referendum on whether to allow nuclear testing (the RDPT and the Tahitian Independence Party) were simply dissolved by President de Gaulle (Firth, 1987). Even today, the nuclear needs of France control local politics in FP. Past President of FP Gaston Flosse was a close personal friend of President Jacques Chirac and supported Chirac's resumption of testing in the mid-1990s. Flosse later sought to relocate the public monument erected in the FP capital Papeete to honor those who suffered from the decades of nuclear testing, moving its location in a public park to being in the center of a traffic roundabout that would make render it inaccessible in 2014, a policy that was internationally opposed and never implemented (Radio New Zealand, 2014). This monument, formally dedicated in 2006 and named the "Place du 2 Juliet 1966" after the date of the first French nuclear test in FP, has frequently been the site of antinuclear protests, and also protests demanding compensation for those who lost property or suffered health effects from the nuclear tests. Flosse's successor, Édouard Fritch would later be overheard stating, "I'm not surprised that I've been called a liar for 30 years. We lied to this population that the tests were clean. We lied" (Adamson, 2018).

How Democracy Helps the Process

Independence has allowed successive governments of the RMI to seek compensation, remediation, and accountability from the United States in a variety of ways. While the United States has been steadfast in resisting any deviation from the agreements reached in the Compact, Marshallese politicians and presidents have pressed their demands in a variety of public fora over a number of decades. While these efforts have not produced material benefits from the United States, they have served to energize and focus Marshallese voters behind the role that politics can play in promoting the interests of those who have suffered from the years of nuclear testing. In the Marshall Islands, among the most important national holidays is Nuclear Victims and Survivors Remembrance Day. This solemn day is on March 1, which is the anniversary of the Bravo Test in 1954. During ceremonies on Nuclear Victims and Survivors Remembrance Day, citizens gather at the capitol building to hear speeches by leading Marshallese politicians, and to express community needs and sentiments (Pacific Islands Forum Secretariat, 2018).

Additionally, the RMI was the lead plaintiff in a series of suits filed against the United States and other NWS citing their lack of action under their obligations as signatories to the Nuclear Nonproliferation Treaty (NPT). The RMI filed suit in the International Court of Justice in The Hague in 2014 asserting that the United States and each of the eight other NWS have failed to meet their obligations to sincerely seek nuclear disarmament as dictated by the NPT (Escritt, 2016). While the suits were thrown out by the court two years later in 2016, these "nuclear zero" lawsuits helped pave the way to concretize the efforts of the series of international conferences on the humanitarian impacts of nuclear weapons, that ultimately culminated in the global mobilization behind the Nuclear Weapon Ban Treaty approved by the United Nations General Assembly last year (Andrews, 2016). Recent RMI President H. E. Hilda Heine has also been a leading global advocate on issues related to global warming and its effects on Pacific Island nations.

In FP, there has been a confluence between independence parties and the antinuclear test movement for many decades. A key step in establishing the nuclear test site in FP and beginning operations was the suppression of popular independence political parties and the jailing of numerous leaders (Fisher, 2013). This practice has endured to the present day. Former FP President Oscar Temaru, who served in the office five different times, is the head of the Union for Democracy, a coalition of five political parties, some of which are primarily focused on independence from France, while others support the position among other platforms. It was under Temaru that the "Place du 2 Juliet 1966" monument was commissioned and dedicated. The nuclear issue and the lack of accountability on the part of France have been employed as an effective organizational factor for the ongoing independence movement in French Polynesian politics (Gonschor, 2007, pp. 213–222).

Temaru has consistently challenged French control of FP, which he has referred to as French-occupied Polynesia (Decloitre, 2006). The French and Paris allied politicians in FP, have opposed him and worked to thwart his capacity to exert political power in FP, even while holding legitimately elected high governmental office. Early in 2018, France's highest administrative court declared that Temaru had violated campaign funding laws and had him removed from the territorial assembly, a charge that was later reversed (PACNEWS, 2018). When asked by Columbia University's *Journal of International Affairs* board about what compensation he feels that FP should seek from France for the decades of nuclear testing, Temura replied, "The only real compensation we're looking for is independence" (JIA Editorial Board, 2018).

Has Democracy Led to a Transformation of the Conflict?

In both the RMI and FP, while democracy has not led to a transformation of the conflict, it has facilitated political avenues that have progressed toward resolution to be robustly embraced by those in the former or current colonial territories. In the RMI, independence has not led to the removal of foreign military bases, nor has it led to the adequate remediation of contaminated lands or compensation of those who have experienced harm during the era of nuclear testing, or as consequence of the radiological fallout and its legacies (Johnston & Barker, 2008). However, democratization has allowed for the RMI to press its case in international fora and courts (Barker, 2004).

In FP, the continued subjective political status of the territory has curtailed any meaningful remediation of the contaminated lands or compensations to those who were harmed by nuclear testing (Rivasi & Aubert, 1999). It has, however, facilitated the emergence of a dynamic independence movement that has vexed French policy implementation and control of the population. While Paris has forcefully pushed back on this movement, continuing, as it had during the overt colonial period, to banish independence leaders from legitimately elected governmental posts, it has been unable to subdue and pacify desires for independence among the Polynesian people (Regnault, 2005, pp. 339–377).

For both the RMI and FP, democratic action can only bring a certain amount of relief. In the RMI, the United States retains the right to operate the RTS on

Kwajalein Atoll for another half a century, a contract that cannot be overturned by democratic action. Additionally, the United States has resisted pressure to further assume any obligation to remediate the former nuclear test site or compensate victims. The singular path to change in FP is to seek independence. The French have consistently hampered and obstructed legitimate independence parties from pursuing independence policies when they are in office. The French retain full control of the former nuclear test site, and, even with the passage of the Morin Law has still offered compensation to only a fraction of the Polynesians who have submitted valid claims.

The Nuclear Ban Treaty passed by the United Nations in 2017 contains language that would obligate nuclear testing nations to fully remediate their former nuclear test sites (United Nations, 2017). None of the NWS are signatories to the treaty, and there is uncertainty about the extent of any legal demands on them to submit to the obligations of a treaty they have not signed, even if it is adopted by the full United Nations. As the unsuccessful lawsuit against the nine NWS by the Marshall Islands reveals, not meeting their obligations under the NPT, to which they are signatories, has not compelled the NWSs to take active steps toward fulfilling those obligations.

What Can the Case Tell Us About Democratization in the Resolution of Conflicts

These two cases reveal some limitations to the resolution of conflicts through democratization. In both cases, steps toward democratic processes have done little to resolve the core conflicts resultant from the decades of nuclear weapon testing. In both cases, these core conflicts are embedded in a deeper colonial legacy. Post-colonial problems and efforts to resolve them through democratic processes are common throughout the world, with various measures of success and justice obtained in various cases. While aspects of the conflicts in the RMI and FP have been resolved through such traditional methodologies, there are specific legacies of nuclear weapon testing that have made these cases unlike many post-colonial struggles for restitution and resolution, or rather, that have positioned them as having dilemmas unique to post-nuclear test sites. This uniqueness has allowed these conflicts to endure, not only because they are not common to post-colonial struggles for justice, but because of the specific problems posed by nuclear weapon testing and radiological contamination. While it is possible, with an intensive investment and commitment of resources to remediate environmental damage from resource extraction activities, such as mining, with radiologically contaminated environments such options are limited.

In former nuclear test sites where the irradiating nation has simply abandoned its test site, such as the abandonment of the Polygon test site in Kazakhstan by Russia after the collapse of the former Soviet Union, there are few paths to resolution. Russia, in this case, simply abdicated responsibility since it is not the national perpetrator, the Soviet Union, anymore. This provided Russia a political resolution that absolved it of any responsibility, but simply left the newly independent Kazakhstan to deal, or not deal, with the radiological legacy by itself (Werner &

Purvis-Roberts, 2006, pp. 461–480). For nations, such as the United States and France, that seek an ongoing military, or in the case of FP, political presence in their former nuclear test site, there comes a delicate balancing act in which remediation is performed, but, because of the physical impossibilities of substantial remediation, never achieved. In such cases, the local government, independent in the RMI, but still partially politically controlled as in FP, finds itself with a limited capacity to demand effective remediation or full compensation.

I would argue that this is not so much the result of political intransigence by the nuclear weapon state, but rather reflects the virtual impossibility of successful resolution. The time frames of liability in relation to nuclear events alter the dynamics of normal political processes, including that of post-colonial relations. It necessitates both a prolonged control of access to contaminated landscapes, and a willingness to adjudicate and seek remediation over such landscapes for centuries. In the RMI, the United States no longer has any control over the former test site locations at Bikini and Enewetak Atolls. These lands have been "returned" to their traditional owners, albeit not in a state that allows continued habitation. The fact of continued large-scale American military operations in the RMI necessitates an ongoing engagement with the nuclear legacy of the United States in the RMI. Thus, the ineffectual remediation of these atolls, along with several atolls contaminated in the Bravo Test that were forcibly evacuated but now returned to traditional owners can essentially be called – theater. In FP, the ongoing military control of the former test site allows the French to avoid any meaningful remediation and continued political control over the government facilitates an abdication from compensating the majority of French Polynesians who were exposed to dangerous levels of radiation during the testing, or whose lands demonstrate ongoing contamination.

Because of these dynamics, the United States and France cannot simply step away from the environmental disasters they created at the test sites but must attempt to cloak them behind the theater of remediation. These are, of course, short-term solutions aimed at forestalling accountability because of the millennia-long periods of time that the environmental catastrophe will endure. In the end, both may simply walk away from their obligations to their former colonial test sites, much as the Russians did, although not with the same excuse of being a different, and therefore not liable, government. There is no example in the world of a nuclear weapon state that has adequately taken responsibility for the ecological consequences of their actions with nuclear weapon production and testing. In the cases of the RMI and FP, it is only the ongoing military needs of the nuclear states that necessitate the insincere theatrics of remediation.

While there has been slow change in the RMI and FP themselves, the history of nuclear weapon testing in the Pacific has had a region-wide effect. A grassroots and powerful antinuclear movement emerged during the 1980s and shaped a number of Oceanic governments. Multiple small, independent nations in the Pacific banded together to support a treaty to make the vast region a nuclear-free region. The Nuclear Free Pacific Conference was held at Suva in Fiji in 1975, followed by a second conference held at Pohnpei, the capital of the Federated States of Micronesia in 1978. A third meeting in 1981 at Kailua in Hawaii led to the establishment of the Nuclear-Free and Independent Pacific. During a fourth conference in Port Vila on Vanuatu the various national groups took additional steps toward concretizing their political opposition to nuclear weapon testing in the Pacific (Salvador, 1999).

In 1986, the Treaty of Rarotonga was signed, establishing the South Pacific Nuclear-Free Zone (SPNFZ). The Treaty has 13 signatory nations, and includes the nation of Kiribati, which had been used for nuclear weapon testing by both the United Kingdom and the United States. Kiribati was the location where the United Kingdom tested all of its thermonuclear weapons (United Nations Office for Disarmament Affairs, 1986). Whereas the RMI supports the Treaty, however it is located in the Northern Pacific Ocean and does not qualify for membership in the treaty cohort. FP, being still under French political control, has not signed the Treaty. The SPNFZ does have "dialogue partners" from outside of the region, and these include the United States, the United Kingdom, and France. France's dialog partner status was suspended in 1995 when it resumed nuclear testing at Moruroa in FP; the status was restored in 1996 after the completion of its test series. The treaty and the meetings that led up to the establishment of the nuclear-free zone did facilitate community building across the vast spaces of the South Pacific, and united Polynesian and Micronesian societies which continued to build a shared sense of post-colonial emergence and ecological self-determination that is ongoing today as the region finds itself on the front lines of global warming (de Ishtar, 1998).

Like the lingering radiation of the nuclear testing itself, it will be hard for both the United States and France to pretend that they are clean in terms of their obligations to remediate their former nuclear test sites. The nuclear legacy is a shadow that never leaves the colonial power no matter how they attempt to illuminate themselves as proactive and responsible in resolving their nuclear pasts on colonial territories.

References

Adamson, T. (2018, November 16). French Polynesian president acknowledges nuclear test lies. *Associated Press*. Retrieved from https://apnews.com

Andrews, S. (2016, March 12). The Pacific nuclear test cases: A tiny Pacific Island nation takes on the world's nuclear powers. *The Diplomat*. Retrieved from https://thediplomat.com

Barclay, K., & Cartwright, I. (2007). *Capturing wealth from tuna: Case studies from the Pacific*. Canberra: Australian National University Press.

Barker, H. (2004). *Bravo for the Marshallese: Regaining control in a post-nuclear, post-colonial world*. Belmont, CA: Thompson Wadsworth.

Barrett, M. (2008). French nuclear testing in the Pacific, 1995-1996, and its fallout for French Australians. *The French Australian Review*, *44*, 25–52.

Begkvist, N., & Ferm, R. (2000). *Nuclear explosions 1945 – 1998 (Report FOA-R-00-01572-180)*. Stockholm: Stockholm International Peach Research Institute (SIPRI).

Bertell, R. (1985) *No immediate danger: Prognosis for a radioactive Earth*. London: The Women's Press Limited.

Brown, A. L. (2014). No promised land: The shared legacy of the Castle Bravo nuclear test. *Arms Control Today*, *44*(2). Retrieved from https://www.armscontrol.org/act/2013_03/No-Promised-Land-The-Shared-Legacy-of-the-Castle-Bravo-Nuclear-Test

Chrisafis, A. (2013, July 3). French nuclear tests 'showered vast area of Polynesia with radioactivity'. *The Guardian*. Retrieved from https://www.theguardian.com

D'Amato, A. (1967). Legal aspects of the French nuclear tests. *The American Journal of International Law*, *61*(1), 66–77.

de Ishtar, Z. (Ed.). (1998). *Pacific women speak out for independence and denuclearization*. Christchurch: The Raven Press.

Decloitre, P. A. (2006, October 27). France replies to Temaru on Tahitian independence. *Pacific Islands Report*. Retrieved from http://www.pireport.org

Department of the Army Historical Summary. (1990). *Department of the Army Historical Summary, FY 1983*. Washington, DC: U.S. Army Center of Military History.

Eknilang, L. (2003). Learning from Rongelap's pain. *Seattle Journal for Social Justice*, *2*(1), 315–321.

Emery, K. O., Tracey, J. Jr, & Ladd, H. S. (1954). *Geology of Bikini and nearby atolls. Geological Survey Professional* Paper 260-A. Washington, DC: US Government Printing Office.

Escritt, T. (2016, March 5). Tiny Marshall Islands takes on nuclear powers in court. *Reuters*. Retrieved from https://uk.reuters.com

Feldman, K. (2018, October 15). Beyond radioactivity: How French nuclear tests changed Polynesia forever. *Equal Times*. Retrieved from https://www.equaltimes.org

Firth, S. (1987). *Nuclear playground: fight for an independent and nuclear free Pacific* Honolulu, HI: University of Hawaii Press.

Firth, S. (1989). Sovereignty and independence in the contemporary Pacific. *The Contemporary Pacific*, *1*(1-2), 75–96.

Fisher, D. (2013). *France in the South Pacific: Power and politics*. Canberra: Australian National University Press.

Glasstone, S., & Dolan, P. (1977). *The effects of nuclear weapons*. Washington DC: US Government Printing Office.

Gonschor, L. (2007). French Polynesia. *The Contemporary Pacific*, *19*(1), 213–222.

Hecht, G. (2012). *Being nuclear: Africa and the global uranium trade*. Cambridge, MA: MIT University Press.

Hendrix, S. (2018, July 7). A scandalous, two-piece history of the bikini. *Washington Post*. Retrieved from https://www.washingtonpost.com

Jacobs, R. (2013). Nuclear conquistadors: Military colonialism in nuclear test site selection during the Cold War. *Asian Journal of Peacebuilding*, *1*(2), 157–177.

JIA Editorial Board. (2018, October 10). Trouble in Paradise: Oscar Temaru on nuclear testing and independence aspirations. *Journal of International Affairs*. Retrieved from https://jia.sipa.columbia.edu

Johnson, G. (2018, July 5). 2023: SEG, Enewetak funding ends. *Marshall Islands Journal*. Retrieved from https://marshallislandsjournal.com

Johnson, B. R., & Takala, B. (2016, September). Environmental disaster and resilience: The Marshall Islands experience continues to unfold. *Cultural Survival*. Retrieved from https://www.culturalsurvival.org

Johnston, B. R., & Barker, H. (2008). *Consequential damages of nuclear war: The Rongelap report*. Walnut Creek, CA: Left Coast Press.

Kahn, M. (2011). *Tahiti: beyond the postcard*. Seattle, WA: University of Washington Press.

Kiste, R. (1974). *The Bikinians: A study in forced migration*. Menlo Park, CA: Cummings Publishing Company.

Lindee, S. (1994). *Suffering made real: American science and the survivors at Hiroshima*. Chicago, IL: University of Chicago Press.

Maclellan, N., & Chesneaux, J. (1998). *After Moruroa: France in the South Pacific*. Melbourne: Ocean Press.
Merlin, M., & Gonzalez, R. (2010). Environmental impacts of nuclear testing in remote Oceania, 1946-1996. In J. McNeill & C. Unger (Eds.), *Environmental histories of the Cold War* (pp. 167–202). Cambridge: Cambridge University Press.
Miller, R. L. (1991). *Under the cloud: decades of nuclear testing*. The Woodlands, TX: Two-Sixty Press.
National Research Council. (1994). *Radiological Assessments for the Resettlement of Rongelap in the Republic of the Marshall Islands*. Washington, DC: The National Academies Press. https://doi.org/10.17226/2352.
Neidenthal, J. (2001). *For the good of mankind: a history of the people of Bikini and their islands*. Majuro: Bravo Publishers.
Nixon, R. (2011). *Slow violence and the environmentalism of the poor*. Cambridge, MA: Harvard University Press.
Pacific Islands Forum Secretariat. (2018, March 16). *Nuclear Victims Remembrance Day in Marshall Islands*. Retrieved from https://www.forumsec.org/nuclear-victims-remembrance-day-marshall-islands/
PACNEWS. (2018, October 19). Temaru set to be cleared in Tahiti election probe. *The Fiji Times*. Retrieved form https://www.fijitimes.com
Radio New Zealand. (2014, June 23). Plan to remove Tahiti nuclear test memorial. *Radio New Zealand*. Retrieved from https://www.radionz.co.nz
Regnault, J.-M. (2005). The nuclear issue in the South Pacific: Labor parties, trade union movements and Pacific Island churches in international relations. *Contemporary Pacific*, *17*(2), 339–357
Republic of the Marshall Islands. (1987). *Marshall Islands Nuclear Claims Tribunal Act (1987)*. Retrieved from http://rmiparliament.org/cms/images/LEGISLATION/PRINCIPAL/1987/1987-0024/MarshallIslandsNuclearClaimsTribunalAct1987_1.pdf
Rivasi, M., & Aubert, M.-H. (1999). *The French nuclear tests in Polynesia: Demanding the truth and proposals for the future: Proceedings of the symposium, 20th February 1999*. Lyon: Centre de documentation et de recherche sur la paix et les conflits
Robie, D. (1987). *Eyes of fire: The last voyage of the Rainbow Warrior*. Philadephia, PA: New Society Publishers.
Robie, D. (2015, July 7). Beyond the Rainbow Warrior – the French Pacific catastrophe. *Pacific Institute of Public Policy*. Retrieved from http://pacificpolicy.org
Ruff, T. (2015). The humanitarian impact and implications of nuclear test explosions in the Pacific region. *International Review of the Red Cross*, *97*(899), 775–813.
Salvador, R. (1999, August 20). The nuclear history of Micronesia and the Pacific. *Nuclear Age Peace Foundation*. Retrieved from https://www.wagingpeace.org
Schull, W. (1995). *Effects of atomic radiation: A half-century of studies from Hiroshima and Nagasaki*. New York, NY: Wiley-Liss.
Shigematsu, I., Ito, C., Kamada, N., Akiyama, M., & Sasaki, H. (Eds.). (1995). *Effects of a-bomb radiation on the human body*. Tokyo: Bunkodo Co.
Smith, A. (2009). Colonialism and the bomb in the Pacific. In J. Schofield & W. Cockroft (Eds.), *A fearsome heritage: diverse legacies of the Cold War* (pp. 51–72). London: Routledge.
Sternglass, E. (1981). *Secret fallout: low-level radiation from Hiroshima to Three-Mile Island*. New York, NY: McGraw-Hill.
Steton, R. L., Schuert, E. A., Perkins, W. W., Shirasawa, T. H., & Chan, H. K. (1956). *Operation Castle: distribution and intensity of fallout*. San Francisco, CA: US Naval Radiological Defense Laboratory.
United Nations. (2017). *Treaty on the Prohibition of Nuclear Weapons* (A/CONF.229/2017/8). Retrieved from https://treaties.un.org/doc/Treaties/2017/07/20170707%2003-42%20PM/Ch_XXVI_9.pdf

United Nations Office for Disarmament Affairs. (1986). *South Pacific Nuclear-Free Zone Treaty*. Retrieved from http://disarmament.un.org

Uriohau, A. (2007, September 28). The Nuclear History of Micronesia and the Pacific. *Whenua Fenua Enua Vanua*. Retrieved from http://uriohau.blogspot.com

Wall, K., Jose, C., & Hinzel, J. H. (2018, February 25). The poison and the tomb: One family's journey to their contaminated home. *Mashable*. Retrieved from https://mashable.com

Weisgall, J. (1980, Summer). The nuclear nomads of Bikini. *Foreign Policy*, *39*, 74–98.

Weisgall, J. (1994). *Operation Crossroads: The atomic tests at Bikini Atoll*. Annapolis, MD: Naval Institute Press.

Werner, C., & Purvis-Roberts, K. (2006). After the Cold War: International politics, domestic policy and the nuclear legacy in Kazakhstan. *Central Asian Survey*, *25*(4), 461–480.

Zorpette, G. (1989, March 27). Raining warheads: Kwajalein Missile Range in Pacific readied for testing of 'Star Wars. *Los Angeles Times*. Retrieved from http://articles.latimes.com

Chapter 3

Democratization, Peace and the Differences Between Asian and Western Approaches: The Case of Cambodia

Makiko Takemoto

Introduction

What is peace? How can democratization be achieved? They are some of the important questions in peace studies. The concept of peace and democratization has their origin in Europe. Are they really globalized? Do we have the same concept of peace in the East and West? In the period of globalization, we must reconsider the answers to these questions.

To discuss the concept of peace and democratization, the case of Cambodia will be analyzed in this chapter. Even though there was an international effort to democratize Cambodia, the democracy established there through the efforts of the international community has been subverted. As reported by many newspapers and TV news programs, the election of July 2018 was undemocratically administered. The Cambodian case is quite important as an example of intervention and the peacekeeping process by the international community in the 1990s and also as one of the examples of the failure of international efforts at democratization. It will be interesting for us to think about the different ways to achieve peace, reconciliation, and democratization from this example. This chapter will examine not only the Cambodian case but also the international influence of the intervention in Cambodia. Especially important in this regard is the Japanese intervention in Cambodia and its influence in turn on the Japanese conception of peace. Similarly, the Chinese influence on Cambodia will be considered in order to make clear the ongoing problems in Cambodia that include the hindrance of democratization and the task of the international society on how to address this issue.

International Perspectives on Democratization and Peace, 43–58

doi:10.1108/978-1-80043-067-920200003

History of the Cambodian Conflict and Civil War

The Roots of the Conflict

The development of Cambodian modern history has been unstable, it was filled with violence, civil wars, mass killings and intervention from foreign countries. Since the nineteenth century, Cambodia was a French colony and became a part of French Indochina that also included present day Vietnam and Laos. During World War II, the Japanese army occupied Cambodia and the country came under the double domination of both Japan and France. In 1945, Cambodia declared its independence from France, which was however rejected. In 1953, Cambodia once more declared its independence and this time around it became an independent country. The independence of Cambodia and Laos in 1953 foreshadowed the French military defeat in Vietnam in 1954 that led in turn to Vietnam being divided into two halves with the north becoming Communist and the south being controlled by a military authoritarian government. The dynamics of the Cold War was played out in Indochina through proxy wars that pitted the West led by the United States and the Communists who were supported by China that had already become Communist in 1949.

From the time of its independence, Cambodia has experienced many political regime types: the Kingdom of Cambodia from 1953 to 1970 (*Sangkum Reastr Niyum* era or Sihanouk era), the Khmer Republic from 1970 to 1975 (Lon Nol regime), Democratic Kampuchea from 1975 to 1979 (Pol Pot regime), Peoples' Republic of Kampuchea from 1979 to 1992, the Kingdom of Cambodia with two co-prime ministers system from 1993 to 1997 as part of a national reconciliation process following international intervention, and the government of the Cambodian People's Party since 1998 (Sasagawa, 2018).

The Cambodian civil war was a long-drawn conflict that lasted more than 20 years from 1973 to 1997. It reflected Cold War dynamics and highlighted the complicated relationships between several parties and politicians. As a small and dependent country, its elite was unable to control the country and its population. And in the face of intervention in the country's domestic politics by larger external powers, the situation became complex and prone to violence. Leading elites sought to buttress their political legitimacy and support through external guarantors that were only too eager to become involved in providing such support as part of a broader regional and global strategy.

In 1953, Cambodia gained its independence from France and Prince Norodom Sihanouk established a new government. Sihanouk, who later became the King and head of state, played an important role in the complex domestic political situation and also in international politics. The first civil war occurred with the peaceful *coup d'état* by General Lon Nol who was supported by the United States, because of Prince Sihanouk's good relations with the Soviet Union and China. The Communist Party of Kampuchea "Khmer Rouge" and Prince Sihanouk established the *Front uni national du Kampuchea* (FUNK) and started to resist the Lon Nol regime. They formed an exiled government in Beijing where Sihanouk had sought and received political asylum. Then, the Khmer Rouge defeated the Lon Nol government with the support of China and FUNK established the state called Democratic Kampuchea. The Khmer Rouge which was led by Pol Pot committed widespread political violence and displacement of the local population under a radical communist ideology that was also ethnically defined. Almost 1.5 million Cambodians such as intellectuals and political opponents were killed through murder, forced labor, starvation and disease. Against the Khmer Rouge, in December 1978, Heng Samrin, who was a military officer and a former member of the Khmer Rouge, established the *Front d'Union nationale pour le salut du Kampuchea* (FUNSK) which was supported by Vietnam and in January 1979, he gained control of Phnom Penh and founded the People's Republic of Kampuchea. However, the civil war did not end with the establishment of this new government. In February 1979, shortly after the Vietnamese invasion and occupation of Cambodia, China launched a month-long punitive expedition against Vietnam partly to assuage the security concerns of Thailand which had sought its alignment against Vietnam. In 1982, the conflict between China and Vietnam influenced Cambodia and the Heng Samrin government was opposed by three anti-Vietnam parties (Pol Pot group, Sihanouk group and Son Sann group, which were communist, royalist and anti-communist respectively). They fought against the Heng Samrin government and the occupying Vietnamese forces. At the broader regional level, this group was also supported by the Association for Southeast Asian Nations (ASEAN) that sought to delegitimize the Vietnamese occupation and proxy government. And in order to achieve that goal diplomatically, ASEAN initially supported the government of Democratic Kampuchea as the legitimate government of the country from 1979 to 1982 at the United Nations. From 1982, the three groups that were united against the Vietnamese-installed Heng Samrin regime held the UN seat and were referred to as the Coalition Government of Democratic Kampuchea (CGDK). This broadened coalition helped to deflect negative international publicity associated with the genocidal policies of the Khmer Rouge.

When we look back at the historical development of the Cambodian conflict, it may be estimated that they were not only political conflicts between Cambodian radical communists, royalists and nationalists but also the Cambodian case can be regarded rather as a reflection of the antagonisms during the Cold War. The politics of Cambodia was strongly influenced by the conflicts between the United States, the Soviet Union and China, then between China and the Soviet Union and lastly the antagonism between China and Vietnam. This is also clear from the fact that peacebuilding could finally be started only with the change in the international political atmosphere which was brought about with the end of the Cold War. In the middle of the 1980s, communist countries started their new and more open policies such as Perestroika in the Soviet Union and Doi Moi in Vietnam. The reduction of financial support by the Soviet Union for Vietnam made it difficult for Vietnam to continue its occupation of Cambodia. Also the political changes of the 1980s especially in Eastern Europe and the Soviet Union eventually brought about the end of the Cold War. It also led to the reconciliation between China and Vietnam, between the United States and the Soviet Union, and between the United States and Vietnam. The *rapprochement* between China and the Soviet Union and the collapse of the Socialist regimes in Eastern Europe were some of the developments that paved the way for the end of the Cambodian civil war (Sasagawa, 2018). The dissipation of antagonisms associated with the Cold War then made the Cambodian situation ripe for international political intervention and settlement.

External Linkages to the Conflict: The International Intervention and its Aftermath

Previous Attempts to Resolve the Conflict

The peacebuilding, reconciliation and democratization processes in Cambodia were realized through international intervention. The first initiative was from Indonesia, a country which has a strong security and military relationship with Cambodia and also led the regional grouping ASEAN. When the Vietnamese army withdrew from Cambodia, Indonesia tried to mediate between the four political parties (Heng Samrin Government, Sihanouk group, Son San group, Pol Pot group) and held unofficial meetings in Jakarta (Jakarta Informal Meetings) in 1987 and 1988. This initiative which was Indonesia's way of regaining its leadership position in ASEAN after having earlier deferred to Thailand on the basis of its security concerns over the Vietnamese occupation of Cambodia was spearheaded by the country's foreign Minister Ali Alatas. However, no agreement was reached between the feuding parties. Nonetheless, this initiative constituted significant progress in that the four parties officially recognized the existence of each other. The Cambodian matter was then brought to the international level for resolution. In April 1989, the Kampuchean People's Revolutionary Party (KPRP) established a new constitution and Cambodia started to change the political and economic system from communism to liberalism. In October 1989, KPRP was renamed to the Cambodian People's Party (CPP) and the party officially gave up the Marxist–Leninist ideology that it had previously adopted. On October 23, 1991, the Paris Peace Accords (Agreements on a Comprehensive Political Settlement of the Cambodia Conflict) were signed by the 4 parties and 18 countries.[1] It effectively signaled the end of the Cambodian-Vietnamese or Third Indochina War.

Indonesia maintained a good relationship with Cambodia and continued to support Cambodian peacebuilding and democratization given its leadership of ASEAN and President Suharto's own new policy of openness in domestic politics. The Indonesian army participated in international operations in Cambodia alongside an international peacekeeping force. Indonesia also endorsed and supported Cambodian membership in ASEAN in April 1999. While ASEAN had hoped to incorporate all countries in the region during its Summit Meeting and

[1]The 18 signatories were as follows: Australia, Brunei, Cambodia, Canada, People's Republic of China, France, India, Indonesia, Japan, Laos, Malaysia, Philippines, Singapore, Soviet Union, Thailand, United Kingdom, the United States, Vietnam, and Yugoslavia.

Thirtieth Anniversary in Kuala Lumpur in 1997 when Laos and Myanmar were accepted as members, the decision was deferred as a result of the outbreak of civil war between the forces of the two co-prime ministers – Norodom Ranariddh and Hun Sen. That conflict was only brought to an end in 1999 following international intervention and mediation.

UNTAC and Cambodia

The interaction between the UN and Cambodia had already existed since the 1950s, Cambodia engaged the UN and became a member of the United Nations Educational, Scientific and Cultural Organization (UNESCO) in 1951. Also, United Nations Children's Fund (UNICEF) started its assistance to Cambodia in 1952, the World Health Organization (WHO) began its involvement in 1953 and the United Nations Development Programme (UNDP) in 1958. According to Fergal Quinn and Kevin Doyle, "UN engagement was part of an overall strategy whereby the autocratic and unpredictable, but undeniably energetic and innovative Sihanouk led Cambodia through a post-independence period of relative peace and prosperity in the late 1950s and the first half of the 1960s" (Quinn & Doyle, 2018, p. 179).

After the Jakarta Informal Meetings, the United Nations took the initiative in the peacekeeping and reconciliation processes in Cambodia. As a result of the second session of the Paris Conference on Cambodia, the United Nations Advance Mission in Cambodia (UNAMIC) was established in 1991. The main mission of UNAMIC was to help the four Cambodian parties maintain their ceasefire. In Resolution 728 (1992) of the UN Security Council, the mandate of UNAMIC was expanded to undertake on an urgent basis a major demining effort in Cambodia, in preparation for a safe, orderly repatriation of Cambodian refugees and displaced people, and to develop a training program for Cambodians in mine detection and clearance and the clearing of repatriation routes, reception centers, and resettlement areas, as well as a program of emergency repairs and rehabilitation of roads and bridges (Osmańczyk, 2003, p. 2408).

In 1992, following the Paris Peace Accords, the United Nations Transitional Authority in Cambodia (UNTAC) was organized and worked for the disarmament and democratization of the country. UNTAC absorbed UNAMIC and the most important task of UNTAC was to hold a free and fair election with the supervision of civil administration. This act differs not only from the former involvement in Cambodia but also the former Peacekeeping Operations (PKO) in which the militaries had mainly supervised the ceasefire processes. UNTAC was regarded as the "second generation of PKO" (Sato, 2010). UNTAC consisted of seven distinct components: (1) human rights, (2) electoral, (3) military, (4) civil administration, (5) civilian police, (6) repatriation, and (7) rehabilitation (Osmańczyk, 2003, p. 2536).

UNTAC was the biggest UN mission at that time. It was strongly supported by the major powers such as France, the United States, Japan and Australia. At its height, in June 1993, UNTAC had a strength of 15,991 military and 3,359 civilian police personnel. There was also provision for an international civilian staff of some 1,150, for 465 United Nations volunteers, and for a local staff of 4,830 supplemented by an international contractual staff and electoral personnel during the election period (Osmańczyk, 2003, p. 2537). In addition, military personnel were despatched from 33 countries.[2]

In May 1993, the first general election was held in Cambodia and about 90% of the electorate voted (Mizumoto, 2003a, 82). However, the Khmer Rouge did not accept the conditions set by UNTAC and boycotted the election and continued to fight against the government. Earlier on it had refused to go into cantonment and be disarmed as required by international intervention. As a result of this unwillingness to accede to the terms of the brokerage, the Khmer Rouge forces moved into the provinces bordering Thailand like Anlong Veng and Preah Vihear. They also maintained an important position in Pailin where the leadership on the organization was located. That election yielded a national reconciliation government with two co-Prime Ministers representing the two major political parties. The royalist party, *Front uni national pour un Cambodge indépendant, neutre, pacifique et coopératif* (FUNCINPEC) won 58 seats, the Cambodian People's Party (CPP) led by Hun Sen got 51 seats, 10 seats for the Buddhist Liberal Democratic Party, and 1 seat for the Molinaka Party (Ishizuka, 2017, p. 33). As a result of the election, a new political system with two leaders (Norodom Ranariddh and Hun Sen) was established in 1993. However, it led to the struggle between the two parties, CPP and FUNCINPEC. The outbreak of this conflict postponed Cambodia's entry into ASEAN from July 1997 to April 1999. It ended when the CPP defeated FUNCINPEC and the seizing of power by Hun Sen in 1998. The Hun Sen government is still in power today after more than 20 years and he has strengthened his position even more. Strong support from China for Hun Sen's authoritarian politics led to the collapse of democracy in Cambodia, which will be examined later.

After the lengthy civil war, not only democratization but also reconciliation between citizens became an important task. Hun Sen's seizing of power has led to several difficult questions to solve, one of the most pressing is the trials against the Khmer Rouge. In 1988, the Khmer Rouge stopped fighting and started the process of reconciliation. They never returned to the battlefield and many of them joined the regular army that effectively ended the Cambodian civil war. UNTAC ended its mission and withdrew from Cambodia after the establishment of the new government and legislative assembly on November 15, 1993. Cambodia declared its independence again and that constituted the official end of the Cambodian Conflict.

UNTAC was regarded as the most successful UN mission at that time. Especially with regards to three points – the introduction of an international cooperation system like the Paris International Conference, the network between

[2]Algeria, Argentina, Australia, Austria, Bangladesh, Brunei, Bulgaria, Cameroon, Canada, Chili, China, France, Germany, Ghana, India, Indonesia, Ireland, Japan, Malaysia, Namibia, the Netherlands, New Zealand, Pakistan, Philippines, Poland, Russia, Senegal, Singapore, Thailand, Tunisia, United Kingdom, the United States, and Uruguay (Ishizuka, 2017, p. 32).

Cambodia, the groups in the conflict and other related countries, and the unified activities of the PKO – UNTAC was very successful when compared with other UN missions (Chino, 2018, pp. 81–85). However, UNTAC drew strong criticism from many countries. The treatment of the Khmer Rouge in particular showed the powerlessness of UNTAC. The Khmer Rouge did not participate in the reconciliation process until the autumn of 1992. They continued their military action, attacked UNTAC and the three opposition parties and obstructed the election campaign. The Khmer Rouge also attacked the civilian police. The staff of UNTAC were often attacked not only by the Khmer Rouge but also by the supporters of CCP (Ishizuka, 2017, p. 33). It was difficult for UNTAC to be trusted by the Cambodian people, because they thought that UNTAC did not take a neutral position on the election. UNTAC showed the lack of the capability in the field of public works, demining and intelligence and it was also criticized for the lack of stabilization and development of democracy in Cambodia. The success of UNTAC was only partial, it was successful in building a new country, but not in building a stable country (Ishizuka, 2017, p. 34).

Japanese Intervention in Cambodia

The International influence on the Cambodian Conflict and civil wars had a strong impact on Japan, especially in the fields of foreign policy and security issues[3]. One of the consequences of its involvement is the Japanese government's hesitation to engage itself in Asian politics. Rather, Japan tries to cooperate with Asian (especially those from Southeast Asia) countries with financial support and Official Development Assistance (ODA) in order to distance itself from its aggression associated with World War II. It is also a form of compensation to Southeast Asia that is the equivalent of war reparations. However, in the case of Cambodia, it was different since Japan participated in the first Paris International Conference. It was the first time that Japan participated in an international peace conference. Japan served as the co-moderator in the third committee. And then in June 1990, the Tokyo Conference on Cambodia was held and the four Cambodian parties participated in it. It was a good opportunity to lead the international discussion on Cambodian peace and reconciliation and was seen as a leading initiative by the UN for the peacebuilding process from 1991. Also, the fact that a Japanese diplomat, Yasushi Akashi, who was the UN Secretary-General's Personal Representative at that time, served as the head of UNTAC and took the initiative in Cambodian peacebuilding, meant Japan undertook an active contribution on this issue, even though Akashi himself worked absolutely as a staff member of the UN (Ishihara, 2017, p. 375) and he did not represent Japan or Japanese interests. His work in Cambodia was held in high regard and later he was appointed as the UN Secretary-General's Personal Representative of the United Nations Protection Force (UNPROFOR) for the resolution of the Yugoslavian Wars.

[3] On Japanese intervention in Cambodia, see for example, Imagawa, 2000; Llewyn, Watson & Kikkawa, 2009; Yamada 2013.

In the Cambodian PKO, the army of the Japanese Self Defense Force (SDF) was sent to Cambodia, it was the first international deployment of the Japanese army after World War II. As already mentioned, because of its past role in the Pacific War, Japan could not undertake political initiatives in Southeast Asia for a long time. However, after the Tokyo Meeting, Japan started to intervene more in international conflicts.

Peacekeeping Operations in Cambodia and Japanese Pacifism: Pacifism as a Global Issue

This change in Japanese politics brought about an intense discussion on Japanese pacifism and peacekeeping operations. The new PKO law was enacted. However, the legality or the illegality of this deployment became a main issue in Japan, because the Japanese Constitution bans military acts in Article 9 of Chapter 2[4] and it is the most important idea which underpinned Japanese pacifism after World War II. The fact that two Japanese civilians were killed in the operation brought criticism on the PKO. Japan's role in the peace process during the Cambodian civil war and its participation in the PKO are regarded as a shift in Japanese politics from a passive role to a more active role including the deployment of its military forces in abnormal cases. It brought about conflict between Japanese pacifism and the country's international contributions. While the Ministry of Foreign Affairs and people who were in this field tend to emphasize the positive side of the Cambodian PKO, and the good relationship between Japan and Cambodia, especially the friendship with Sihanouk, Japanese NGOs and peace movements saw the danger of the revision of the Constitution including Article 9 in the Cambodian case.

Also, after Hun Sen came into power in 1998, Japan continued to support Cambodia. Since March 1999, Japan helped Cambodia especially in the field of the construction of law and the judicial system, for example to establish new civil laws. Japan played an important role in the Khmer Rouge trials, donating 21.6 million dollars to its cost of 56 million dollars (Makita, 2018, p. 53). Not only with monetary support but also with its support for infrastructure, industry and human security issues, Japan became the largest supporter of Cambodia (Ministry of Foreign Affairs of Japan, 2008; Kimura, 2017, p. 51). It is also deeply involved in the provision of health and educational infrastructure in the country.

---

[4]Chapter 2. (Renunciation of War) Article 9 of the Japanese Constitution: Aspiring sincerely to an international peace based on justice and order, the Japanese people forever renounce war as a sovereign right of the nation and the threat or use of force as means settling international disputes. (2) In order to accomplish the aim of the preceding paragraph, land, sea, and air forces, as well as other war potential, will never be maintained. The right of belligerency of the state will not be recognized (*Eibun Taiyaku Nihonkoku Kenpou* [English Translation: Japanese Constitution], Tokyo: Chikuma Shobo, 2011, p. 24).

Entry and Impact of Democratization: Successful Peacebuilding and Unsuccessful Democratization?

Internal Problem for Reconciliation and Democratization

It seemed that Cambodian democratization was accelerated by the support of UNTAC and international interventions, however it was not an easy task. One of the biggest problems was the issue of the Khmer Rouge. The Khmer Rouge, which was a group of radical xenophobic communists, committed mass killings during the civil war and around 1.5 to 1.7 million people were killed. Until 1991, the Khmer Rouge was regarded as the only legitimate government by the UN and countries such as China, the United States, Japan and members of ASEAN and participated in the Paris meeting and signed the peace agreement. However, it did not accept the intervention of UNTAC and refused its program, namely the participation in the election, the disarmament and demobilization. The Khmer Rouge continued to fight. After the election, the new government outlawed the Khmer Rouge and it led in turn to an internal power struggle within the group. As a result of the persistent persuasion and negotiation by UNTAC and some countries, half of the Khmer Rouge defected to the national army in 1996 and surrendered themselves to Hun Sen. In 1997, Pol Pot, the former leader of the Khmer Rouge, was arrested and the next year he was dead. He is believed to have been assassinated by other top cadres of the organization.

In the long-term, the conflict in Cambodia and the massacres by the Khmer Rouge were terrible atrocities which must be overcome by the people in Cambodia. The judicial process and reconciliation after the genocide by the Khmer Rouge became an important issue. The government agreed to establish the Extraordinary Chambers in the Courts of Cambodia (ECCC) with the UN and they were called to investigate the case of the massacres by the Khmer Rouge since 2006. The responsible members of the Khmer Rouge were prosecuted for violations of international law, especially for genocide and crimes against humanity and war crimes.

The other hindrance of the progress of democratization is Hun Sen himself, and that became one of the issues of concern among the international community. Hun Sen was one of the members who fled from the Pol Pot group to Vietnam and became a leader after Heng Samrin, and is regarded as a capable politician and charismatic leader. Yasushi Akashi, the head of UNTAC, once called Hun Sen "Cambodian Gorbachev" in his diary (Akashi, 2017, p. 44). Hun Sen played the main role with King Sihanouk (Ishihara, 2017, p. 371) in the reconciliation and democratization process in Cambodia and the first initiative of the Paris Meeting was started by these two men. After the victory against Norodom Ranariddh in 1997, Hun Sen won the elections in 1998 and 2003 and affirmed his authority. The former charismatic King, Sihanouk's death in 2012 brought more power to Hun Sen and CPP too. The monarchy in the country no longer played the same symbolic role and much of its power and prestige dissipated over time. This displacement of a traditional source of power and brokerage in the country naturally favored Hun Sen and his continued consolidation of political power.

While Hun Sen and CPP strengthened their power, the opposition party, the Cambodia National Rescue Party (CNRP), was established in 2012. The party was founded as a merger between the Sam Rainsy Party and Human Rights Party led by Kem Sokha. CNRP made a breakthrough and it got 55 seats (44%) in the election of 2013. Regime change was not possible, because CPP gained 68 seats (48%) at this election, however CNRP showed its ability to become the rival of CPP within a seemingly dualistic competition for power and influence (Sasagawa, 2018, p. 203).

Against the rising popularity of CNRP, Hun Sen and CPP tightened control on the freedom of speech year by year. On July 13, 2015, the National Assembly bulldozed the Law on Associations and Non-Governmental Organizations, which can be used to control the activity of NGOs. In 2017, one year before the general election, CPP escalated its oppression of CNRP. Kem Sokha, who was a member of the National Assembly and the leader of CNRP, was arrested on a charge of treason in September 2017. Many CNRP members and other activists have been arrested or they had to flee from Cambodia to another country, in order to avoid unwarranted arrest. In November 2017, CNRP was forced to dissolve and the members of the party were banned from politics for five years. In the election of 2018, the freedom of journalists was also controlled. Because of the lack of the biggest opposition party CNRP, CPP won an overwhelming victory in the election by default. The international society criticized this undemocratic election and is worried about the regression of Cambodian democratization (Yonekura, 2018; Kumaoka, 2018). The UN is expected to push Cambodia for further democratization, however, as Quinn and Doyle argue, Hun Sen has demonstrated the limits of UN authority, both moral and physical, within the borders he controls. (Quinn & Doyle, 2018, p. 202). Younger Cambodians, and the political opposition, look to the UN as a partner and as a means of protection from the worst excesses of Hun Sen's authoritarian style of government (Quinn & Doyle, 2018, p. 203), and if Hun Sen and the CPP had lost power in the election in 2018, the UN could have supported Cambodian democratization again, but it was not realized.

In addition to these problems related to democracy, the persecution of minorities is a big issue in Cambodia. People from Thailand or Vietnam are often discriminated against and attacked in Cambodia and it is criticized as a violation of human rights (Sato, 1994). Cambodia and Thailand are in rivalry over political and cultural issues such as the Angkor monuments. It is a precarious factor in the stability of the bilateral relationship between these two proximate neighbors. In fact in 2010 and 2012, both countries came close to widespread violent conflict over the control of territory around the Preah Vihear Temple complex (Sasagawa, 2018, pp. 202–203). And it was Indonesia and its charismatic Foreign Minister Marty Natalegawa who interceded and brokered the dispute to prevent its escalation. Control of territory and its defence is an emotional issue in both countries and the fact that both countries are prone to nationalistic rhetoric with the armies deployed across the border makes the situation extremely combustible. Some of the territory that constitutes present day Cambodia were actually ceded by Thailand through the Anglo-French Treaty of 1896 in order for the country to retain its sovereignty when coping with aggressive British and French colonial occupation of the wider region in mainland Southeast Asia.

External Problem for Democratization in Cambodia: Influence of China and Conflict Between Japan and China

After its recent economic development, China became the strongest financial supporters of Cambodia and with this support (Uemura, 2018). Cambodia is one of the important countries for the Chinese Belt and Road Initiative (BRI), which is a strategy to develop Chinese infrastructure and investment from East Asia to Europe and beyond as well as to strengthen Chinese influence in the world (Toyo Keizai, 2018b). Recently, many Chinese enterprises have made inroads into Phnom Penh, notwithstanding opposition by other countries like the United States. China does not demand democratization as a precondition of its support and its aid and investment policies have traditionally been decoupled from conditionalities unlike that of most Western countries that require the observation of fundamental human liberties and a democratic political regime. The EU criticized Hun Sen and the results of the general election held in July 2018, however he ignored his international critics and remained secure with significant Chinese financial support. Unlike the EU, Japan has continued its monetary support after the election. The aim of the Japanese government is the stabilization of Cambodia, not just democratization, and that position is criticized by Japanese NGO activists and politicians (Toyo Keizai, 2018a; Fujita, 2018; Takahashi, 2018). This issue is viewed as problematic not only for Cambodian democratization but also for peace and democracy in Asia in general.

The case of democratization in Cambodia and the involvement of China and Japan show how difficult it is to realize peace and democracy in Asian countries. Authoritarian politics are more powerful in Asian countries than in Europe, democracy can easily become authoritarian, which is what happened in Germany in 1933. Until now, the UN tried to strengthen the democratic governance following European model of democracy, rules of law and the plural party system in countries which were established after conflict or civil war (Hasegawa, 2018, p. 205). Culturally, it is regarded as the heritage of Greek democracy, Roman laws, and the concept of human rights which were developed through the experience of the French Revolution as well as the discussions on peace and humanity after the Nazi holocaust against the Jews. The Cambodian case shows that even if such a system is introduced, it is perhaps difficult to realize democracy without the relevant cultural roots and regular nourishment and support for such values and attendant institutions to propagate them. Additionally, the seeming conflation of state security with regime security and in particular the security of leading politicians of these regimes has also posed problems in the introduction of universal norms modeled after Western experiences.

Recently, it has been pointed out that European countries have lost their interest in PKO (Ishizuka, 2017, p. 176). The race for Cambodia between China and Japan without the surveillance of Europe has led to a struggle for supremacy in Asia in general. Today, Europe has many problems with democracy in its own countries, and therefore, it is quite difficult for European countries to think about Asian peace and democratization. Consequently, we need to reconsider whether peace and democratization in the sense of the Western European consensus can remain as the global standard.

Conclusion: Contributions from the Case Study on Cambodia

This chapter on peace, pacifism and peacekeeping as it applied to Cambodia shows that "peace" is still quite a vague concept. In the nineteenth century, when peace movements such as civic movements began in Europe (at first in the Anglo-Saxon countries), "peace" simply meant "the absence of war" and "war" simply meant conflict between countries. This early operational definition has changed in the twentieth century such that peace now means freedom from violence, fear and danger, it also includes democracy and humanity. It can be argued that this broader concept of positive peace has been developed in the modern history of Europe with the Enlightenment, the French Revolution, socialist movements, two World Wars and the discussion on human rights and humanity after the German holocaust. Even though every culture in the world has a word for peace from ancient times, the concept of "peace" and especially "peacekeeping," which we now use in international politics, reflects the European experience and concepts derived from it. The peacekeeping operations by the UN in the Asian and African regions may bring an end to violent conflicts, however it is often very difficult to bring peace in its broader meaning (democratization, liberalism, etc.) in other areas. This effort continues to be an ongoing process in countries like Indonesia while it is regressing in other countries like Thailand. Strong cultural norms and practices and locally unique conditions appear to play a role in the onset of peace in the broader sense. Structural norms and leadership considerations are also crucial for the establishment and sustenance of evolving democratic ideals.

We find the same problem with the "peace" achieved in Cambodia. Did peace really come to Cambodia? What are the other consequences of UNTAC and the peacebuilding process by the international community other than the procedural elections in the formation of government? The overthrow of the genocidal the Khmer Rouge regime is regarded as "peace" in the primary original meaning, in other words, the absence of war. The peacekeeping process of UNTAC has been evaluated in various ways from negative, "qualified" positive to positive (Ishizuka, 2009; Peou, 2017; Quinn & Doyle, 2018). The democratization in Cambodia has developed as far as it was expected to go. As a result of the civil war after the first election in 1993, Hun Sen was elected as Prime Minister and he still holds that appointment. According to one survey conducted in 2004, only 30% of the Cambodian people assessed UNTAC positively (Ishizuka, 2009, p. 197).[5] As demonstrated in this chapter, the Hun Sen government suppressed journalism and the freedom of speech in the general election in 2018. Corruption in politics and the gap between the rich and the poor are problematic issues in Cambodia. Have we ended one civil war only to facilitate the emergence of an authoritarian government as its replacement?

---

[5]Originally in: *Japanese Ministry for Foreign Affairs, Prevention of Conflicts: The Reality and Future*, March 2005.

The success and failure of UNTAC influenced the other UN missions. Katsumi Ishizuka pointed out that the UN mission failed to bring democratization to Timor-Leste and one of the reasons for this failure is that the lessons of peacebuilding in Cambodia were not applied (Ishizuka, 2009). Timor-Leste, which was a Portuguese colony, was invaded by Indonesia in 1975 and was forced to be under the effective control of the Indonesian government. Its President Suharto oppressed the people in Timor-Leste, it especially targeted and killed participants in the independence movement. The military authoritarian government dealt with insurgency and separatist movements through military force just like in Aceh and Papua as well. However, when the Suharto regime collapsed due to the democratization of Indonesia in 1998 that was in turn triggered by the Asian financial crisis the year before, his successor, B. J. Habibie opted for a referendum on independence for East Timor. The agreement for the referendum was signed by Timor-Leste, Portugal, Indonesia and the UN and following this agreement, the United Nations Mission in East Timor (UNAMET) was established. After the referendum, the United Nations Transitional Administration in East Timor (UNTAET) was organized in 1999 in order to facilitate the independence and the construction of the structure of governance thereafter. On May 20, 2002, Timor-Leste declared its independence as the first independent state in the twenty-first century (Ministry of Foreign Affairs of Japan, 2009). UNTAET ended its mission and the United Nations Mission of Support to East Timor (UNMISET) was established for further support for Timor-Leste in order to facilitate the new country's transition into independence. It seemed that the governance and security of Timor-Leste became stable with the peaceful election in 2007. However, in February 2008, both President Jose Ramos-Horta and the Prime Minister Xanana Gusmao were attacked by rebel soldiers. This was regarded as the failure of the democratization by the UN mission. Ishizuka explained the four lessons which should be learnt from UNTAC and the failure of the Cambodian democratization referring to the research by Trevor Findlay, Lise Howard, Michael Doyle and James Schear. According to Ishizuka, the first lesson is on rapid deployment and preparedness. The rivalry over the leadership of Cambodia's peace process between France and Australia, the delay of logistics preparation, the difficulty in managing UNTAC in addition to two other UN operations in Somalia and Yugoslavia, and the subsequent slow procedures for deciding budgets for UNTAC resulted in UNTAC's late deployment. UNTAC lost the proper momentum for effective operations and that was one of the biggest flaws of the Cambodian mission. The second lesson to be learnt is the difficulty for UN peace operations to ensure a sufficiently neutral political environment for the election. The third lesson is the significance of civilian components including civil police in peacekeeping and transitional missions. The fourth lesson is the so-called "exit strategy," UNTAC is criticized for its early withdrawal from Cambodia (Ishizuka, 2009, pp. 201–203). The UN mission in Timor-Leste should have learnt these lessons. Ishizuka suggested a learning curve from the Cambodian case as follows:

> UN peace-building will not be successful even if it is financially and physically improved, unless it learns lessons from previous missions. However, it is not enough. Peace-building is a more

> human-related mission than traditional peacekeeping. Such a mission should pay more attention to the cultural aspect of indigenous people in host governments. UN culture should also be reconsidered if it does not meet the demand for current post-conflict peace-building. (Ishizuka, 2009, p. 217)

What brings peace and peacebuilding to Asian democracies? It is an important case not only for Cambodia and Timor-Leste, but also other countries such as Myanmar. The reconciliation process in Cambodia is still ongoing. As well as the reconciliation, the democratization of Cambodia must be developed by educating people in order to let them learn about human rights and positive peace. Only then can positive peace be nourished in a sustained manner so that it becomes a permanent feature of political reform with attendant structural changes and habits.

There were many conflicts in the twentieth and twenty-first centuries and these conflicts were very often untouched by the international community under the guise of self-determination and non-intervention. The end of the Cold War made the new interventionism possible since basic agreement has been reached on the need of governments to provide and protect its citizens (Mizumoto, 2003b, p. 179). Additionally, the international community led by the UN has become galvanized to legally authorize such interventions. A similar situation involved Japan and its discussion on "proactive pacifism." However, many scholars have pointed out that interventionism leads to standardization or Westernization by the UN and great powers. Ishizuka wrote

> The UN, which has been highly influenced by western culture, regarded free and fair elections and referenda as a significant stepping stone to democracy, whereas such elections and referenda were traditionally nonexistent and culturally new for host governments. Furthermore, many states which accept post-conflict peace-building led by the UN have culturally gained their governing position through violently overthrowing an oppressive predecessor. (Ishizuka, 2009, p. 217)

In the Cambodian case, the UN and UNTAC could contribute to the end of the war, but they could not bring peace in the broader sense of the word. In this regard, for true peace to obtain it must have an enduring quality for which structural changes and procedural norms are necessary to create a positive environment and conducive culture.

References

Akashi, Y. (2017). *Kanbojia PKO nikki. 1991nen 12gatsu – 1993nen 9gatsu [My Cambodian PKO diary: 1991.12-1993.9]*. Tokyo: Iwanami Shoten.

Chino, K. (2018). *Sengo kokusai chitsujono owari [The End of the postwar international order]*. Tokyo: Rengo Shuppan.

Fujita, Y. (2018, September). Kanbojia – Minshushugi no shi [Cambodia: Death of democracy]. *Masukomi shimin, 596*, 56–59.

Hasegawa, S. (2018). *Kokuren heiwa kouchiku Funsou no nai sekai wo kizuku tameni naniga hitsuyou ka [UN Peacebuilding: What we need for constructing a world without conflict]*. Tokyo: Nihon Hyoron Sha.

Imagawa, Y. (2000). *Kanbojia to nihon [Cambodia and Japan]*. Tokyo: Rengo Shuppan.

Ishihara, N. (2017). "Kaisetsu" [Commentary on the Diary of Yasushi Akashi]. In A. Yasushi (Ed.), *Kanbojia PKO Nikki. 1991nen 12gatsu – 1993nen 9gatsu [My Cambodian PKO diary: 1991.12-1993.9]* (pp. 369–378). Tokyo: Iwanami Shoten.

Ishizuka, K. (2009). A comparative analysis on UN peace-building. *Kyoei Daigaku Kenkyu Ronshu [Journal of Kyoei University], 7*, 195–221.

Ishizuka, K. (2017). *Ke-su de manabu kokuren heiwa iji katsudou. PKO no konnan to chousen no rekishi [The United Nations Peacekeeping Operations]*. Tokyo: Souseisha.

Kimura, A. (2017, October). "Kanbojia wa chugoku ni kawareta noka" [How China "buys" Cambodia]. *Kaigai Jijo [Journal of World Affairs], 65*(10), 49–59.

Kumaoka, M. (2018, March). Kanbojia de naniga okite irunoka [What is happening in Cambodia?]. *Sekai Nippo*. Retrieved from http://www.worldtimes.co.jp/

Llewelyn, J., Walton, D., & Kikkawa, G. (2009). *A pacifist state in a hostile region: Japan and post-war conflict in Southeast Asia*. New York, NY: Nova Science Publishers, Inc.

Makita, M. (2018). *Funsou shuketsu gono Kanbojia. Kokugun jotai heishi to shakai saitougou [Cambodia after the end of the conflict: Demobilized soldiers of the armed forces and social reintegration]*. Tokyo: Sekai Shiso Sha.

Ministry of Foreign Affairs of Japan. (2008, August 5). Japan's support for the democratization of the general election in Cambodia. *Ministry of Foreign Affairs of Japan*. Retrieved from https://www.mofa.go.jp/mofaj/press/pr/wakaru/topics/vol3/index.html

Ministry of Foreign Affairs of Japan. (2009, April 22). Current status and issues of East Timor, the first independent country in the 21st century. *Ministry of Foreign Affairs of Japan*. Retrieved from https://www.mofa.go.jp/mofaj/press/pr/wakaru/topics/vol36/

Mizumoto, K. (2003a, March). UNTAC kara 10 nen go no Kanbojia – Heiwa kochiku heno kadai [Cambodia, Ten years after UNTAC: Tasks for peace-building]. In Japan Institute of International Affairs (Ed.), Conflict Prevention *(2002 Report commissioned by the Ministry of Foreign Affairs)* (pp. 76–88). Tokyo: Japan Institute of International Affairs.

Mizumoto, K. (2003b). UNTAC no seika to shinsei Kanbojia no kadai [Outcome of UNTAC and Tasks of New Cambodia]. In Hiroshima Peace Institute of Hiroshima City University (Ed.), *Jindo kiki to kokusai kainyu: Heiwa kaifuku no shohosen [Humanitarian crisis and international intervention: Formulae for restoring peace]*. Tokyo: Yushindo.

Osmańczyk, E. J. (2003). *Encyclopedia of the United Nations and International Agreements* (3rd ed., edited and revised by A. Mango). New York, NY: Routledge.

Peou, S. (2017). Peace through Democracy and Justice? Legacies and lessons from the case of Cambodia. *Asian Journal of Peacebuilding, 5*(1), 89–110.

Quinn, F., & Doyle, K. (2018). Cambodia and the United Nations 1980-2000 (and Beyond). In T. O. Smith (Ed.), *Cambodia and the West, 1500-2000* (pp. 177–209). London: Palgrave Macmillan.

Sasagawa, H. (2018). Kambojia – Naisen no kizuato, fukko no meian [Cambodia, Scar of Civil Wars and the Bright and Dark Sides of Reconstruction]. In K. Shimizu,

K. Tamura, & T. Yokoyama (Eds.), *Tounan Ajia Gendai Seiji Nyumon (Kaiteiban) [Introduction of South East Asian Modern Politics (Revised Edition)]* (pp. 185–208). Kyoto: Minerva Shobo.

Sato, Y. (1994, February). Ajia no jinken koujou wo mezashite. Kanbojia (UNTAC) no keiken kara [Toward the Improvement of Human Rights in Asia: from Experiences in UNTAC]. *Buraku Kaiho, 369*, 38–47.

Sato, Y. (2010, January). 'Ho no shihai' no jirenma. Kanbojia no ho seibi shien no kadai to tenbo [Dilemma of Rule of Law: Tasks and Perspectives of the Support for Law and Development in Cambodia]. *Horitsu Jiho, 82*(1), 11–16.

Takahashi, S. (2018). Interview: Uchikudakareta hitobito no negai. Minshuka shita hazuno Kanbojia de kyofuseiji ga futatabi [Interview: Wish of dejected people. A second reign of terror in Cambodia, the country which appears to have been democratized]. *Manabu, 738*, 6–12.

Toyo Keizai. (2018a, April 3). Garden Editorial. Kanbojia no dokusai wa dorehodo hidoi noka [How terrible is the Cambodian dictatorship?]. *Toyo Keizai.* Retrieved from https://toyokeizai.net/articles/-/214981

Toyo Keizai. (2018b, October 30). Garden Editorial. Nihonjin ga shiranai Kanbojia "Dokusaika" no genjitsu [The reality of the dictatorship in Cambodia, which is unknown to the Japanese people]. *Toyo Keizai.* Retrieved from https://toyokeizai.net/articles/-/246151

Uemura, M. (2018, August). Kanbojia no wahei-minshuka to nihon [Japan and Reconciliation and Democratization in Cambodia]. *Toki no horei, 2056*, 86–90.

Yonekura, Y. (2018, August 10). Tatoeba sekaide ima – Cambodia – Saidai yato fuzai de yoto assho [World News Frontline: Cambodia. Overwhelming Victory of the Ruling Party in the Absence of the Biggest Opposition Party]. *Shukan kinyobi, 1196*, 44–45.

Yamada, H. (2013). "Hito" ga heiwa wo tsukuru. Kanbojia wahei kousho ni okeru nihon no sekkyoku gaikou ["Human beings" building peace. Japanese active diplomacy in the peace negotiations in Cambodia]. In C. Fukutake, A. Horiba, *Genba fi-rudo karano heiwa kouchiku ron [Theory of peacebuilding from the killing fields]* (pp. 19–43). Tokyo: Keiso Shobo.

Chapter 4

Democratization and Its Impact on Ethnic Conflict and Peace in Myanmar

N. Ganesan

Introduction

Ethnic conflict is deeply rooted in Myanmar and owes its origins to the uneven colonization of the country and negative domestic political developments in the post-independence period. Ethnicity and religion as well as majority–minority divides have all contributed to the conflict and made it complex and deeply embedded in the local landscape. The process of democratization that began in the country in 2010 has generally helped to ease ethnic conflict and has resulted in a structured political response to end the conflict. However, this is still very much a work in progress and not all the ethnic armed groups have signed on to the peace process. Fighting continues unabated especially in the northern Shan and Kachin states and the military that controls important ministries is also above parliamentary scrutiny. Hence, there are structural factors associated with the 2008 constitution that have led to the persistence of the conflict as well.

Roots of the Conflict

Ethnic conflict in Myanmar has long and deep historical roots. The country's population has traditionally been heterogeneous like many countries in the wider Southeast Asian region. In fact, the British catalogued a total of 135 ethno-linguistic groups in the country prior to the outbreak of World War II in 1939. This diversity was especially true of the highland areas where many of the ethnic minorities resided. Most of the ethnic groups are broadly from the Tibeto-Burman or Sino-Tai ethnic groups from Yunnan province in China.

British colonization of the country had a strong impact on ethnicity and its politicization. The British who fought three Anglo Burmese Wars to gradually subdue the country opened the country's borders to migration from the Indian sub-continent. In fact, Burma as it was then called was ruled from British India

International Perspectives on Democratization and Peace, 59–73

doi:10.1108/978-1-80043-067-920200004

until 1937 and policy initiatives toward the country were piece meal (Taylor, 2007, p. 70). British colonization had a number of other major consequences. The first of these was the reification of ethnicity and the use of ethnicity for administration and cataloguing of the population. Ethnicity became highly politicized as a result of this policy and the locals have historically regarded themselves as being colonized in the first instance by the British and subsequently by South Asians (Taylor, 2015). The country was also subdivided into seven states that carried the names of the major ethnic groups. However, the British were only able to subdue and colonize the lowland areas that were predominantly home to the dominant Bamar ethnic majority that accounted for some two-thirds of the population. These lowlands that came to be called Ministerial Burma were subjected to direct colonial rule. The highlands that were forested were conveniently avoided owing to the difficult terrain as well as the threat of malaria. Consequently, the colonial authorities generally signed peace treaties with the highlanders in order to contain them, and they were subjected to the more indirect "frontier areas administration." However, many highlanders like the Chin and the Kachin in particular were recruited into the Burma Army given the British preference for martial races that were deemed more hardy and fit for soldiering. What this policy effectively meant was that large units of the Burma Army had ethnic battalions rather than general troops. And from early on the majority lowland Bamar tended to look down on the highlanders and viewed them as inferior inhabitants who were culturally and developmentally backward. This led in turn to a majority–minority divide that later became ensconced in the post-independence period. And since political power was generally wielded by this majority, the minorities felt a deep sense of suppression and resentment.

The British distrusted the Bamar ethnic group as well since many of the early military recruits and elite were trained by the Japanese and fought against the British. This was certainly true of the Thirty Comrades including General Aung San who led them. The distrust became stronger on account of recruiting soldiers from the highland minorities who were regarded as more trust worthy and physically able. After the War when the British announced a policy of withdrawing from colonized areas in acknowledgement of their shrinking empire Aung San convened the Panglong Conference in 1947. This meeting sought to bring the highlands and ethnic minorities into a workable union in the post-independence period given the geographical and structural fragmentation that existed. The terms of reference at the Conference that was attended by elite representatives of the major minority groups were accommodative and liberal. Aung San promised the possibility of secession from the union if untoward developments occurred for some of the groups to break away from the union. Unfortunately for him though, he was assassinated prior to actual independence in 1948. The country's political situation then became much more divisive and polarized especially when Bamar ethnicity was combined with Buddhism as part of a new and more powerful identity. This new identity also meant greater alienation for non-Buddhists many of who were highlanders.

In the post-independence period when parliamentary rule was practiced, the country's politics began to deteriorate and ethnicity and religion became major issues for political mobilization. By the 1950s, the U Nu government began taking sides with the Bamar-Buddhist majority and the ethnic minorities became disenfranchized. Territorial and administrative consolidation of the country was already weak since ethnic militia controlled many of the highland areas and a Kuomintang army detachment from the Chinese civil war was trapped in the Shan states. China was determined to defeat this army while the United States covertly supported it as part of a broader policy of the containment of communism during the Cold War. Consequently, the political situation deteriorated to the point where the military staged its first coup against the civilian government in 1959 and administered a caretaker government for 18 months before returning power to the civilian government. Then citing a continuing deteriorating situation, Ne Win staged the second coup in 1962 and imposed a military authoritarian regime on the country that lasted until 1988. Hallmarks of the military government were the adoption of a radical socialist model for the economy and the nationalization of industries (Tin, 2007, pp. 114–115). This development led in turn to the flight of both capital and trained professionals from the country further worsening the situation. Additionally, the government also practiced a foreign policy of passive neutrality obtained through isolationism. Political power and control of the country was practiced through the Burma Socialist Programme Party (BSPP) that was formed in 1963.

The collapse of the military authoritarian BSPP government in 1988 coincided with a number of other developments that led in turn to a historical conjuncture with path dependent trajectories for future developments. The first of these was a student-led protest movement clamoring for democracy. The transitional government initially tolerated the protests before subduing it violently leading to some 3,000 deaths (Kyaw Yin Hlaing, 2013, pp. 242–243). It was also at this time when Aung San Suu Kyi returned to Burma in order to care for her ailing mother. She would be viewed as an icon of democracy by activists in the country and went on to form the National League for Democracy (NLD) and compete in the 1990 elections. She won an overwhelming victory that was however not acknowledged by the military. Separately, in 1989, the Burma Communist Party (BCP) collapsed and led to the formation of two newer large ethnic armed groups in the United Wa State Army (UWSA) and the Myanmar National Democratic Alliance Army (MNDAA – Kokang). Both these groups were the sword arms of the BCP and ethnically Chinese as well. In order to contain the new situation, the government began to sign bilateral ceasefire agreements with the ethnic armed groups (Steinberg, 2001). These agreements were on liberal terms that included control of a contiguous geographical area, the retention of arms and a requirement for the military to serve advance notice when entering such designated safe areas.

Previous Attempts to Resolve the Conflict

The earliest attempts to resolve the ethnic conflicts coincided with the collapse of the BSPP government, student-led uprisings for democracy and Aung San Suu Kyi's return to Myanmar. During this turbulent period of political transition, the military government simply thought that it would be prudent to stabilize the domestic political situation and conserve state resources to deal with all the internal challenges. In a sense, it was a way to stave off the problem to be dealt with more comprehensively in the future. Hence, beginning with the two early bilateral ceasefire agreements, the military government went on to consolidate the process by signing another 14 such agreements to bring the total to 16 arrangements and these agreements included almost all the major ethnic armed groups. The last three groups to sign such ceasefires were the Karen National Union (KNU), Chin National Front and the Karenni National Progressive Party (KNPP) in February 2012 (Ganesan, 2015). The early leading architect of these arrangements was General Khin Nyunt who was head of Military Intelligence and Prime Minister before he was abruptly removed from power in October 2004. The process however continued under the leadership of the military government that was headed by General Than Shwe.

There were a number of other domestic and international political developments that affected Myanmar during this period. The first of these were the national elections won by the NLD that were ignored. Secondly, beginning from the 1990s, the military junta began to arrest large numbers of members of opposition political parties and political dissidents. The annulment of the elections and the violent suppression of the student movement led in turn to a surge of anti-government sentiments and also strengthened the ethnic armed groups that often-provided sanctuary for some of the exiles along the border areas. And from 1994, the Than Shwe government announced the onset of a roadmap to democracy that led to national conventions that sought to engage the ethnic groups. These meetings led in turn to the 2008 Constitution that the government proclaimed was ratified by a hastily concluded referendum in December and in the aftermath of Cyclone Nargis that claimed about 130,000 lives earlier that year. Internally, Suu Kyi was often placed under house arrest especially after the Depayin incident in June 2003 that led to violence against her political supporters by local militia groups. The detention of large numbers of members of the political opposition and dissidents led to a wide-ranging sanctions regime that was imposed by the international community. Consequently, the military authoritarian regime that was in power until 2009 lacked both domestic and international political legitimacy.

The government then decided to hold a national election based on the 2008 Constitution and the military leaders who were in power until then stood down from their official leadership of the country. The election was won by the Union Solidarity and Development Party (USDP) that was supported by the military and had morphed from the corporatist peak labor organization, the Union Solidarity and Development Association. Leading opposition parties boycotted the elections and the USDP won handsomely in the election. The newly formed government was helmed by a large number of high-ranking military officers who traded their uniforms for civilian garb and became ministers in the new government led by President Thein Sein. He undertook a slew of liberal reforms that included broad based amnesty for members of the political opposition and exiles and introduced a much more liberal political climate. And in exchange for these positive developments in the country, the international community slowly began to disband the sanctions regime (Ganesan, 2013).

In 2012, the new government allowed Suu Kyi to register the NLD for the April by-elections and the NLD then secured 43 out of the 45 seats that it contested making it the leading opposition party in parliament and setting the stage for the NLD's overwhelming victory in the 2015 November election that paved the way for it to form a new government and lead parliament from April 2016. A clause in the 2008 Constitution prohibits locals with spouses or children holding foreign citizenship from occupying the office of the President. In order to bypass this quirk and lead the party and parliament the position of State Counselor was created and Suu Kyi currently exercises power through that office. Her confidant Htin Kyaw was appointed as the first President and his successor and current President is Win Myint. The 2008 Constitution allows for the military to appropriate 25 per cent of all seats in state and regional parliaments as well as the federal government in Naypyitaw. Additionally, the military is not subjected to parliamentary scrutiny and also controls the Ministries of the Interior, Border Areas and Defence. Consequently, there are provisions within the 2008 Constitution that structurally empowers the military and protects its independent standing within the country. In fact, there is even a proviso for the military to take power from an elected civilian government should it think such action necessary to safeguard the national interest (Taylor, 2009, pp. 489–499). In this regard, the military views itself as being above politics and a national institution that protects the best interests of the state and its citizens.

It was the Thein Sein government that continued the process of attempting to broker a more long lasting and structured peace agreement with the ethnic armed groups. Invoking executive powers the new government established the Myanmar Peace Center (MPC) in October 2012 to centralize the peace process (Ganesan, 2014). The government aimed to legitimize the bilateral arrangement at the regional and state levels in the first instance and then convene a Nationwide Ceasefire Agreement (NCA) that would include all the 16 ethnic armed groups that it had been dealing with. It however refused to deal with newer groups and organizations that did not have standing armies. Eventually, the government persuaded 8 out of the 16 armed groups to sign on to the NCA in October 2015 just before it turned over power to the new NLD-led government. This was done with great fanfare in the capital Naypyitaw and in the presence of international dignitaries that included United Nations Secretary General Ban Ki Moon. The KNU was the largest armed group among the signatories. The non-signatories were collectively grouped in the United Nationalities Federal Council (UNFC) although the largest armed group, the UWSA, remained aloof from all these developments arguing that its early bilateral ceasefire agreement was working well and no further agreements were needed. Hence structurally, it was a bipolar situation for the most part although the bilateral agreement with another large armed group, the Kachin Independence Organization/Army (KIO/KIA) collapsed in June 2011 leading to renewed fighting in the northern state.

There were three other armed groups that the military refused to recognize and sign bilateral agreements with. This was partly because they were of recent vintage but also because they had brazenly attacked the northern towns of Laukkaing in March 2015 (Myanmar National Democratic Alliance Army – MNDAA) and Muse (KIA, Arakan Army (AA) and MNDAA) in October 2016. Shortly afterwards in December 2016, all of these groups and the UWSA announced the formation of the Northern Alliance and their withdrawal from the UNFC. This new organization was led by the UWSA and announced its disagreement with the terms of the NCA as constituted and called for a new dialogue process. And in the meantime, both the signatories and non-signatories of the NCA regularly consulted on their policy positions going forward and such meetings were typically held in Chiangmai in Thailand.

When the new NLD government came into power it recalibrated the peace process. It formed a new National Reconciliation and Peace Center (NRPC) and moved the office from Yangon to Naypyitaw. It then appointed Dr Tin Myo Win, Suu Kyi's personal physician and confidant as the new government's interlocutor and began a new series of meeting called the twenty-first Century Panglong Conference, harkening to the meeting held by General Aung San with the ethnic leaders in 1947 (Ganesan, 2018). Naturally, this initiative carried both promise and peril since the ethnic groups revisited the liberal terms offered earlier including the possibility of secession from the Union and a federal system that guaranteed freedom and equality to all. Since the new government was sworn into power, three such meetings have taken place and although the stated intention of the government is to hold two such meetings each year at 6 months interval there have been inevitable delays. The government's publicly stated goal is to be able to wrap up the process of national reconciliation with the ethnic armed groups by 2020 when its current term expires. Additionally, the government is also hoping to revise the 2008 Constitution in tandem with the peace talks in order to move the process forward as part of a broader national agenda. The military however does not appear enthused with this idea and has indicated in no uncertain terms that the 2008 Constitution and territoriality are sacrosanct. The latter assertion is meant to preclude the possibility of secession from the Union. The other sticking point since the third such meeting in July 2018 is over the creation of a national army and how to integrate the ethnic militias into it. While the ethnic armed groups are interested in what they have called security sector reforms the military has been pushing for disarmament, demobilization, and reintegration.

Finally, in order to underline the importance of ethnicity for the new government, a new Ministry of Ethnic Affairs was created even though the total number of ministries was reduced from 33 to 22. Importantly, the new Minister for Ethnic Affairs is always a member of the ethnic minority from the state or region. And since the 2008 Constitution privileges the central government in the appointment of Chief Ministers, the NLD government has been able to nominate such appointees even in the states where it did not secure a majority in the local legislature. And this was the case with Shan and Rakhine states where home-based ethnic parties defeated the NLD in the state legislatures. The hope of the government is that such structural reforms will allow it to place ethnicity as an important national issue for structural attention and also to try and win the support of the ethnic minorities for its more holistic approach to governance. As of now, ethnic political parties rather than the USDP which is allied with the military pose a greater electoral challenge to the NLD. And the military is not only allied with the USDP but also often has a position that is independent of the government. Recent statements from the ethnic armed leaders appear to suggest that it is the military that is intransigent in the dialogue process and seems to want to gain the upper hand. The government is viewed as powerless to go against the position of the military although Suu Kyi has publicly noted that she hopes to persuade the military to introduce changes to the constitution.

External Linkages to the Conflict and Peace Process

There has always been an external dimension to the ethnic conflict and related peace process in Myanmar. The earliest external linkages for the ethnic armed groups were the countries that were proximate to where they were located. And many of these groups were located in areas well beyond government control and often in rugged terrain bordering neighboring countries. The northern armed groups like the Wa, Kokang Shan and Kachin groups have always maintained linkages with China (Ganesan, 2017a). Given the fact that some of these groups have been in existence for almost six decades many of them have also evolved their own political and economic arrangements. Such arrangements often included harvesting the country's abundance of natural resources like jade, gold, amber, and teak. Many of these products found ready markets in nearby countries like China and Thailand. And the location of these groups also meant that cross border linkages were established early on.

Hence, groups like the Shan State Army-South (SSA-S) and the KNU were located close to the Thai–Myanmar border and the groups from Nagaland and Chin state often operated across the border in India as well. In fact, previous Thai governments that pursued a buffer policy against Myanmar given the historical animosity between the two countries were known to support the KNU and the SSA-S (Chachavalpongpun, 2005; Ganesan, 2010, pp. 17–18; Maung Aung Myoe, 2002). The fighting between government troops and these armies also meant that there were a large number of ethnic refugees across the border in Thailand. In fact until today in 2019, there are more than 90,000 Myanmar refugees in Thailand most of whom have Karen ethnicity and have lived in refugee camps for decades in Mae Hong Son and Tak provinces across the border. Many of them were displaced when the military fought pitched battles with the KNU before seizing their major bases of Kawmoora and Manerplaw along the Thai–Myanmar border between 1993 and 1995. While large numbers of them have previously been settled in third countries like Australia, Canada and the United States through the United Nations High Commissioner for Refugees (UNHCR) such countries have been far less willing to accept such refugees since the changes in domestic politics from 2010.

China's linkages with groups like the Wa and the Kokang go back to the days of the BCP and are therefore much more deeply embedded historically. The cultural and ethnic similarities also make these groups identify more with China. And China has stepped up its role in being an intermediary in the peace process as well. The appointment of Senior Envoy for Asian Affairs Sun Guoxiang to mediate the dispute between the Myanmar government and military on the one hand

and the ethnic groups from the Northern Alliance since 2016 is a clear indication of China's not only continued but increasingly growing role in the peace process (Ganesan, 2018). The formalization of the peace process and the creation of the MPC by the Thein Sein government also brought with it more external linkages. The European Union and Norway in particular were leading sponsors and financiers of the peace process from early on. Japan has also made significant contributions through state agencies as well as NGOs like the Nippon Foundation that supports the large number of Internally Displaced Persons (IDPs) in Kachin and Shan states. International organizations like the United Nations and its affiliated agencies have also apportioned a role for themselves in the peace process and maintain an institutional presence in the country.

Both the Thein Sein and Suu Kyi governments have sought to engage the international community in the peace process as stakeholders in order to give the process greater momentum and legitimacy. The ethnic armed groups also prefer the internationalization of the process in the hope that they will be dealt with fairly and in a transparent manner. They are also hopeful that such measures will lead to greater progress and accountability from both the government and the military. In the past and under an isolationist government, the military was able to act at will and away from the prying eyes of the international community. Such gestures by the international community also perform an important legitimating function for the government in power and enhance its prestige both domestically and abroad. The military on the other hand is not always enthused with such internationalization since it places the process under greater scrutiny and reduces its advantageous domestic position in power terms.

In fact that is exactly what happened when the military conducted clearance operations in Rakhine state following the coordinated terrorist attacks by the Arakan Rohingya Solidarity Association in August 2017. The result was the displacement of more than 730,000 Muslims from Rakhine state to Bangladesh where they now languish as refugees. And this development is over and above the 140,000 displaced persons currently held in squalid detention centers following an outbreak of violence against Muslims in Rakhine in 2012. While the United Nations and humanitarian aid agencies have documented widespread and systematic use of violence and torture against the displaced Muslim community in Bangladesh, the military rejects the findings and has exonerated itself based on its own findings. In fact the International Court of Justice (ICJ) ruled in January 2020 that the Myanmar government undertake measures to protect the Rohingya community from genocidal activities. The case was brought against Myanmar by Gambia that represented the Organization of Islamic Cooperation. That decision was also rejected by the Myanmar government albeit Suu Kyi did make a spirited defence for the country at The Hague where the trial took place. Notwithstanding the loss her defence has significantly empowered her politically and may win her greater support in the November 2020 elections. Myanmar has also consistently denied access to UN observers and fact-finding missions and has banned the UN Special Rapporteur on Myanmar Yanghee Lee from visiting the country accusing her of biased reporting. There appears to be little hope of the refugees being repatriated back to Myanmar in the near future given international assessments that Myanmar is unable to guarantee a safe return and living conditions with dignity. In fact, the word Rohingya is forbidden and not used in Myanmar where they are simply and derogatorily referred to as Bengalis with the attendant connotative value that they are illegal immigrants from across the border. There is also the domestic fear that the acceptance of this identity would in turn allow them to make claims based on being one of the original ethnic groups in the country that would then entitle them in turn to benefits afforded to the other groups. The civilian government in Myanmar is also powerless to deal with the military on account of its independence and immunity from parliamentary oversight.

Entry and Impact of Democratization on the Conflict

Democratization has had a positive impact on the ethnic conflict in Myanmar in a number of ways (Ganesan, 2017b). Most importantly, the process has become a structured issue and part of the national agenda. While there have been differences in the approach of the Thein Sen and Suu Kyi led governments on how to engage the groups and structure the process, both elected governments have sought to contain the process and try to resolve it through negotiations. In this regard, the process has been brought into the open and widely publicized. Such publicity creates transparency to the process which was previously shrouded in secrecy and brought it into the public domain. In fact, the NLD-led government publicly announced that the ethnic peace process was the most important agenda item for the government when it took office (Ganesan, 2017c). The appointment of Suu Kyi's confidants to broker the process also indicates a degree of personal involvement and commitment.

A more liberal political environment has also resulted in a broader engagement of ethnicity as an important national issue. The media has access to developments related to the peace process and more recently NGOs and political parties with representatives in parliament have also been included as observers to broaden the process. Another positive development is that the ethnic armed groups themselves have been able to appropriate the positive developments associated with democracy like political contestation and structured representation in local and federal legislatures. Hence, all such groups invariably have a registered political party to compete in the elections as well to take advantage of the process. They therefore pursue a two-pronged approach with an armed group engaged in the protection of their interests and a political party to elect representatives to the regional and federal legislatures. And the inclusion of international sponsors and participants to important achievements in the peace process also leads to positive and independent output to further the process.

Notwithstanding these positive contributions not all the benefits from democratization have been successfully harnessed. And part of the reason for this has to do with the 2008 Constitution that privileges the role of the military in the domestic political process. Since the military is not subjected to parliamentary oversight and does not subscribe to civilian supremacy the government in power often does not have control over the peace process. And this is especially true where active conflict obtains like in Shan and Kachin states. In the most recent development, the military has announced a four months long ceasefire in the northern and northeastern areas in order to move the peace process forward. However, this unilateral ceasefire only obtained after the KNU withdrew from participation in the peace process in October citing a lack of progress. Since the KNU served to anchor the peace process as the largest armed group to sign the NCA, there was a very real sense that the process itself was becoming untenable. The Revolutionary Council of the Shan States (RCSS) was another signatory that withdrew from the peace talks. Additionally, the KNPP that had earlier expressed willingness to sign on to the NCA has held back for some years now accusing the military of violence and encroachment into its territory. Consequently, it is arguable that the unilateral ceasefire is simply a way for the military to make the NCA signatories regain confidence in the peace process.

And in the middle of this ceasefire, fighting has now spread to Rakhine state where the AA is trying to establish bases. It has led coordinated assaults against border police posts and also attacked military columns. This group that was previously headquartered in Laiza in Kachin state is a rather new armed group that was nourished and supported by the KIA. As a result of this background and its attempts to eke out new territory to control, the military has engaged the group robustly. After its coordinated attacks against police posts in January 2019 that left 14 policemen dead, even the government has called for the group to be crushed. Hence, a new theater of conflict has now opened up in the west where the local Rakhine Buddhist community already has deep seated hatred for the Bamar majority that it holds responsible for its suppression and underdevelopment.

Attempts to revise the constitution that favors the military by the government can easily be thwarted since such revision requires a super majority of 75 per cent of votes in parliament. And with 25 per cent of the seats being held by the military that typically votes as a bloc, such a prospect does not appear to be forthcoming. Additionally, control of the three important ministries that are involved with control over territory and administration of it are also controlled by the military. Consequently, it is arguable that the government is presented with some serious structural hurdles in its attempts to broker peace.

Conflict Transformation from Democratization

There appears to be some limited amount of transformation of the ethnic conflict in Myanmar. In the past, most of the ethnic armed groups were generally friendly toward each other since they all had common grievances against the military government in power. Consequently, they often helped each other and found common causes to bind themselves together as well. And some of these sentiments continue to linger on. So for example, the original two groups among the signatories and the non-signatories and the manner in which they were clustered around common goals and aspirations suggested such sentiments. Similarly, the Northern Alliance that was formed in late 2016 has also held a common position during negotiations and refuses to be dealt with on a bilateral basis. While strategically it makes sense from the point of having a common platform in its dealings with the government and the military there appears to be shared sentiments among the groups. In fact, they have insisted and held to this collective position which has recently borne fruit since the military has in 2019 agreed to deal with the Northern Alliance as a group after informal meetings in China (Nan Lwin Hnin Pyint, 2019). Additionally, it is noteworthy that both the signatories and the non-signatories have always consulted with each other and tried to present a common front regardless of their structural situation with the military and the government. Such meetings are normally held in Chiangmai, Thailand where many of the groups had their representatives in the past. Government negotiators from the NRPC often engage these groups in Thailand informally in order to suss out the situation prior to formal talks in Naypyitaw. And this informal mechanism is sometimes referred to as the Bangkok Process. The Northern Alliance tends to do this either in Panghsang in Wa state or Kunming in China which is easily accessible to groups operating in the Shan and Kachin states in the north. Such talks often involve Chinese officials and interlocutors as well.

Notwithstanding this general understanding and camaraderie among the ethnic armed groups it should be noted that fighting has broken out among themselves as well. Such fighting has occurred between signatory groups among themselves as well as between signatory and non-signatory groups. So for example there have been numerous clashes between the RCSS and the Ta'ang National Liberation Army (TNLA) that represents the Palaung ethnic group. And more recently the RCSS also had skirmishes with the Pa O National Organization. Such conflicts are typically over control of territory and unannounced troop movements. The problem is complicated by the fact that different ethnic groups often cohabit in a particular area leading to contested claims for control. In fact prior to and shortly after independence the Burmese Army had ethnic battalions owing to the British preference for highlanders who were regarded more hardy and physically stronger. Hence in the early years after independence for example, the government used the Kachin Rifles against the KNU when they almost seized power in Rangoon. Similarly, the Kachin and Chin Rifles were used in engagements against the stranded Kuomintang Army and the BCP. Hence there is a history of the state using different ethnic groups against each other leading to a measure of general solidarity among the ethnic armed groups against the Bamar majority and the military.

It should also be noted that the violence against Muslims in Rakhine state is an old and historical issue that has little to do with the domestic ethnic armed groups. This fight is essentially against what the locals and in particular the Buddhist Rakhines consider illegal immigrants from neighboring Bangladesh. And since Rakhine state is extremely poor such tensions are exaggerated. Previous governments and the military have been involved in violence against the Muslims and this conflict is also ethno-religious in nature and can draw on extremist Buddhist sentiments within the country and the monastic order. The second angle to this conflict is that Rakhine ethnics do not regard the Bamar majority favorably as well since the state was home to an ancient kingdom that was destroyed by the Burmese. And it is for this reason that Rakhine political parties drawing on regionally anchored sentiments and loyalties are able to easily defeat the NLD in state elections. And there appears to be some measure of local support for the AA that is currently seeking a foothold in the state as previously mentioned (Lawi Weng, 2019). In fact, the AA has thus far made the most audacious call in expressing a political preference for a confederation-styled arrangement rather than a federal state – a demand that was swiftly rejected by the military (Nyein Nyein, 2019). And different and competing conceptions of what constitutes federalism is another major sticking point between the military and the ethnic armed groups. While the military views it as way of maintaining territoriality and sovereignty in the traditional Westphalian sense for the ethnic armed groups it is a way of formalizing areas under their control including the right to a private army. In fact even the signatories to the NCA have thus far not agreed to the disbandment of their armies which they regard as necessary insurance against a predatory Bamar majority and a hostile military that is keen to usurp territorial control over ethnic areas and appropriate its natural resources.

Contributions from the Myanmar Case Study

The Myanmar case study offers many interesting lessons with regard to how the process of democratization can move a peace process forward. The most important lesson is that democratization allows for a centralized and structured response to the peace process. It is able to directly engage with the stakeholders and involve them in efforts to broker peace. The state is able to draw on public resources and personnel in order to entrench, establish a measure of ownership of the process, and ensure its continuity. Importantly, state-sponsored attempts to broker peace also helps to raise the international profile of the conflict and peace process and draw international goodwill and sponsorship for the process. These domestic and international efforts can enhance the political legitimacy of the government and earn it much goodwill and recognition. Nonetheless, democratization itself cannot bring about peace and the willingness of the concerned parties is important in order to move the process forward.

During the last three years when the NLD-led government has been in power, the levels of political violence has spiked considerably. And there are a number of reasons for this development some of which are related to democratization and some others not. The military's decision to aggressively engage the smaller groups like the MNDAA, TNLA, and AA that have brazenly attacked it and border towns close to China is part of the reason. The military's attempts to take control of resource rich areas in Kachin state previously controlled by the KIA is another reason for the uptick in fighting. And finally, the recent attempts by the AA to secure a foothold in Rakhine state has also led to heavy fighting and the displacement of some 100,000 civilians. And while the government genuinely works toward peace the military remains in control of conflict zones and border areas. As a result of such de facto control, the government is often unable to control the process at the ground level.

Democratization also has the potential to aggregate differences and sharpen distinctions between groups. Under the previous military authoritarian government, there was harsh suppression of civil liberties including freedom of speech and association. However, many of these structural impediments were removed after 2010 leading to greater articulation of not just differences but also animosity between groups. This is most marked in the aggregation of extremist Buddhist rhetoric against the Muslim minority in the country. In this regard, democratization does not necessarily offer a consistently positive trajectory in the resolution of differences and may in fact bring it into sharper focus especially during political contestation. Owing to such developments, ethnic political parties offer stiff resistance to the NLD and as mentioned earlier such parties control the local legislature in Rakhine and Shan states. This development and the ability of the central government to appoint a chief minister in the state regardless of its local electoral performance have also exaggerated differentials. There is the widespread perception in these states that the central government tries to control and oppress the ethnic minorities even after losing in the local elections. And with ethnic groups now pushing for greater political consolidation in order to gain greater coordination and leverage in the 2020 elections ethnicity continues to be deeply politicized. Additionally, such politicization thwarts the democratic spirit of resolving differences peacefully.

Like all configurative case studies, the Myanmar case is unique unto itself as well confirming the theoretical tradeoffs between specificity and generalizability in the study of comparative politics. The large number of ethnic armed groups fighting against the government and the deeply embedded nature and length of the conflict makes it unique and difficult to draw parallels with other countries. It also makes the situation much less amenable to resolution given the splintered nature of the process and large number of actors. Agreement from many actors is simply that much more difficult to obtain. While democratization has consolidated and started the peace process, it is by no means certain to be able to bring an end to the conflict. And even if the current or future government succeeds in doing so it will take a long time to succeed. The narrowing of differences between the government and the military on the one hand and the ethnic groups on the other is the most important requirement going forward in order for strategic convergence of interests to obtain. And the independence of the military and its structural claims to power also make a common position even on the government's side that much more difficult. The long tradition of isolationism since the 1960s also makes political elite and the military suspicious about the intentions of even well-meaning external efforts at mediation. And interestingly, within the broader Southeast Asian region, it is military strongmen turned politicians who have displayed the greatest ability to bring an end to civil wars peacefully. In 1996, Fidel Ramos was the first Philippine President to sign a peace agreement with the Moro National Liberation Front and its leader Nur Misuari. The pact finally fell apart after Nur Misuari's governorship of the Autonomous Region of Muslim Mindanao ended but nonetheless the fact that it was a first agreement and one that worked for five years was in itself a significant achievement then. Similarly, it was Susilo Bambang Yudhoyono in Indonesia who brought an end to the conflict with the *Gerakkan Aceh Merdeka* (GAM – Free Aceh Movement) through political dialogue, disarming and then democratization. GAM successfully transformed itself into a political party, *Parti Aceh,* and then went on to win the elections held in the province in 2005.

And finally, in the case of Myanmar it was President Thein Sein who was the architect of the NCA in October 2015 after consolidating on the earlier bilateral peace agreements. In this regard, the evidence from the ground is counter-intuitive in that ex-military strongmen have had the greatest success in bringing violent regional conflicts to an end using diplomacy and autonomy as tools. Democratization and transformation of the conflict into peaceful contestation was also possible in two of the three cases in Indonesia and the Philippines. In the case of Myanmar where the situation is much more complex, democratization has only met with limited success thus far.

References

Chachavalpongpun, P. (2005). *A plastic nation: The curse of Thainess in Thai-Burmese relations*. Lanham, MA: University of America Press.

Ganesan, N. (2010). Myanmar's foreign policy towards its near neighbours. *International Studies Review*, *11*(1), 1–24.

Ganesan, N. (2013). Interpreting recent developments in Myanmar as an attempt to establish political legitimacy. *Asian Journal of Peacebuilding*, *1*(2), 253–274.

Ganesan, N. (2014). The Myanmar peace center: Its origins, activities, and aspirations. *Asian Journal of Peacebuilding*, *2*(1), 127–141.

Ganesan, N. (2015). Ethnic insurgency and the Nationwide Ceasefire Agreement in Myanmar. *Asian Journal of Peacebuilding*, *3*(2), 273–286.

Ganesan, N. (2017a). Changing dynamics in Myanmar's ethnic peace process and the growing role of China. *Asian Journal of Peacebuilding*, *5*(2), 325–339.

Ganesan, N. (2017b). Democratization and its implications for the resolution of ethnic conflict in Myanmar. *Asian Journal of Peacebuilding*, *5*(1), 111–129.

Ganesan, N. (2017c). Appraising Myanmar's democratic transition and evolving challenges. *Japanese Journal of Political Science*, *18*(1), 196–215.

Ganesan, N. (2018). Taking stock of Myanmar's ethnic peace process and the third twenty-first century Panglong peace conference. *Asian Journal of Peacebuilding*, *6*(2), 379–392.

Ganesan, N., & Kyaw, Y. H. (Eds.). (2007). *Myanmar: State, society and ethnicity*. Singapore: Institute of Southeast Asian Studies.

Ganesan, N., & Kim, S. C., (Eds.). (2013). *State violence in East Asia*. Lexington, KY: University Press of Kentucky.

Kyaw, Y. H. (2013). The four eights democratic movement and political repression in Myanmar. In N. Ganesan & S. C. Kim (Eds.), *State violence in East Asia* (pp. 231–256). Lexington, KY: University Press of Kentucky.

Myoe, M. A. (2002). *Neither friend nor foe: Myanmar's relations with Thailand since 1988*. Singapore: Institute for Defence and Security Studies, Nanyang Technological University.

Nyein, N. (2019, January 18). AA must give up goal of confederation: Myanmar military. *Irrawaddy News*. Retrieved from https://www.irrawaddy.com

Pyint, N. L. H. (2019, February 5). Government agrees to meet Northern Alliance as a Group. *Irrawaddy News*. Retrieved from https://www.irrawaddy.com

Steinberg, D. I. (2001). *Burma: The state of Myanmar*. Georgetown, Washington DC: Georgetown University Press.

Taylor, R. (2007). British policy towards Myanmar and the creation of the 'Burma Problem'. In N. Ganesan & K. Y. Hlaing (Eds.), *Myanmar: State, society and ethnicity* (pp. 70–95). Singapore: Institute of Southeast Asian Studies.

Taylor, R. (2009). *The state in Myanmar*. Honolulu, HI: University of Hawaii Press.

Taylor, R. (2015). *Refighting old battles, compounding misperceptions: The politics of ethnicity in Myanmar today (ISEAS Perspective No. 12)*. Singapore: Institute of Southeast Asian Studies.

Tin, M. M. T. (2007). *State dominance in Myanmar*. Singapore: Institute of Southeast Asian Studies.

Weng, L. (2019, February 12). Many Arakanese embrace AA's presence. *Irrawaddy News*. Retrieved from https://www.irrawaddy.com

Chapter 5

The Peace Process in Sri Lanka: The Challenges for Democracy After Decades of Civil Conflict and Terrorism

Raquel Duque

Introduction

The "pearl of the Indian Ocean," as Sri Lanka is known, went through a long-lasting ethno-political internal conflict between the 1970s and the early 2000s that involved the Tamil minority group and the national government and military. Tamil groups claimed to being marginalized in their social and political rights by the country's successive governments – which were composed mostly of Sinhalese (the main ethnic group) – since the independence of Sri Lanka from the British, in 1948. Among different secessionist groups, the Liberation Tigers of Tamil Eelam (LTTE) became prominent and the violence perpetrated by both the violent groups and the security forces resulted in tens of thousands of victims, internally displaced people and exodus and resettlement in other countries, and massive property damage. The LTTE laid claim to a Tamil State (the Eelam) and fought for the independence of two specific regions of the Sinhalese territory, the North and the East, where most of the Tamil population was (and still is) concentrated. The national authorities fought back to guarantee the unitary state.

The oldest democracy in Asia (DeVotta & Ganguly, 2018) experienced a civil war between 1983 and 2009 with moments of escalation of violence followed by moments of appeasement as well as attempts for a negotiated solution. A ceasefire was finally reached in 2009 with the victory of the government forces over the separatists, allowing the country to enjoy a pacified environment since then.

In 2019, 10 years after the end of hostilities, it is time to write on Sri Lanka. Hence, through a qualitative analysis and using secondary data, this chapter follows the subheadings suggested by the editor and starts by analyzing the roots of the Sri Lankan conflict; then examines the attempts to resolve the conflict; it

International Perspectives on Democratization and Peace, 75–90

doi:10.1108/978-1-80043-067-920200005

investigates the external linkages that influenced the course of the conflict; next it studies the role of democracy in the resolution of this conflict; it highlights the contributions from the Sri Lankan case before some concluding remarks.

The Roots of Sri Lanka's Civil Conflict

Sri Lanka is a semi-presidential republic with approximately 21 million inhabitants, 80 per cent of whom live in rural areas and the remaining 20 per cent live in cities (Peiris & Arasaratnam, 2018). There are a variety of ethnic groups, the largest one is made of Sinhalese, with 15 million people (who are mainly Buddhists), the second biggest group is Tamil[1] with about three million people (who live predominantly in the North and East of the country and are mostly Hindu), and the third main group consists of Muslims who are approximately 1.9 million people (and the majority live in the South-eastern part of the country), the remaining population belong to other ethnic groups of smaller representation (Department of Census and Statistics, 2012).

The Tamils claim to being the target of discrimination since independence from British rule (proclaimed on February 4, 1948) when the new political structures – in order to fully establish an independent, democratic and representative Sri Lanka – were controlled by the Sinhalese (the majority of the population). At the heart of the Tamil criticisms was a set of measures that favored the largest ethnic group at the expense of themselves and other minorities. Some of those measures encompassed (i) the decision to make Sinhala the official language of the country, in the mid-1950s; (ii) the adoption of Buddhism as the national religion; and (iii) changes in higher education that reduced access to Tamils (Ross & Savada, 1988).[2] In turn, the Sinhalese understood these legal changes as the necessary response to the oppression they suffered during British colonial times that benefited the Tamils (Bajoria, 2009).

Throughout the decades of 1950s, 1960s, and 1970s, the Tamil resentment increased and fueled the desire for independence or self-government in the Tamil-dominated areas (of the North and East) which was channeled into the Tamil United Liberation Front (TULF), created in the 1970s (Rotberg, 1999). In 1976, the LTTE emerged from the TULF and in the following decade became the dominant militarized Tamil group among others such as the Tamil Eelam Liberation Organization, the Eelam Revolutionary Organization of Students (EROS) and the Eelam People's Revolutionary Liberation Front.

The LTTE undertook a set of practices that allowed it to survive in open conflict against the military for 26 years, often introducing innovative elements in the landscape of intra-state conflicts, including the use of suicide bombers,

[1]To further understand the origins of Tamil population, see Rathi (2017).

[2]The second and third examples were part of the Constitution of Sri Lanka of 1972, the second constitution since the independence and a fundamental document because it changed the name of the country from Ceylon to Sri Lanka, declaring it a republic and a unicameral National State Assembly.

recruitment of child soldiers and women, and financial support from the Tamil diaspora around the world (International Crisis Group, 2012, p. 3). The insurgents also directed their violence to the assassination of key politicians, such as Jaffna Mayor Alfred Duraiappah in 1975; Indian Prime Minister Rajiv Gandhi in 1991; and President Ranasinghe Premadasa in 1993 (BBC News, 1991). The LTTE came to be considered as a terrorist group by the Sri Lankan authorities and by India, the United States, the European Union, Canada, and other countries. Data collected precisely on the number of terrorist incidents from 1983 and 2009 in Sri Lanka show a total of 1.128 with the death toll higher than 6.000 victims (National Consortium for the Study of Terrorism and Responses to Terrorism (START), 2019). Besides, this group managed to maintain an administrative and institutional organization in the territory it controlled in the North, especially in Mullaitivu and Kilinochchi districts, that was parallel to the one of the central state (International Crisis Group, 2012, p. 3).

The more intense the LTTE violence the more assertive the response was from the government with the passage of laws to strengthen the country's security. A clear example of this occurred in 1971, when the state of emergency declared to deal with the Sinhalese Marxist–Leninist youth movements served not only to respond at that moment to the Tamil separatists but also to maintain that state of exception for six consecutive years (Tambiah, 1986, p. 14). Another example was the approval of the Prevention of Terrorism Act (1979) that extended powers to the level of detention until 18 months without resort to judicial review or without access to relatives or lawyers which had an initial duration of three years but in March 1982 was permanently integrated into Sri Lankan legislation (Pavey, 2008). Hence, in their urge to contain violence, law enforcement forces (who were mostly Sinhalese) committed abuses and generated a sense of impunity felt by the Tamils that worsened the tension and foreshadowed the beginning of the civil war. This, in fact, started in July 1983 after the LTTE attacked a military escort, killing 13 infantrymen in the Jaffna district – the largest casualty figure among security forces until then (Senaratne, 1997, p. 44). This episode triggered a retaliation from the Sri Lankan authorities and the Sinhalese population that resulted in riots, persecution and assassinations of Tamils, along with looting and destruction of Tamil homes and businesses in different cities (Tambiah, 1986, p. 21). Given the magnitude of the attack against the soldiers, the LTTE was subjected to severe punishment. The then President Junius Richard Jayawardene announced a series of wide-ranging measures to limit Tamil secessionist ambitions that included the interdiction of all Tamil pro-independence movements and declared that those individuals with secessionist aspirations would lose their civil rights and be "banned from holding office and prevented from practicing a profession" (Pavey, 2008). The Parliament, also pursuing the limitation of the scope of action of Tamil politicians prone to independence, approved an amendment to the Constitution requiring all Members of Parliament to take an oath of loyalty in favor of a unitary Sri Lanka (Senaratne, 1997, pp. 40–50).

The Sri Lankan armed conflict witnessed campaigns of violence among the different secessionist Tamil groups that disputed the leadership to represent the Tamil cause, and between these groups and national security forces. In nearly three decades, the toll of victims reached an estimated number of 80,000–100,000 fatalities – among Tamil rebels, soldiers, police, and civilians (Humanity House, 2017). Both the Sri Lankan military and the LTTE are accused of having committed human rights abuses. On the military side, there are accounts of "enforced disappearances, violent crackdowns on protestors in various towns and extrajudicial punishment" (International Crisis Group, 2012, p. i), and shelling of "no fire zones" as well as hospitals and food distribution lines during the final stages of the war (United Nations, 2011). On the LTTE side, the list includes abduction, conscription, suicide bombers, and the use of child soldiers (Bajoria, 2009; Puri, 2016, p. 35).

The Sri Lankans who survived this ferocious armed conflict

> suffered from prolonged periods of violence and physical insecurity, repeated displacement, loss of land and livelihoods, food insecurity, and the destruction of physical infrastructure [...] serious unresolved issues of psycho-social trauma, sexual violence, and the culture of impunity. (de Mel & Venugopal, 2016)

This is a country with deep wounds regarding the integration of ethnic minorities in the public sphere and to overcome this will take time, but mainly, will require the adoption of balanced reconciliation measures. The commitment to find a solution to the ethnic conflict through the devolution of power to North East Sri Lanka must be consequent and from the lines of the Lesson Learnt and Reconciliation Commission Report released by the Government of Sri Lanka in December 2011, plans must be put in place.

The Attempts for a Negotiated Solution

The conflict in Sri Lanka witnessed different periods of intensified violence that are classified as the Eelam Wars: the first from June 1983 to July 1987; the second from June 1990 to January 1995; the third from April 1995 to February 2002; and the fourth from July 2006 to May 2009 (Puri, 2016, pp. 32–35; Yusoff et al., 2015, p. 512). In the course of these wars, various attempts were made to restore peace by internal and external actors (seeking to act as mediators, namely India and Norway) (see Fig. 1).

The first initiative to bring war to an end came from India (which has a significant Tamil community in the South and was concerned about the violence in Sri Lanka) in the summer of 1985 when it organized a meeting in Bhutan with delegations from the Sri Lankan government and the main Tamil groups. Their stances were incompatibles for most of the issues and the peace talks did not come to fruition. A couple of years later, though, Prime Minister Rajiv Gandhi and Sri Lankan President Jayewardene signed the India–Sri Lanka Agreement to Establish Peace and Normalcy in Sri Lanka on July 29, 1987. To accomplish this plan, an Indian Peace Keeping Force (IPKF) was deployed in the North and East of Sri Lanka to stabilize the regions and to disarm all Tamil militant groups (Cronin, 2009, p. 58). However, the Indian force was involved in the fighting

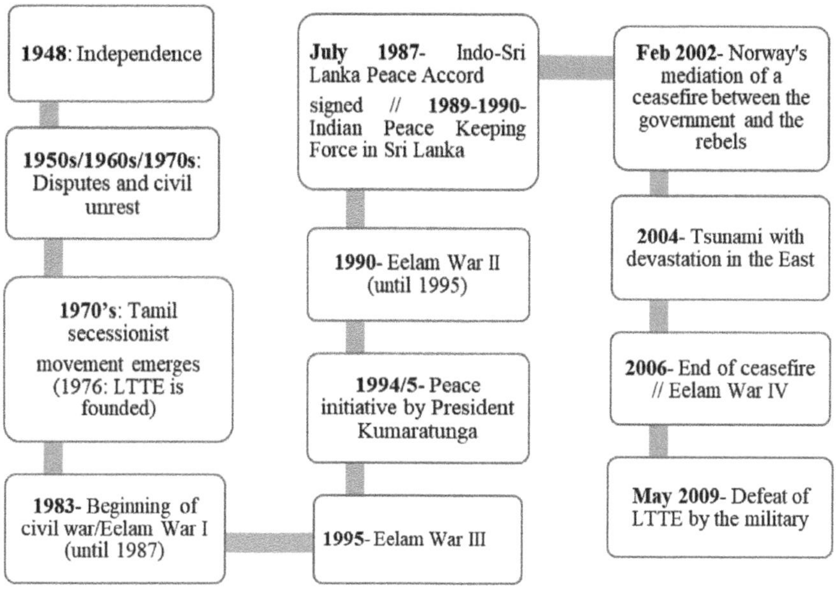

Fig. 1. Timeline of Key Events in Sri Lankan Conflict.

with the LTTE and the casualties kept rising, surpassing 1,000 which became decisive to India to cease the mission in March 1990 (Puri, 2016, p. 31). At the same time, the President of Sri Lanka, Ranasinghe Premadasa, began a new round of negotiations with the LTTE but it was insufficient to prevent the continuation of violent clashes, and so, in June 1990 the Second Eelam War began. During this war a series of assassinations of high-profile figures took place, namely that of Indian Prime Minister Rajiv Gandhi in May 1991 and then President Premadasa in May 1993 (Bose, 2007, p. 29). In fact, the assassination of Rajiv Gandhi led India to classify "the LTTE as a terrorist organization in India, and its leader, Prabhakaran, became a wanted man in India" (Destradi, 2010, p. 9).

The second peace effort was attempted in late 1994 by then President Chandrika Kumaratunga which resulted in a ceasefire in January 1995. However, on 19 April the LTTE attacked two navy gunboats (SLNS *Sooraya* and SLNS *Ranasuru*) and two military planes, killing a total of 97 people (Human Rights Watch, 1996) which resulted in a heavy military retaliation from the government that included land and air attacks in Jaffna Peninsula – a LTTE controlled area – forcing the rebels to move to the forests on the north of Sri Lanka and from 1995 to 2002 the country went through the Third Eelam War (Bose, 2007, pp. 36–39).

The third attempt to resolve the armed conflict was again initiated by President Chandrika Kumaratunga in January 2000 with the invitation of Norway to mediate a peace settlement between the Sri Lankan government and the LTTE that would grant autonomy for the North and East under a federal system (Lunstead, 2007, p. 15; Reliefweb, 2003). Political instability in the Sri Lankan government delayed the long-waited moment but the ceasefire agreement was finally signed on February 22, 2002, foreseeing a monitoring mission to accompany the progress of the ceasefire which lacked the means to enforce compliance.[3] Peace talks progressed the following months with several rounds in Thailand and Japan, but in April 2003 the LTTE withdrew from the negotiations on the grounds that it had been excluded from a preparatory meeting in the United States (a country that put the group on the list of terrorist organizations) (Destradi, 2010, p. 10). The group continued targeting the police and the military in the North and East of the country and resisting the counter-offensives of the government (Cronin, 2009, p. 60).

During this time of confrontations but still before the beginning of the Fourth Eelam War, Sri Lanka's foreign minister, Lakshman Kadirgamar, was assassinated (in August 2005) which strengthened the government's response against the LTTE. The elections held in November 2005 installed Mahinda Rajapaksa as the new President of Sri Lanka who was anti-LTTE. Even though he was from the Sri Lanka Freedom Party (SLFP) – one of the two major Sri Lankan parties – he obtained the support of a peculiar alliance: the communist party Janatha Vimukthi Peramuna (JVP – People's Liberation Front) and the nationalist Buddhist monks-controlled party Jathika Hela Urumaya (JHU – National Heritage Party). A harsh approach against the LTTE followed from this coalition and between 2006 and 2009 the conflict reached the most violent and deadly peak between the two sides. The United Nations estimated the rather largish number of 40,000 civilians killed during this period alone (United Nations, 2011, p. 41). The military forces progressively won territory from the LTTE until victory was proclaimed on May 18, 2009 and the death of LTTE leader, Velupillai Prabhakaran was declared. The efforts of Sri Lankan authorities paid off, but together with the increasing commitment of the government and the military to defeat the LTTE and with improvements to the Sri Lankan Army and Navy (to which the financial support from China was significant), other aspects have contributed to the government victory, namely the "defection of key personnel from the LTTE, significant reductions in LTTE external funding (…), and fallout from the 2004 tsunami" (Smith, 2010, p. 42) – which affected mostly areas dominated by the LTTE and the credibility of the LTTE was damaged by allegations of corruption concerning the distribution of humanitarian aid (Fernando, 2009; Puri, 2016, p. 35).

Whereas the initiatives to a peaceful settlement of the conflict are meritorious, they also show the existence of several hindrances that delayed a swifter and more adequate end. First, the engaging attitude of the LTTE for dialog with the Sri Lankan government was utilitarian in its essence because the secessionist group considered these stages as extra time "to enhance its own position, re-arm, and alienate its competitors" (Cronin, 2009, p. 59). Second, whoever held government office faced antagonism every time there was a prospect to achieve a peace agreement: either by the "LTTE together with sympathetic Tamil forces and nationalist Sinhalese forces" (Shinoda, 2011, p. 15) or by major Sri Lankan

---

[3]With the worsening of hostilities in May 2006, the mission saw its task hard to accomplish and ended completely in 2008.

political parties that strategically differentiated their position – to be inclusive and appeasing toward the Tamil claims or, on the contrary, more restrictive and inflexible – according to their place in power or in the opposition (Shinoda, 2011, p. 15). Third, the promotion of alignments with different countries allowed the Sri Lankan governments to intensify or de-escalate the conflict against the LTTE through the years – a closer relationship with China and Pakistan in the former or with European countries in the latter (Shinoda, 2011, p. 17).

External Linkages

The studies on internal armed conflicts demonstrate the existence of an external component which can be as diverse as other states, humanitarian organizations, international media, peacekeeping forces and non-governmental organizations. In Mary Kaldor's words, this is the result of "the intensification of global interconnectedness – political, economic, military and cultural" (Kaldor, 2012, p. 4). Although the antagonism between Tamils and Sinhalese was predominantly domestic, there have been external linkages that have influenced the conflict and these can be divided into the following: (i) regional neighbors, such as India, and other countries; (ii) the diaspora; and (iii) the relationships with other insurgent groups.

The interest of India, the giant neighbor, in the Sri Lankan conflict is hardly surprising. India is the major regional power in South Asia and a significant number of Tamils – about 69 million citizens, equivalent to almost 6 per cent of the Indian population (Office of the Registrar General, 2011) – live in its southern province of Tamil Nadu. This region received thousands of Tamil refugees – who were seeking shelter given their family or identity ties – during the ethnic riots against the Tamil population in Sri Lanka throughout the 1950s, 1960s, 1970s, and 1980s (Destradi, 2010). Many of these refugees remained in Tamil Nadu province and kept following closely the progress of the Sri Lankan political situation. The LTTE also used this Indian region to develop its network of operations, and in the 1970s and 1980s, India even supported the group with training, supplied weapons, and financed the LTTE (Bajoria, 2009; Destradi, 2010; Gunaratna, 1997). This support ceased years later though with the Indian leadership of Rajiv Gandhi.

Given the negative experience of the IPKF in Sri Lanka and the assassination of Prime Minister Rajiv Gandhi by a LTTE suicide bomber in 1991, and the subsequent classification of the LTTE as terrorist group, which made it difficult to negotiate with the separatists, India changed its approach toward its southern neighbor. Nevertheless, India sought a negotiated solution and a peaceful outcome to the ethnic conflict that would comprise a unitary, sovereign and integrated Sri Lanka where minorities would have their rights respected – and that could mean the implementation of a federal system in Sri Lanka (Destradi, 2010, p. 12). This stance reflected India's own fear of independentist spill-over effects. From 2007 onward, the attitude of India changed, and it became closer to the Sri Lankan government due to the latter's *rapprochement* to Chinese investments and financial and military support. Therefore, India suppressed LTTE networks in the province of Tamil Nadu, and developed military cooperation and supplied military equipment to the Sri Lankan government (Destradi, 2010, pp. 13–15). Thus, for security reasons (both domestic and regional), India kept a close eye on what was happening in Sri Lanka.

Other countries have influenced the course of the conflict. China is one of them, not for having the same domestic interests as India but for geopolitical interests – to broaden the scope of action in South Asia. In March 2007, China and Sri Lanka signed an agreement for the construction of the port of Hambantota, in the South of Sri Lanka with China financing 85 per cent of its total cost (US$360 million) (Financial Agreements, 2007). In the military domain, China became the main weapons provider of Sri Lanka between 2002 and 2009 with a total of 212 deliveries (with the higher number of deliveries taking place in between 2006 and 2008 with figures reaching 49, 48 and 59 deliveries, respectively). Israel was the second biggest exporter with 133 deliveries to Sri Lanka, and India being the third biggest supplier with a total of 41 deliveries registered in 2006, 2007, and 2008 (10, 21, and 11, respectively) (Stockholm International Peace Research Institute (SIPRI), 2019). The military aid from China was a great boost for the Sri Lankan government winning the war.

The analysis of the first type of external linkages (regional neighbors and other countries) must also include the role of the United States which was a discreet actor during the 1980s and 1990s and was also supportive of Sri Lanka's "sovereignty and territorial integrity as well as its democratic institutions and socio-economic development" (Vaughn, 2011, p. 4). In terms of USAID, for a 50-year period (1956–2006) Sri Lanka received approximately "$2 billion, which is an average of $40 million per year, a substantial amount" (Lunstead, 2007, p. 12). But, unlike India or China, the United States lacked strategic interests in Sri Lanka – in terms of military bases, Sri Lanka does not benefit from a strategic location compared to other Asian countries such as the Philippines, for example. Sri Lanka does not constitute a relevant trading partner either. Furthermore, the Sri Lankan-origin community in the United States is residual and does not have a significant impact on US domestic politics. Nevertheless, a combination of two elements made the United States look at Sri Lanka more enthusiastically. First, the September 11, 2001 terrorist attacks altered the US posture because the mindset was to prevent any terrorist group to achieve its goals through terrorism (Lunstead, 2007, p. 5), and the LTTE was listed as a terrorist organization, so it would be important to strengthen the government side and make Sri Lanka a role model. Second, in 2002, the prospects of peace with the ceasefire agreement mediated by Norway was a positive sign to the United States – evidence of this is attested to by the evolution of the Foreign Military Financing program "(the program under which the U.S. provides grants to other countries for the purchase of U.S. military equipment)" which was non-existent before the peace process and in 2004 it reached $2.5 million (Lunstead, 2007, p. 17).

The second external linkage that influenced the Sri Lankan conflict is the Tamil diaspora which represented a vital pillar in the survival of the LTTE – with the idea that only the creation of a separate state would guarantee this ethnic group peace and security (Gunaratna, 1997). Although some of the Tamils in the diaspora supported the LTTE, the group used intimidation against these communities to collect funds, for example by extorting money to guarantee the security of family members in Sri Lanka or to pay for ransoms of wealthy Tamils kidnapped in Sri Lanka (Bajoria, 2009). Charitable organizations were also created as a front to provide funds for the LTTE, and all "these forms of funding have made the LTTE one of the wealthiest militant organizations in the world" (Bajoria, 2009). The United Kingdom was the destination of much of the Tamils and this country concentrated most of pro-LTTE organizations, like newspapers and centers that disseminated news from Sri Lanka – these were usually sources of propaganda for the LTTE in Europe, North America and other parts of the world (Gunaratna, 1997).

In addition, external linkages also comprised the relationship of Tamil groups with other insurgent groups such as the Polisario Front (Morocco), Palestinian groups, the Kurdistan Workers' Party (PKK), and Islamists groups (Gunaratna, 1997; Jayasekara, 2009). Not only the LTTE but also the EROS, established ties with the Palestine Liberation Organization (PLO) to receive military training in PLO camps in Lebanon in the 1970s (Jayasekara, 2009). In the 1990s, the LTTE purchased 11 surface-to-air missiles from the PKK and in the first decade of the twenty-first century, the LTTE developed relations with al-Qaeda-affiliated groups in Africa and Asia (Jayasekara, 2009). This internationalization enabled the LTTE to withstand the counter-offensives of the Sri Lankan authorities.

The Role of Democracy/Democratization in the Resolution of the Sri Lankan Conflict

Democracy is a system of government with some relevant and indispensable elements that deserve to be outlined here. The first element is that the people are entitled to choose those who they want to represent and govern them and do so through elections which must be regular, free and fair, and offer a plurality of candidates. Such a democratic system allows the people to hold their leaders accountable for their policies and their conduct in office – thus maintaining their own legitimacy. The basic principle is the consent of the governed. The second element relies in the participation of the people in politics (understood broadly, encompassing civic life as well). Strong democracies are those with strong civil societies and these mean a "social 'glue' [that] also supports moderation among political parties and provides unofficial fora for interaction outside the formal structures of democracy" (Sisk, 2003). The third element consists of human rights guaranteed to all citizens, especially in fragmented societies where non-discriminatory policies are crucial (Premdas, 1997). Finally, the fourth element is the rule of law, and the certainty of all citizens that the laws are equally applied regardless of race, gender, religion, and political views, among other frequent factors of discrimination.

In a democratic society, there are competing interests which require a negotiation process to reach a decision on the issue, sustainable compromises and accommodation of grievances. In deeply divided societies, especially those seeking to escape "intractable conflicts" (Sisk, 2003), democracy is difficult either to implement or to maintain for several reasons: first, "parties in conflict lack the inherent trust needed for democracy to prosper" (Sisk, 2003) – it is a complex task to ask adversaries (who have been ferocious enemies for years or decades) to erase hatred from their memory and automatically start a dialogue and work together without reservations. It is crucial to acknowledge that time is needed and so is political will to guarantee that the basics of democracy are respected. Then, "majority rule can mean majority tyranny" (Sisk, 2003) – to exercise power is a delicate art, in fact, to represent the majority and still integrate the minorities is a hard task. To keep a good balance is the key, but very complex though, even more when identity aspects dominated the conflict, such as ethnicity did in Sri Lanka. Lastly, "the persistence of deep divisions" (Sisk, 2003) may hinder democracy. In the case of Sri Lanka, the ethnic divisions and claims for self-determination and independence persist and despite the acknowledgement for autonomy effective steps are not taken, it is very difficult to have a lasting peace. If the "basic consensus on a future of living together" (Sisk, 2003) is lacking, then democracy is condemned.

But, is democracy possible in deeply divided societies? One must believe the answer is yes. Sri Lanka was founded on democratic principles when the civil war started and is a case in point that when serious problems are neglected, they fuel conflicts. Hence, it is essential to address them as soon as possible to avoid the resumption of war. To encourage local-level politics (municipal, provincial or regional) and public participation (Lederach, 1997) might be a positive solution to Sri Lanka – where communities felt isolated from the decision-making process.

How does Sri Lanka fair in relation to democratic norms? The performance of this country in international assessments that scrutinize democracy or freedom is positive. In the Democracy Index,[4] in 2017, Sri Lanka scored 6.48 points (out of 10) – by comparison, the highest score belonged to Norway with 9.87 points (The Economist Intelligent Unit, 2017). The Freedom House Index, which assesses political rights and civil liberties annually in 195 countries,[5] awarded Sri Lanka, in 2018, a score of 55 (out of 100) corresponding to the status of "partially free" (Freedom House, 2018).

Sri Lanka is a democracy that like so many others has been engulfed in a long-lasting internal conflict which has jeopardized the social peace. Looking at the most recent elections, in 2015, they have empowered moderates on both the Sinhala and Tamil sides of the ethnic divide with popular mandates for peacebuilding and governance reform. The alliances formed during elections transcended traditional political party rivalries, and the government has been formed with a new cross-party political alliance: President Maithripala Sirisena and Prime Minister Ranil Wickremesinghe headed the two largest parties, the SLFP and the United National

---

[4]This is done by *The Economist* in 167 countries, and there are 60 indicators under evaluation such as political participation, electoral process, civic liberties, etc., in a scale from 0 to 10.

[5]The assessment may conclude that the country is in one of three situations: free, partially free or non-free.

Party (UNP), respectively. The main Tamil party, the Tamil National Alliance (TNA) was not part of the ruling coalition but backed those in power.

Sri Lanka was also able to restore political institutions at local provincial and national levels with democratically elected bodies within few years of the end of civil war. The election held in 2013 in the northern provincial council was viewed as a new chapter in post-civil war transition process (Srinivasan, 2013). These political circumstances were unprecedented, and they provided an important window of opportunity for peace to obtain. However, some accounts from the ground show that there is still work to do. The International Crisis Group reports indicate that "the almost entirely Tamil-speaking north is now dotted with Sinhala sign-boards, streets newly renamed in Sinhala, monuments to Sinhala war heroes" (2012, p. ii). Also worrying is the movement of Sinhala settlers; the resistance of the military to give back occupied land to its owners in these areas; and the construction of Buddha statues in Tamil and Muslim communities. These are the kind of actions that give rise to resentment. The widespread belief that there is a deliberate government policy to "Sinhalise" the north expresses a deep-seated fear among many Tamils that they are losing control over their own communities, land and resources, and through this, ultimately, losing their collective identity and political presence (International Crisis Group, 2012, p. 17).

Moreover, religious minorities remain at risk. According to Human Rights Watch, in September 2017, Rohingya Muslim refugees were victims of threats made by Buddhist extremists and had to be taken into protective custody by authorities, and violence against Muslim homes and businesses have been recurrent in the South (Human Rights Watch, 2018, p. 507). Furthermore, serious legal and humanitarian questions persist about the treatment of those detained for suspicion of being LTTE ex-combatants – who are denied due process and access to independent monitoring (United Nations, 2011, p. 47).

Additionally, recent political events suggest a period of uncertainty about the future of the country and the consolidation of the peace process given the fact that on the evening of October 26, 2018, President Sirisena appointed the ex-President Mahinda Rajapaksa as Prime Minister, creating a government parallel to what was operational in the country at the time (Daily FT, 2018). The dismissed Prime-minister, Wickremesinghe, continued in Temple Trees, the official residence of the prime minister, and contested the lawfulness and constitutionality of the act. In Sri Lanka,

> a prime minister can only be removed when he or she ceases to be a member of parliament such as for failing to meet criteria to be an elector or candidate, when a vote of no-confidence is passed, or when he or she chooses to resign. (The Guardian, 2018)

None of these conditions were met. Besides, the

> constitution also makes it abundantly clear that the president cannot dissolve parliament until the body has served four-and-a-half of its five-year term. The current parliament was elected in August 2015. (DeVotta & Ganguly, 2018)

It is relevant to note that former President Rajapaksa brings bad memories to Tamils and other minorities given his nationalist pro-Sinhalese Buddhist alignment, hard-line approach against the LTTE, increasingly authoritarian positions (DeVotta, 2018), corruption and a history of "degradation of the rule of law institutions" (Ginsburg & Huq, 2018, p. 27). Fortunately, though the situation was resolved amicably later with the previous status quo reinstated and a potential coup averted.

Contributions from the Case Study

The study of the peace process in Sri Lanka is complex and stimulating at the same time. The advances and setbacks, the intricate webs of actors, and the speed of events make this small country a peculiar, and inexplicably, scarcely analyzed case by Western scholars. From the various relevant aspects, this chapter will focus on two: the characteristics and the evolution of the conflict, on the one hand, and the relationship between democracy and conflict, on the other hand.

Considering the literature, specifically the definition of the Uppsala Conflict Data Project, an armed conflict consists of

> a contested incompatibility that concerns government or territory or both where the use of armed force between two parties results in at least 25 battle-related deaths. Of these two parties, at least one is the government of a state. (Gleditsch et al., 2002, pp. 618–619)

In our case-study, there is a clear contested incompatibility that concerns territory: Tamil groups demanded for the secession or autonomy of the North and East of Sri Lanka to form the Tamil Eelam/State. A more detailed category from this definition would frame the Sri Lankan conflict as an internationalized internal armed conflict that "occurs between the government of a state and internal opposition groups with intervention from other states" (Gleditsch et al., 2002, p. 619). Such interference may be exemplified by the role of India which has supported either the rebels or the national authorities according to its interests. The post-Cold War geopolitical changes had implications for the Sri Lankan conflict. As most conflicts ceased to be proxy wars and the intra-state conflicts became the most common, the search for regional solutions to conflicts seemed the right way to go and, therefore, regional organizations turned into the privileged fora for conflict management (Destradi, 2010, p. 7). However, in the absence of such an organization in the regional context of Sri Lanka, the question is whether the conflict in Sri Lanka would have had another outcome and earlier (still in the 1990s, for example) if the South Asian region had an organization with a security mandate such as the North Atlantic region has North Atlantic Treaty Organization (NATO)*.

*This is an intergovernmental alliance of military scope and constituted by means of a treaty (the North Atlantic Treaty, signed on April 4, 1949), which established the principle of collective defense, according to which the member states of that alliance agree with the mutual defense in response to an attack by any entity outside the organization.

The second aspect also raises a question: since Sri Lanka's independence is concomitant with the founding of democracy in the country, how could the latter have responded to avoid exacerbating minority inequalities and to have given rise to the separatist terrorism that plunged the country into a bloody civil war? The question remains valid in 2019. Several steps can be taken to prevent the resurgence of violence, the first being based on power sharing. As mentioned in the previous pages, democracies sustain themselves with power delegation and in Sri Lanka this can be materialized with decentralization from the capital to the Northern and Eastern Provinces – to the provincial and local councils (Fernando, 2009). Doing this has two consequences: (i) it fosters cooperation – "politicians from opposite sides of the aisle in local councils are often more willing to work together to get things done than national politicians" (Fernando, 2009) and (ii) it strengthens Sri Lankan democracy – because it makes it "more accountable and responsive to people's needs" (Fernando, 2009). A second step resides in safeguarding human rights which are a pillar of any democracy.

For all that was said, it is fundamental to address the structural causes of the conflict which goes beyond the end of the armed conflict. Sri Lanka must apply a multi-facetted approach that includes ethnic, religious, territorial, and constitutional issues for an enduring peace.

Conclusion

This chapter followed the guidelines proposed by the editor of this volume for more consistency and is divided into five parts, in addition to the introduction and the conclusion. The first part examined the roots of the Sri Lankan conflict and pointed to several key conjunctures. At the time of the independence of the state from British rule, and instead of taking advantage of that moment to solve existing issues (related to the rights of the minorities) with reasonable and sustainable formulae, there were mutual accusations between the Sinhalese and the Tamils (and other minorities as well) of discriminatory behavior and laws. Violence escalated on both sides and culminated in a civil war with approximately 100.000 deaths and hundreds of thousands displaced and large numbers with severe trauma as well.

The second part was devoted to the (meritorious) efforts to achieve peace, but showed that the conflict ended with the implementation of classic war tactics of unlimited force against everything and everyone in the conflict areas. The IPKF and the ceasefire agreements after the second Eelam War and the third Eelam War between the government and the rebels failed. The government and the LTTE intensified the combat and progressively the government became victorious culminating in killing the historical leader of the separatist group, Velupillai Prabhakaran, and defeating the remaining fighters.

The third part focused on the external linkages of the conflict and the role of India, China and the United States was emphasized given the importance of these countries at particular moments of the conflict and their alignment with and support of the government of Sri Lanka. Also, the diaspora and the ties of the LTTE with other insurgent groups were analyzed and this aspect exposed their importance in turn for the survival of the LTTE.

The role of democracy in the resolution of the conflict constituted the fourth part and in theory, the main elements of a democracy seem suitable and robust to solve emerging problems in a country, but as the case has demonstrated, reality is often more complicated. Sri Lanka is a deeply divided society and the 1978 Constitution that adopted the system of proportional representation – which was designed to give minority parties more influence in national politics – should have met the needs of the minorities but that was not the case and war erupted five years later. Democracy is tested every day and pluralism, true electoral competition, human rights, decentralization of power, and moderate institutions (Diamond, 1995) still must be the goals to pursue and to abide by.

The final part presented the contributions of the case study and it is worth noting that Sri Lanka has not benefited from regional organizations' support to deal with the conflict as the new post-Cold War era was expected to in terms of the peace dividend. It received aid from certain states instead. An important date has just lapsed: May 19, 2019 marked 10 years since the civil war in Sri Lanka ended and the country still needs to address important issues (such as a thorough and impartial investigation on human rights abuses during the war, both by the LTTE and the government forces) that are crucial to guarantee a sustainable peace. Attention has to be focused on the steps that will be taken in the short-term and these should be thoughtful and responsible in order to guarantee the population that the next decades will foster hope, peace and democracy.

References

Bajoria, J. (2009, May 18). *The Sri Lankan Conflict*. Council on Foreign Relations. Retrieved from http://www.cfr.org

BBC News. (1991, May 21). 1991: Bomb kills India's Former Leader Rajiv Gandhi. *BBC News*. Retrieved from http://news.bbc.co.uk/onthisday/hi/dates/stories/may/21/newsid_2504000/2504739.stm

Bose, S. (2007). *Contested lands: Israel-Palestine, Kashmir, Bosnia, Cyprus, and Sri Lanka*. Cambridge, MA: Harvard University Press.

Cronin, A. (2009). *How terrorism ends*. Princeton, NJ: Princeton University Press.

Daily FT. (2018, November 6). Sri Lankan Press Freedom Crushed Following Mahinda Rajapaksa's Return. *Daily FT*. Retrieved from http://www.ft.lk/news/Sri-Lankan-press-freedom-crushed-following-Mahinda-Rajapaksa-s-return/56-666213

de Mel, N., & Venugopal, R. (2016, March). *Peacebuilding Context Assessment – Sri Lanka 2016*. Colombo: United Nations Sri Lanka.

Department of Census and Statistics. (2012). *Census of Population and Housing of Sri Lanka, 2012 – Table A3: Population by district, ethnic group and sex*. Retrieved from http://www.statistics.gov.lk/PopHouSat/CPH2011/Pages/Activities/Reports/FinalReport/Population/Table%20A3.pdf

Destradi, S. (2010, December). *India and the Civil War in Sri Lanka: On the Failures of Regional Conflict Management in South Asia (GIGA Working Paper No. 154)*. Hamburg: GIGA.

DeVotta, N. (2018, December 3). Sri Lanka's crisis of democracy. *East Asia Forum*. Retrieved from http://www.eastasiaforum.org

DeVotta, N., & Ganguly, S. (2018, November). Asia's oldest democracy takes a hit. *Foreign Policy*. Retrieved from https://foreignpolicy.com

Diamond, L. (1995). *Promoting Democracy in the 1990s: Actors and instruments, issues and imperatives*. Washington, D.C.: Carnegie Commission on Preventing Deadly Conflict.

Fernando, N. (2009, May 5). Sri Lanka: Rising to the challenges after the war. *East Asia Forum*. Retrieved from http://www.eastasiaforum.org

Financial Agreements. (2007, November 8). Financial agreements signed for Hambantota Port Project. *Daily News*. Retrieved from http://archives.dailynews.lk/2007/11/08/bus12.asp

Freedom House. (2018). Freedom in the World 2018: Democracy in crisis. *Freedom House*. Retrieved from https://freedomhouse.org/report/freedom-world/freedom-world-2018#anchor-one

Ginsburg, T., & Huq, A. (2018). Democracy's 'Near Misses'. *Journal of Democracy*, *29*(4), 16–30.

Gleditsch, N., Wallensteen, P., Eriksson, M., Sollenberg, M., & Strand, H. (2002). Armed conflict 1946–2001: A new dataset. *Journal of Peace Research*, *39*(5), 615–637.

Gunaratna, R. (1997). *International & regional security implications of the Sri Lankan Tamil insurgency*. London: International Foundation of Sri Lankans.

Human Rights Watch. (1996). *World Report 1996*. Retrieved from https://www.hrw.org/reports/1996/WR96/Asia-08.htm#P735_195262

Human Rights Watch. (2018). *World Report 2018*. Retrieved from https://www.hrw.org/world-report/2018

Humanity House. (2017, January 23). Disasters and conflicts: Sri Lanka. Civil War, 1983–2009. *Humanity House*. Retrieved from https://www.humanityhouse.org/en/rampen-conflicten-sri-lanka-burgeroorlog-1983-2009

International Crisis Groups. (2012, March 16). Sri Lanka's North 1: The denial of minority rights. *International Crisis Groups*. Retrieved from https://www.crisisgroup.org/asia/south-asia/sri-lanka/sri-lanka-s-north-i-denial-minority-rights

Jayasekara, S. (2009). Tamil Tiger Links with Islamist Terrorist Groups. *International Institute for Counter-Terrorism*. Retrieved from https://www.ict.org.il

Kaldor, M. (2012). *New and old wars. Organised violence in a Global Era*. Cambridge: Polity Press.

Lederach, J. P. (1997). *Building peace: Sustainable reconciliation in divided societies*. Washington, D.C.: United States Institute of Peace.

Lunstead, J. (2007). *The United States' role in Sri Lanka's peace process 2002–2006*. Asia Foundation website. Retrieved from https://www.asiafoundation.org/resources/pdfs/SLSupplementarytoSCA.pdf

National Consortium for the Study of Terrorism and Responses to Terrorism (START). (2019). *Global Terrorism Database – Number of incidents occurred in Sri Lanka between 1983–2009* [Database]. Retrieved from https://www.start.umd.edu/gtd

Office of the Registrar General (2011). *Census of India 2011*. Retrieved from http://www.censusindia.gov.in/2011Census/C-16_25062018_NEW.pdf

Pavey, E. (2008, May 13). The massacres in Sri Lanka during the Black July riots of 1983. *Online Encyclopedia of Mass Violence*. Retrieved from https://www.sciencespo.fr

Peiris, G. H., & Arasaratnam, S. (2018). Sri Lanka. *Encyclopaedia Britannica*. Retrieved from https://www.britannica.com/place/Sri-Lanka

Premdas, R. (1997). *Public Policy and Ethnic Conflict* (UNESCO MOST Discussion paper series No. 12, document code: SHS.97/WS/13). Retrieved from UNESCO digital library website https://unesdoc.unesco.org/ark:/48223/pf0000111316?posInSet=1&queryId=N-EXPLORE-e743322f-6808-4a41-86de-f78cc352a6c4

Puri, S. (2016). *Fighting and negotiating with armed groups: The difficulty of securing strategic outcomes*. Oxon: Routledge

Rathi, N. (2017). 'Indian Tamils' of Sri Lanka and Sri Lankan Tamils: Here is the difference. *The Indian Express*, May 16. Retrieved from https://indianexpress.com

Reliefweb. (2003, April 30). Sri Lanka peace talks and related event – Timeline. *Reliefweb*. Retrieved from https://reliefweb.int/report/sri-lanka/sri-lanka-peace-talks-and-related-events-timeline

Ross, R., & Savada, A. (1988). *Sri Lanka: A country study*. Washington D.C.: GPO for the Liberty of Congress. Retrieved from http://countrystudies.us/sri-lanka/

Rotberg, R. I. (Ed.). (1999). *Creating peace in Sri Lanka: civil war and reconciliation*. Washington, D.C.: Brookings Institution Press.

Senaratne, J. P. (1997). *Political Violence in Sri Lanka, 1997-1990: Riots, Insurrections, Counter-insurgencies, Foreign Intervention*. Amsterdam: VU University Press.

Shinoda, H. (2011). *Politics of Peace Processes in Sri Lanka: Reconsidered from domestic, international and regional perspectives (IPSHU English Research Report Series No.25: Peacebuilding in South Asia)* (pp. 129–155). Hiroshima: Hiroshima University.

Sisk, T. D. (2003, August). Democracy and conflict management. In G. Burgess & H. Burgess (Eds.), *Conflict information consortium*. Boulder, CO: University of Colorado. Retrieved from http://www.beyondintractability.org/essay/democ-con-manag

Smith, N. A. (2010). Understanding Sri Lanka's defeat of the Tamil Tigers. *Joint Force Quarterly*, *59*(4), 40–44.

Srinivasan, M. (2013, September 17). Northern province polls, A new chapter for Sri Lanka: (updated version 2016, June 02). *The Hindu*. Retrieved from https://www.thehindu.com

Stockholm International Peace Research Institute (SIPRI). (2019). *SIPRI Arms Transfers Database - Importer/Exporter TIV Tables – TIV of arms exports to Sri Lanka, 2002–2009* [Database]. Retrieved from https://www.sipri.org/databases/armstransfers

Tambiah, S. J. (1986). *Sri Lanka: Ethnic Fracticide and the dismantling of democracy*, London: I. B. Tauris & Co. Ltd.

The Economist Intelligent Unit. (2017). *The Economist Intelligence Unit's Democracy Index* [Database]. Retrieved from https://infographics.economist.com/2018/DemocracyIndex

The Guardian. (2018, October 27). Sri Lanka in turmoil after prime-minister Wickremesinghe sacked. *The Guardian*. Retrieved from https://www.theguardian.com/world/2018/oct/27/sri-lanka-in-turmoil-after-prime-minister-wickremesinghe-sacked

United Nations. (2011, March 31). *Report of the UN Secretary-General's Panel of Experts on Accountability in Sri Lanka*. Retrieved from http://www.un.org/News/dh/infocus/Sri_Lanka/POE_Report_Full.pdf

Vaughn, B. (2011, June 16). *Sri Lanka: Background and U.S. relations* (Congressional Research Service RL31707). Retrieved from https://fas.org/sgp/crs/row/RL31707.pdf

Yusoff, M. A., Hussin, N., Sarjoon, A., Efendi, D., & Azmier, B. (2015). From the era of Civil War to peace and democratization: Sri Lanka in transition. *The Social Sciences*, *10*(4), 510–519.

Chapter 6

A Democratic Tradition as the Background to Armed Conflict: The Paradox of the Colombian Case?

Margarita Cuervo Iglesias

Introduction

On the evening of October 5, 2016, a crowd holding lit candles marched in silence toward the Plaza de Bolívar, the main square of the Colombian capital, Bogotá. With the motto "¡Acuerdo ya!" (Agreement now!), thousands of people joined in the demonstration called by students demanding the country's political leaders to reach a consensus to continue with the peace process with the "Fuerzas Armadas Revolucionarias de Colombia" (FARC, "Revolutionary Armed Forces of Colombia"). Barely two days had passed since the plebiscite in which a narrow majority rejected the contents of the peace deal reached between the government and the guerrilla that took up arms against the state in 1964.

In the course of that march, two generations gazed at each other with some amazement, perhaps seeking an expression of hope. On the one hand, there was the generation that lived through the escalation of violence in the 1980s, while Colombia witnessed the first peace negotiations; as students at the time, they led the movement that allowed the election of the National Constituent Assembly in 1990. On the other hand, there were those who were born in the final decades of the twentieth century, when amnesties for guerrilla groups occurred parallel to the drug trafficking boom and the expansion of democracy. Nowadays, after 30 years of peace processes, they, like their fellow Colombians, have never known their country to be free from violence.

"Peace is a right and duty that must be obligatorily enforced" – so reads article 22 of Colombia's political constitution. Without a doubt, this is one of the unfulfilled promises of the 1991 Constitution, the one with most guarantees ever

International Perspectives on Democratization and Peace, 91–111

doi:10.1108/978-1-80043-067-920200006

in force in this country that refers to itself as Latin America's oldest democracy,[1] but where the society has been polarized on the difficult path toward peace.

Over two years after the ceasefire with the FARC, the situation is rather complex. The implementation of the agreements advances slowly while the war persists with other irregular groups that have taken the control of or are still disputing areas from which this guerrilla group has withdrawn. In parallel, the number of threats and murders targeting social leaders, victims and former combatants has increased in areas with weak state presence.

Although the Colombian case is rather particular, it also offers the opportunity to explore interactions between democracy, conflict and peace at an intrastate level. In fact, it shows that the relationship between democratization and conflict resolution at a domestic level is not always linear since, unless the structural causes undergirding the confrontation are dealt with, the consolidation of democracy will also be hindered. This chapter provides a brief account of the context and background of the armed conflict in Colombia and the efforts toward its resolution, before explaining the role that democratization has played in conflict transformation. The chapter ends with some final observations and lessons learned based on the studied case.

An Internal Conflict with Deep Roots, Multiple Actors, and Staggered Attempts to Achieve Peace

Decades of internal conflict in Colombia, multiple actors and causes in complex interactions, as well as several attempts for conflict resolution have led some scholars to classify this as an intractable case (Arnson, 2005; Kriesberg, 2004). Indeed, left-wing guerrilla groups, paramilitary organizations, and drug traffickers have threatened the rule of law in a democratic regime with a relatively stable economy.

Figures cannot fully portray the dreadful consequences of war on society. However, they provide an initial perspective to understand why issues such as transitional justice or the political reintegration of ex-combatants trigger high levels of polarization, as happened in the 2016 plebiscite. Since 1985[2] 7.7 million have been internally displaced due to the armed conflict (UNHCR, 2018). According to the Historical Memory Group, the war has left a death toll of 220,000 and approximately 25,000 have been recorded as missing; there have been

---

[1]At least on a formal level, as recalled by Leal (2018, p. 99). This statement is based on the formation of political parties at the end of the 1840s, the holding of regular elections and on the fact that Colombia has survived the twentieth century without dictatorships, with the exception of that of Rojas Pinilla (1953–1957).

[2]This year was approved by the Colombian Congress in 2011, following the "The Victims and Land Restitution Law," as the year to start the quantification of the conflict victims. The purpose of this was to provide for reparation measures that also included victims affected by assassinations, terrorism by drug cartels and the Palace of Justice siege.

almost 30,000 cases of kidnapping and more than 11,000 people have been victims of anti-personnel mines (Grupo de Memoria Histórica (GMH), 2013).

Numerous contributions[3] have facilitated an understanding of the conflict in Colombia, yet finding effective formulae for its resolution has proven more than difficult. Before discussing the recent process with the FARC, the following section describes the factors associated with the emergence of the conflict, as well as its main international linkages and effects. The section ends with a brief account of lessons learned from previous conflict resolution attempts in the country.

A Confrontation Rooted in Structural Problems That Are Aggravated by Violence: The Vicious Circles of the Armed Conflict in Colombia

Due to its length, the armed conflict in Colombia has undergone several transformations, and thus, the factors that originally gave rise to the conflict currently coexist with others that have perpetuated it (Gutiérrez & Sánchez, 2006; Rettberg, 2002). For instance, when discussing the historic roots of the conflict, some authors trace these to the nineteenth century, when the foundations of the land distribution model and the delegation of governing powers were established in favor of local elites, generating a rural conflict that has continued to influence the war to the present day (González et al., 2003; Legrand, 1986; Robinson, 2013; United Nations Development Programme (UNDP), 2011). However, taking into account the emergence of the first guerrilla groups, the origins of the confrontation arose between 1948 and 1958, a period marked by intense inter-party violence, and also initially linked to land ownership issues and unattended social transformations (Bejarano et al., 1997; Pizarro, 1991a, 1996a; Montenegro & Posada, 2001).

During "La Violencia" (The Violence), as this period was named, the Armed Forces were politicized and got involved in massacres and assassinations of both liberals and conservatives. Its final phase was marked by the only dictatorship in Colombia's contemporary history: General Rojas Pinilla came to power in 1953 in order to remedy the increasing violence and was subsequently removed by a Military Junta in 1957 (Hartlyn, 1984). Both the military coup and its conclusion were consented to by the leaders of the two political parties, who later agreed to share and alternate government every 4 years for the next 16 years, as a formula in order to end the cycle of violence (Deas, 2003, p. 78).

This agreement on shared government, known as the National Front, formally terminated in 1974 but it was only until the 1980s that it was totally dismantled, thus preventing alternative political movements to access any government position (Hartlyn, 1988). This exclusion from the political regime in turn legitimated

[3]It is worth highlighting the contributions from the research groups commissioned by Colombian governments in order to understand the phenomenon of violence at different historic moments, such as Guzmán, Fals Borda, and Umaña (1964), Sánchez (1987) or more recently, the Historic Commission on the Conflict and its Victims (Comisión Histórica del Conflicto y sus Víctimas, 2015, febrero).

the discourse of the classical guerrilla groups that emerged in the sixties and the so-called "second-generation" guerrilla groups in the seventies and eighties[4] (Nasi, 2012; Vargas, 2000).

Two facts complicated this scenario. On the one hand, the 1966 Defence Statute opened the way for "civil defence organizations" to confront violence, a problem that increased with the subsequent proliferation of self-defence groups (Duncan, 2006; Gutiérrez & Barón, 2006; Romero, 2003). On the other hand, the rise of drug trafficking in the 1980s as a source of financing for the conflict, the drug cartels with their private armies and, after their dispersion, the consolidation of the paramilitary phenomenon constituted an additional source of destabilization of the state at the end of the century (Camacho, 2002; Gutiérrez & Barón, 2006).

Therefore, the existence and persistence of irregular groups for decades in some regions derives from deeper structural problems such as precariousness or even lack of presence by state institutions throughout the territory (Palacios, 1999). In other words, the Colombian state is still on the way to consolidating a key issue for democracy: the monopoly of the legitimate use of violence.

Thus, in a sort of vicious circle of violence, the conflict is rooted in and at the same time reinforces the marked regional and social exclusion as well as the failure of the central state to effectively and legitimately delegate power at all local and departmental levels. Precisely in some of these areas where the armed confrontation has historically taken place, the conflict has deepened inequality by particularly affecting the local population. This has in turn led to the coexistence of "para-state" illegal organizations that regulate the economy, justice, and life in general (Acemoglu & Robinson, 2012; Duncan, 2009).[5]

The existence of such para-states has allowed criminal organizations not only to transit and control routes for the flow of all kinds of illicit goods, but also to take refuge in territories on the other side of the border. Among other factors, these are some of the effects of the conflict beyond the domestic realm.

From Regional Impacts to the Strategic Internationalization of the Conflict

Although primarily domestic, the emergence of guerrillas in Colombia and the first decades of the confrontation were marked by the context of the Cold War (Pizarro, 2002). The Cuban revolution and the Sino-Soviet split between the main communist parties in the late 1950s and early 1960s significantly influenced the ideological foundations of the insurgent groups (Vargas, 2000, p. 10). Colombian

---

[4] 1964 saw the emergence of the FARC and the "Ejército de Liberación Nacional" ("National Liberation Army," ELN), a group that is still active; the "Ejército Popular de Liberación" ("Popular Liberation Army", EPL) arose in 1967 and most of its combatants demobilized in 1991. Five other guerrilla groups emerged after this initial generation and all demobilized during the period of democratic expansion at the end of the twentieth century.

[5] This argument has been developed extensively in Gehring and Cuervo (2014).

military forces, for their part, began a process of adjustment in accordance with the irregular warfare strategies developed in the United States. The participation of an infantry battalion that served alongside with the United States in the Korean War marked a milestone for the Colombian Army. This forged a close relationship of military cooperation with the United States, a country that has since then strongly influenced the development, structure and doctrine of the Colombian military (Dávila, 1999; Dufort, 2017; Pizarro, 1996b).

Subsequently, the intensification of the war, the exponential growth of coca cultivation, and the humanitarian and governance crisis in the mid-1990s, led academics and practitioners to highlight the spill-over effect of the Colombian crisis across its borders in neighboring territories. Colombia's "weak state" or "partial collapse" of the state was identified as a source of regional instability (Bejarano & Pizarro, 2005; Mason & Tickner, 2010). The exodus of Colombians displaced by violence to other countries in the region, as well as binational crises over cross-border security issues has also been part of the regional effects of the conflict (Ramírez, 2004). And although the current situation is far from what it was at that time, borders remain areas of high vulnerability and governance problems (Molano & Zarama, 2016). In particular, Venezuela and Ecuador have been territories used by illegal armed groups as a strategic rearguard (Carrión, 2016; Idler, 2012; Rodríguez & Ito, 2016).

Indeed, the confrontation has had direct effects on the region, but as Borda (2012, p. 32) explains, Colombian governments have also actively sought to discursively align the armed conflict with the interests of possible allies in the international arena, in search of military support and political backing. Although this had already been the case in the past, it has become a recurrent practice since the late 1990s.

In this respect, an important milestone was the formulation and implementation of the Plan Colombia (1999–2016). This plan was initially formulated during the Pastrana administration (1998–2002) with the idea of being a "Marshall Plan" in which governments from all over the world could cooperate in the reconstruction of zones affected by war in this South American country as well as alternative development programs to eradicate illicit crops. In its original version, the Plan Colombia proposed not only a military aid component but also a strategy for stabilization and comprehensive institutional and economic consolidation of the country. However, it only received financial and technical support from the US Government,[6] mainly for the war on drugs in an initial phase and subsequently, after the peace talks with the FARC broke down, also for counterinsurgent warfare.

In this regard, the events of 9/11 had a trigger effect. The "global war on terrorism" served as a backdrop for the "strong hand" discourse that emerged after

[6]Until 2016, Colombia had invested USD $1.3 million on the military component of the Plan; the United States invested USD $9.6 million during the same period. For each 10 USD invested, 7 were allocated to military aid and 3 to economic and social development (DNP, 2016).

the failed peace process with the guerrillas that ended in February 2002. As a consequence, the political platform of Álvaro Uribe, who proposed to relentlessly fight the now called "narco-terrorists groups," gained broad support throughout the country and led him to win presidency in that year (Borda, 2007; Pizarro, 2003).

The development of peace dialogs has also received support from international allies. The 1990s saw a series of negotiations outside national territory facilitated by guarantor states that hosted talks between the Colombian government and various guerrilla groups. These include the peace talks in Caracas in 1991 and Tlaxcala in 1992, when the FARC, the ELN, and a dissident faction of the EPL attempted a joint negotiation with the government under the Simón Bolívar Guerrilla Coordinating Board. Germany also hosted dialogs between the government and the ELN in 1998, when talks took place in the cities of Mainz and Würzburg. In this *rapprochement*, not only the German government but also the Episcopal Conferences of both countries played an important role.

The most recent peace process with the FARC also received significant international support, including Norway's role as guarantor and mediator of the process from the outset, but also the important work of the United Nations verification mission, which constantly monitors the implementation of and compliance with the Havana Agreements. The support of the governments of Cuba and Venezuela was also decisive. Indeed, for historical and ideological-affinity reasons, the participation of both countries as guarantors served to increase the credibility of the negotiations from the perspective of the FARC. Moreover, although the cycles of negotiations took place in Havana, the first conversations at the secret stage took place near the border in Venezuelan territory. The tensions and *rapprochements* between the Colombian and Venezuelan governments, as well as the crisis in the latter, were the backdrop for a necessary yet sometimes uncomfortable relationship for the negotiation (Ramirez, 2017). This conflict and its resolution, however, remain fundamentally a Colombian issue –and certainly not a simple matter with so many parallel intervening factors and previous failed attempts. However, some lessons obtained from the road to peace and they are outlined below.

Between a Negotiated Solution and Military Defeat: An Incomplete Peace

Since 1981, when the first peace commission was created in Colombia, the resolution of the armed conflict has been part of the government agenda and, though not always continuous, these efforts have generated a cumulative progress toward that purpose. However, due to the persistence of other actors in confrontation, when achieved, peace has only been partial (Bejarano, 2010; Nasi, 2007). Moreover, decades of multiple and failed attempts to achieve sustainable peace have generated high levels of polarization in the society, to the extent that Colombians seem to dispute each other on the road to peace.

Indeed, a peace agreement is not equivalent to conflict resolution, since the latter implies the transformation of structures linked to the deep roots of a violent conflict (Boutros-Ghali, 1992; Galtung, 1976), but the different attempts to end the conflict in Colombia have been part of its transformation. In this respect, some valuable scholarly contributions assess the experiences of previous peace processes, such as the recent work of Pizarro (2017) and Villarraga (2015), or those that describe and analyze the first peace processes, such as García Durán (1992), Ramírez and Restrepo (1989), to cite just a few examples.

Between 1984 and 2018, 16 peace negotiations took place with illegal armed groups in Colombia; within these, there were five attempts with the FARC and four with the ELN, in addition to the demobilization processes of other smaller guerrilla groups that emerged in the 1970s and 1980s. This also includes the justice and peace process of the United Self-Defence Forces of Colombia (AUC) under the Uribe administration. As Pizarro (2017, p. 342) recalls, more than a peace process, the paramilitary group submitted to the framework of the Justice and Peace Law that allowed the demobilization of more than 31,000 combatants between 2003 and 2006.

The accumulation of efforts, successes and failures over decades, were undoubtedly an important basis for achieving the recent peace agreement with the FARC. In a way, these are "staggered" peace processes (Bejarano, 2010). For example, in the Gaviria administration (1990–1994) four guerrilla groups demobilized after the pioneering process with the M-19 movement under the preceding government; the latter, in turn, participated in the 1991 Constituent Assembly.

In addition, without the military modernization that began in the late nineties, it would not have been possible to further regain military control and security in areas that until then had no state presence, as occurred during the first Uribe administration (2002–2006). Moreover, without these advances, it would have been difficult to consolidate state presence in some of these regions during his second presidency (2006–2010) or to strategically weaken the guerrilla groups and later initiate peace negotiations under the Santos administration (2010–2018). Indeed, one of the lessons learned from this process is that institutional continuity and adjustment within the military sector has been key to provide the strategic conditions to negotiate peace (Pizarro, 2018). The difficulty, however, has been to accompany military presence in the territories to be recovered with that of civil state institutions.

Challenges on the road to conflict resolution have also stemmed from particular ways of approaching the negotiation processes or even the nature of the counterpart. For example, maximalist approaches to negotiation, with excessively broad or participatory agendas, have usually resulted in the impossibility of reaching an agreement. In addition, the levels of fragmentation within the guerrilla groups as well as ideological rigidity and sectarian conflicts within their factions have also spoiled negotiated peace in the past (Pizarro, 2017). Moreover, the guerrillas have more than often entered negotiations with no will to reach an agreement, therefore instrumentalizing peace talks as a platform for strengthening military power and gaining international legitimacy (Nasi, 2012). As discussed in the next section, democracy consolidation has also played a role in transforming the conflict and has been part of the peace agenda during the past three decades.

Democracy and Peace Processes in the Midst of Violence: Unsteady Progress Toward Conflict Resolution

In addition to considering lessons learned from previous peace negotiations, the recent process with the FARC began by recognizing three fundamental features in relation to democratic consolidation in Colombia. First, decades of violence had particularly affected certain regions and populations for whom democracy has not become effective (Jaramillo, 2013). Second, the peace process should aim at closing those gaps and consolidating rule of law throughout the country. Finally, that this should be done within the legal framework of the 1991 Constitution and not by creating a new one, as demanded by the FARC, since it already contained an unfulfilled promise of democracy expansion and guarantee of fundamental rights (Bermúdez, 2018, pp. 58–59).

The first part of the next section describes key milestones in the road toward consolidating democracy and achieving peace in Colombia. It then briefly explains the recent negotiation process, describes in broad terms the peace accord between the government and FARC, and its overall implementation. Finally, it specifically deals with the agreement provisions for political participation and political reincorporation, aspects explicitly related to the role given to the expansion of democracy in this recent peace process.

Violence and Peace at the Turn of the Century: Democratization Did Not Lead to Peace But Paved the Way for Future Endeavors

The late 1980s and early 1990s marked a crucial moment for democracy and conflict transformation in Colombia. The governments of President Barco (1986–1990) and, afterwards, Gaviria offered amnesties to different guerrilla groups and facilitated the reincorporation of five of them. In addition, democratization delegitimized violence as a means to fight political exclusion (Bermúdez, 2018; Nasi, 2007; Pizarro, 2018).

In fact, the political movement "Alianza Democrática-M19" (M-19 Democratic Alliance) that emerged after the demobilization of that guerrilla group participated with 19 of the 72 constituents that were elected by popular vote to draft the new constitution.[7] Although the movement was diluted in the following years due to a lack of electoral results, today some of its former militants are still active politicians at national and local levels.

One of the main changes brought about by this process to strengthen democracy in Colombia was the broad proclamation of fundamental rights and the creation of the Constitutional Court as the safeguard for compliance with the 1991 Charter. So was the figure of the "tutela" or protective action, to which citizens can appeal when their fundamental constitutional rights are violated

[7]Considering they had not yet demobilized, seats with the right to speak but not to vote were granted to two representatives of the EPL guerrilla group, one of the Quintín Lame Armed Movement and one of the Workers' Revolutionary Party.

or threatened by the action or omission of any public authority. Participatory democracy, decentralization, and the popular election of governors were also part of this process.

An important change toward consolidating democracy during the Gaviria government occurred in the area of civil-military relations. Indeed, Colombia did not make the transition from a dictatorship to democracy, but a relatively high level of autonomy had been granted to the military in the past decades, and it was therefore necessary to expand civilian control over it (Borrero, 2006). Although this issue encountered great resistance within the Constituent Assembly and civilian management of the security and defence sector is still a pending issue on the agenda for consolidating democracy, the Gaviria government implemented fundamental initial reforms in this sense (Pizarro, 1991b; Schultze-Kraft, 2012).

This period of democratization paradoxically coincided with an escalation of political violence. At the national level, three presidential candidates (two of them from AD-M19) and two former candidates were assassinated. At the local level, 162 mayors and 420 councilors were assassinated between 1986 and 2003, without counting the dozens who were kidnapped and hundreds who were threatened (Bermúdez, 2018). But illegal armed groups not only perpetrated crimes against politicians and public officials; they also exerted pressure and violence to influence citizens' votes. On many occasions, they also prevented the population from exercising their civil and political rights, or the authorities even had to suspend elections in some municipalities due to public order problems (Nasi, 2012).

During these years, it was not possible to achieve a peace accord either with the FARC or with the ELN.[8] These groups, alongside with paramilitaries and drug traffickers, continued in a confrontation that destabilized democracy, deepening the legitimacy and governability crisis in the country (Murillo & Valdivieso, 2002). That is why some claim that Colombian democracy went from being "restricted" before the 1990s to afterwards being "besieged" by external factors that impeded its proper functioning (Bejarano & Pizarro, 2005).

Thus, not only did the democratization of the 1990s fail to solve the conflict, but the latter has further affected the democratic exercise and prevented the full enjoyment of the rights enshrined in the constitution (Nasi, 2007). Moreover, the decentralizing spirit that accompanied the democratic opening-up had the undesired effect of facilitating, through armed pressure, the control of public finances and local politics by illegal armed groups in regions where they disputed with the state the control of territory and population (Barberena, 2013). This caused a perverse effect and, although the guerrillas also exercised this type of influence and political violence, the phenomenon had its most absurd episode in the framework of the justice and peace process with the AUC, when paramilitary leaders claimed that they had influenced the election of 35 per cent of members of the Congress (Lewin, 2014).

It can therefore be said that the democratic expansion at the turn of the century did not contribute to the resolution of the conflict (Nasi, 2007), but it did

---

[8]Only one faction of this guerrilla group demobilized at that time.

to its transformation and to accompanying staggered peace efforts as described above. This also served to undermine the discourse of violence as a way out of exclusion used by the guerrilla groups and offered a framework for the recent negotiation with the FARC based on the constitutional guarantees existing since 1991.

The Peace Process with the FARC 2012–2016: A Necessary But Insufficient Step in the Resolution of the Conflict in Colombia

Colombia's governments have attempted to achieve a negotiated peace with the FARC on four occasions since 1984. The fifth attempt, which ended with its demobilization in 2017, began with an exploratory stage at the beginning of the Santos administration. First, with a confidential exchange of correspondence and later through secret talks, initial steps were taken to agree on a joint agenda and negotiation methodology published on an official announcement in August 2012.

The dialogs were formally initiated in Oslo in October 2012, and, after 51 rounds of conversations in Havana, the parties reached a definitive bilateral ceasefire in August, 2016. The "Final Agreement to End the Armed Conflict and Build a Stable and Lasting Peace" (Oficina del Alto Comisionado para la Paz (OACP), 2016) specifically provides guidelines and measures regarding the points on the agenda agreed by the negotiating parties: a more inclusive rural and regional development; expansion of democracy in general and guarantees for the political reincorporation of the demobilized group; a model of transitional justice and reparation for the victims; the solution to the drug trafficking problem; and with respect to its public endorsement, implementation and verification (OACP, 2016).

However, in a more general sense, the peace accord recognizes the need to promote social and regional inclusion as key factors for the consolidation of peace, as well as some fundamental measures contemplated in the 1991 Constitution that have not been implemented (Bermúdez, 2018). "Territorial peace" and "closing gaps" were terms used by the government to emphasize the need to resolve the country's fragmentation problems, the exclusion of regions particularly affected by the conflict and the precarious governance in those areas as a cause of persistent violence (Departamento Nacional de Planeación (DNP), 2014; Jaramillo, 2014). In addition, the peace process offered a window of opportunity to operationalize the Constitution's principle of participatory democracy as a way to reverse cycles of violence and exclusion and thus strengthen the state's legitimacy.

Submitting the peace dialogs to a predetermined agenda and strict confidentiality was the result of lessons learnt in past failed negotiation processes. However, this secrecy also undermined the public acceptance of the agreement. Among other reasons, it was due to a failure of the government to communicate the contents of the agreements to the general public and to reach out to sectors that were critical of the process (Gehring & Cuervo, 2016). A public opinion survey in 2015 already predicted what happened in the plebiscite: a large majority of Colombians supported peace with the FARC but objected to concessions in terms of justice and political participation of this group (García, Montalvo, & Selligson, 2015).

Thus, when 50.2 per cent of voters rejected the agreement in October 2016, the government delegation met with representatives of different political and social groups that led the "No" campaign to listen and take into consideration their criticisms and proposals. In a record term of one month, the delegates renegotiated in Havana the new agreement with the FARC and, finally, the Congress unanimously approved the definitive agreement in December, 2016.[9]

The next step was the demobilization of ex-combatants and the laying down of 7,132 weapons during the first six months of 2017, a process supported by the German government (Bundesanstalt Technisches Hilfswerk (THW), 2017). For the first time in Colombia, a disarmament process had a rate of 1 weapon per combatant –something unusual when compared to other experiences worldwide (Fundación Ideas para la Paz (FIP), 2017). Although it is estimated that around 1,500 ex-combatants are now dissidents, this first step and the de-escalation of the armed conflict were undoubtedly positive steps.

However, as is common in the post-demobilization phase, the first months were a critical phase. A rapid response plan after the bilateral ceasefire was considered a priority, including a security strategy and putting in place civil institutions to regain control of the areas from which the FARC had withdrawn. However, this did not happen in many areas – or at least not successfully enough – among other things, due to the lack of physical infrastructure and public services.

Furthermore, as the Kroc Institute for International Peace Studies [10] (2018) has recently reported, compared to other comprehensive peace agreements, the process in Colombia has an average implementation rate after the first 18 months. In addition, there are different levels of progress within the peace deal: actions have been implemented in 61 percent of the provisions (21 per cent of which have been met in full) but no action has been taken in the other 39 per cent. The smallest progress can be found in the comprehensive rural reform and political participation provisions, a point dealt with below.

Democracy Expansion and Political Reincorporation: Progress, Difficulties in Implementation, and Resistance to Change

The points dealing with "Political participation: A democratic opportunity to build peace" and the "Reincorporation of the FARC-EP into civilian life" are the two aspects of the agreement most explicitly related to the expansion of democracy (OACP, 2016). The document contemplates three main approaches in this sense: the need for the political system to be more inclusive; the importance of

[9]Although modifications were made, not all "no" points were included in the new agreement. The Democratic Centre party, led by former President Uribe and a strong opponent of the agreement's contents throughout the negotiations, abstained from voting.

[10]This research center has been officially commissioned to monitor the implementation of the agreements.

guaranteeing the safety of those who will be politically active; and encouraging the participation of social organizations in democracy.

During the negotiation, government delegates insisted that the agreement would signal a roadmap toward sustainable peace but that it would be up to the Congress to discuss and approve the specific reforms to achieve it (Bermúdez, 2018). This underscores the negotiators' confidence in the democratic institutions, but the legislative process also distorted some of the aspects linked to political participation, which so far is one of the points with the lowest implementation level.

Indeed, the same Congress that unanimously approved the final agreement in December, 2016, then distorted and finally torpedoed key reforms to improve the political system and expand democracy during the following months (Misión de Observación Electoral (MOE), 2018a). This apparent contradiction is not only due to the fact that the political support for the Santos government diluted at the end of his administration, parallel to increasing objections from political groups critical of the agreement (Rettberg & Quiroga, 2014). It also shows a strong resistance to change by political elites against achieving fairer rules and greater representation for excluded citizens and regions.

A clear example of this is the reform bill to increase transparency within the political system. After going through the legislative process, the project suffered a distortion that even reversed issues that had already seen improvements in the previous years. Given this scenario, the government decided to shelve the reform project, considering that it was not coherent with the spirit of expanding democracy and transparency initially intended (MOE, 2018a, p. 20).

Something similar happened with the mechanism called "Transitory Peace Circumscriptions" which sought to further promote the ideal of decentralization of the 1991 Constitution (Bermúdez, 2018). Recognizing that there are populations particularly and historically affected by violence, excluded from national politics despite their wealth in resources and territory, the agreement provided for a mechanism so that these regions would have guaranteed seats in Congress during the following eight years. This was intended to compensate for the low representation and the impact violence had had on these populations, spread over one third of Colombia, with a wealth of natural resources and indigenous reservations as well as community councils for African descendants, but representing only 7 per cent of the electoral census (MOE, 2018a, p. 21). However, the bill did not achieve the necessary votes and ended up sinking for lack of parliamentary support.

One aspect in which progress has been made concerns the statute for guaranteeing the exercise of political opposition – something also contemplated in the 1991 Constitution but which had not been materialized. Although its implementation has been more formal up to now in terms of formulating procedures and its regulation, more of its results will be seen in the 2019 local elections, particularly in terms of greater visibility in the media (Huertas, 2019).

Regarding the political reincorporation of the FARC, this point mainly contemplated guarantees of participation and political representation for the new political party, as well as security measures to protect its members. Although formal progress has been made, in practical terms there is still resistance to change. The "Revolutionary Alternative Force of the Common" (FARC), as the former guerrilla fighters decided to call their new political party, has legal status and funding for its operation and its center of thought. It also had been granted funding for the 2018 election campaign, but in practice this did not work properly, because the financing system initially demanded prerequisites that the newly formed party did not meet, there were obstacles in the financial sector preventing the administration of resources of a political organization with guerrilla origin, and a lack of timely communication between state institutions and financial institutions (MOE, 2018b).

As for the guarantees of protection and physical security, there were not only threats against the candidates who campaigned for the presidential and parliamentary elections in 2018, but also murders: five members of the FARC party were killed, making this the political group with the highest number of victims of this type of political violence in the election year.

In general, the points regarding the consolidation of democracy and the political reincorporation of the FARC had a relatively low level of implementation until late 2018. The local elections of 2019 will be an important checkpoint regarding the financing guarantees and the security of candidates from the newly created political party, but also for the protection of political and civil rights of all Colombians. Otherwise, there will be the perception that, in the end, it was not possible to expand democracy or reduce the conflict convincingly, and that the peace agreement came with promises and expectations still "to be fulfilled" like those of the 1991 Constitution. In the following and final section, a brief review is made of the possible lessons of the Colombian.

"Without a State There Will Be Neither Peace Nor Democracy"[11]

Without a doubt, the situation in Colombia is far from being that of a "stateless" country. But there are many "Colombias" –and not only the one that separates Bogotá as capital in a highly centralized country from the rest of the territory. A state on the way to consolidate rule of law and democracy for all its citizens coexists with illegal parallel states able to dispute and assume control in specific areas of the country.

As is usually the case in protracted conflicts, these tend to generate the perception of being impossible to solve due to their cyclical nature and the capacity of trigger factors to reinforce their complexity (Ramsbotham, Woodhouse, & Miall, 2015). Colombia has not been an exception to this, but a mid- and long-term perspective allows us to assess progress and reflect on possible points of entry to transform it. In this final section, some lessons from the Colombian case are shared in terms of democratization processes and the resolution of domestic conflicts.

Firstly, *silencing the guns does not equal conflict resolution, but this step allows to recognize and address other key problems in the peacebuilding and democracy consolidation agendas.* Proof of this came in 2018, when Colombia experienced

[11]This is how Palacios (1999) titled his text on violence and peace in Colombia (original in Spanish: "Violencia y paz: sin Estado no habrá paz ni democracia").

the first elections without the FARC in more than six decades. The level of electoral risk due to violence factors was the lowest since 2006[12] and, compared to the 2014 elections, that risk was eliminated in 79 municipalities (MOE, 2018a). In that sense, although the elections were not entirely peaceful and there is still much to be done in terms of protecting and guaranteeing civil and political rights, there has definitely been a positive change in the scenario.

Among other things, because of the existence of the conflict and, in particular, the guerrilla groups have for years been used to justify various problems in the country that sometimes interact with violence, though these have much deeper roots. In fact, sometimes violence and turmoil serve to support exclusionary social orders, insofar as they offer a kind of "curtain" hiding other problems that remain invisible (Acemoglu & Robinson, 2012, pp. 368–402). For example, the debate over corruption began to occupy a more central place in Colombia's public agenda in the last two years. This is certainly not a new phenomenon but moving toward peace allows us to appreciate other obstacles hindering the consolidation of a democratic political system (MOE, 2018a, pp. 30–31).

Symbolically, social networks widely echoed the phrase "before, the bridges were taken down by guerrilla groups, now they fall because of corruption" in November 2017, when a bridge collapsed due to flaws in design, killing nine people. Although it is undoubtedly an exaggeration and cannot be generalized, it is at least a sign that Colombians' perception of the country's problems is changing.

Furthermore, as the title of the recent Democracy Observatory special report on attitudes and perceptions of citizens in post-conflict rural areas suggests, silencing weapons allows us to hear voices that have historically been ignored.[13] The study is based on surveys and focus groups conducted in 2017 and 2018 in regions prioritized for the implementation of the agreements because over the years they have been affected by violence and the presence of the FARC. In terms of needs and concerns perceived by the population in these regions, corruption and lack of infrastructure have begun to gain relevance compared to the conflict and the guerrilla fighting. And although the levels are still relatively low compared to the national sample, the perception that security is now being provided by the public forces and no longer by the FARC has increased (Observatorio de la Democracia [Democracy Observatory], 2018a, p. 113).

Secondly, Colombia shows, as in other cases, that *democracy alone not only does not lead to the resolution of conflict, but also, in contexts of state fragility, citizens cannot fully exercise democracy*. A third of the violence against social leaders in the country and 40 per cent of the violence against the community action councils (MOE, 2019) occurs in those areas where the recently demobilized guerrilla group used to operate. These communal organizations are precisely those that enjoy greater trust on the part of the resident population, far more than the

---

[12]The first year these data were recorded.

[13]Silenciar las armas, oír las voces: Colombia Rural Posconflicto [Silence the weapons, hear the voices: Postconflict Rural Colombia]. *Obervatorio de la Democracia (Democracy Observatory)*. Retrieved from https://sitios.obsdemocracia.org/

political parties and the Congress, the last ones on the list (Observatorio de la Democracia [Democracy Observatory], 2018b, p. 52). In addition, the percentage of those expressing a high level of support for the system, political tolerance and a commitment to democracy has decreased in the last two years (Observatorio de la Democracia [Democracy Observatory], 2018b, p. 28).

These data underscore the importance of supporting the implementation of the agreements to meet the expectations generated in populations that have been systematically excluded from peace, democracy, and socio-economic development. But it also highlights the worrisome situation of insecurity and lack of guarantees for political, social and community leaders in Colombia. As for the violence that occurred against political leaders around the last electoral process, all parties were victims of threats and killing of political leaders in 2018 but the FARC was the most affected (27 per cent of assassinations) (MOE, 2019).

Additionally, according to official sources,[14] there were 343 murders of social leaders and human rights advocates between January 2016, and August 2018. "What a tremendous contrast: as the casualties of war descend, the victims of peace grow," reflected recently Gonzalo Sánchez, former director of the National Centre for Historical Memory and a pioneer in the study of the conflict in Colombia (Sánchez, 2018).

Neither the Santos government nor that of the current president, Iván Duque (2018–2022), has taken a clear stand against this type of violence or to generate a strong institutional response, and even the Ministers of Defence in both administrations made statements in which the problem was minimized or attempted to link the victims with criminal activities. At the moment of writing this chapter, it is evident that there is a systematic practice following the struggle for territorial control, with at least two clear trends. First, murders are occurring with greater intensity in areas where illicit crops are grown: 74 per cent of selective murders in 2018 occurred in municipalities with this problem (MOE, 2018). Second, the victims are community leaders, volunteers working on illicit crop replacement projects, and people claiming the return of their land (Prem, Rivera, Romero, & Vargas, 2018).

This study leads to a third important message left by the Colombian case in terms of the importance of guaranteeing security for the population throughout the territory and what is required for a comprehensive response for conflict resolution, not only by the military, but also from civil institutions. In other words, dilemmas such as "peace or military solution" and "negotiation or firm hand" are false dichotomies that only contribute to increasing levels of polarization and lead to partial institutional responses. Here, it is worth remembering that the road toward disarmament and demobilization of the FARC was marked both by the military's weakening of the guerrilla forces and the parallel exploration of a negotiated peace. Not in vain did President Uribe charge his peace commissioner with the task of exploring dialogues with the ELN and the FARC before the end of his mandate in 2009.

Similarly, when addressing issues such as state weakness and the need to prioritize state monopoly on violence, this includes but transcends a security policy

---

[14]The official figure is a total of 164 murdered leaders until the middle of December 2018 (Defensoría del Pueblo, 2019).

and implies a broad reform (Schultze-Kraft, 2010, 2012). In areas where homicides are occurring, there is not only a lack of military or police presence; the judicial system lacks institutional tools and officials, physical infrastructure is precarious and basic social services are not covered. It seems an obvious lesson, but of course not an easy one and demands a direct and committed involvement of the civil authorities in managing the security and defence sector in accordance with transparent democratic parameters.

In this regard, although this topic deserves much deeper reflection and analysis, the reform of the security and defence system is also an important part of the consolidation of a democracy, as is the civil authorities' capacity to control and manage the sector in general and the Armed Forces in particular. In Colombia, this task is still pending and a high priority issue (Leal, 2018). For example, the doctrine reform and the restructuring of the armed forces was not part of the Havana agenda, but the military themselves put in place a transformation process, among others, in order to participate in international missions within the context of a global partnership with the North Atlantic Treaty Organization (NATO). However, neither the relevant institutions of the executive, nor the legislative or the civil society, have played an active role in this institutional change.

Tensions in the Transition and Hope on the New Generations to Keep Walking the Road Toward Peace: Conclusion and Final Reflections

Following the night of the plebiscite in October 2016, thousands of FARC ex-combatants and the members of the Colombian public forces guarding them in the areas destined for their pre-demobilization concentration, lived hours of anxiety. While thousands of Colombian citizens marched and demanded that the political class reach a compromise so as not to sink the peace process, both armed groups, accustomed to seeing the other as the enemy in battle, decided to respect the ceasefire.

With their actions on the field but also in Havana, the active members of the military and police assigned by the government to negotiate the end of the conflict with the guerrilla delegates, decided to protect a peace that in Bogota seemed to be hanging by a thread.

"It's just that Bogotá is very far from Colombia" as a member of the guerrilla delegation in Havana said (Bermúdez, 2018, p. 44). Maybe because of that, and because those who fought and suffered in the war sometimes seem more willing to make peace,[15] there was no return to confrontation with the FARC and members

---

[15]In this regard, Pizarro (2018) recalls the decisive nature of the participation of officers on active service in the negotiations with the FARC and it has been documented how their participation was fundamental in the negotiation of the DDR point and verification. Likewise, in the public opinion survey of the Obervatorio de la Democracia [Democracy Observatory] (2015), the areas affected by the conflict showed more favorable attitudes in support of the process with the guerrilla groups compared to the national sample.

of the state forces generated protocols to continue with the process while the renegotiation took place with the approval of the government.

Such a statement, which could also have been uttered by a communal leader, a victim or a member of the armed forces, contains the essence of the problem of governance –where the center does not govern in the periphery – and of a conflict that "coexists with, and is nourished by, other long-standing structural failures" (Schultze-Kraft, 2010, p. 289). Here, it is worth emphasizing that recognizing the existence of structural factors linked to the existence of conflict, as has been done in this chapter, does not justify, in the manner of "objective causes," the use of violence as a means to bring about changes in a social order. But this allows to take a different view in which *the armed conflict in Colombia, rather than the main problem, is a symptom, among others, of deep structural failures linked to the consolidation of the rule of law*, democracy and social and regional inclusion – in short, a deficit of governance. In Colombia, violence has contributed to the deepening of these problems, to the extent that it has served as a "veil" to overshadow or put in the background other problems that must be addressed in order to strengthen democracy and the rule of law.

Thus, achieving legitimate monopoly on violence and the effective presence of civil institutions of the state at the local and regional level will be a precondition for consolidating democracy and enabling the resolution of conflict based on pluralism. Without a doubt, Colombia has made progress along this long road, but it will require the commitment of present and future generations to continue in that direction and not yield in those areas where democracy is already entrenched.

References

Acemoglu, D., & Robinson, J. (2012). *Why nations fail: The origins of power, prosperity and poverty*. New York, NY: Crown.

Arnson, C. (2005). Third parties and intractable conflicts: The Case of Colombia. In C. Crocker, F. O. Hampson, & P. Aall (Eds.), *Grasping the Nettle: Analyzing cases of intractability*. Washington, DC: United States Institute of Peace Press.

Barberena, V. (2013, junio 2). Descentralización en Colombia: 25 años preparando el territorio para la paz. *Razon Republica*. Retrieved from http://www.razonpublica.com

Bejarano, A. M. (2010). Conflicto prolongado, múltiples protagonistas y negociaciones escalonadas. In A. Rettberg (Ed.), *Conflicto armado, seguridad y construcción de paz en Colombia* (pp. 43–96). Bogotá: Ediciones Uniandes.

Bejarano, J. A., Echandía, C., Escobedo, R., & Queruz, E. (1997). *Colombia: inseguridad, violencia y desempeño económico*. Bogotá: Fondo Financiero de Proyectos de Desarrollo, Universidad Externado de Colombia.

Bejarano, A. M., & Pizarro, E. (2005). From 'Restricted' to 'Besieged': The changing nature of the limits to democracy in Colombia. In F. Hagopian & S. Mainwaring (Eds.), *The Third Wave of Democratization in Latin America. Advances and setbacks* (pp. 235–260). Cambridge: Cambridge University Press.

Bermúdez, A. (2018). *Los debates de La Habana: una mirada desde adentro*. Bogotá: Fondo de Capital Humano para la Transición Colombiana, Instituto para las Transiciones Integrales (IFIT).

Borda, S. (2007). La internacionalización del conflicto armado después del 11 de septiembre: ¿la ejecución de una estrategia diplomática hábil o la simple ocurrencia de lo inevitable? *Colombia Internacional*, *65*, 66–89.

Borda, S. (2012). *La internacionalización de la paz y de la guerra en Colombia durante los Gobiernos de Andrés Pastrana y Álvaro Uribe. Búsqueda de legitimidad política y capacidad militar*. Bogotá: Ediciones Uniandes.

Borrero, A. (2006). Los militares: los dolores del crecimiento. In F. Leal (Ed.), *En la encrucijada. Colombia en el siglo XXI* (pp. 113–146). Bogotá: Ediciones Uniandes, Norma.

Boutros-Ghali, B. (1992). *An Agenda for Peace. Preventive diplomacy, peacemaking and peace-keeping* (A/47/277/S24111). United Nations website. Retrieved from http://www.un.org/ga/search/view_doc.asp?symbol=A/47/277

Bundesanstalt Technisches Hilfswerk (THW). (2017, September 24). *Bundesinnenminister dankt dem Technischen Hilfswerk für seinen Einsatz bei der VN-Friedensmission in Kolumbien*. Retrieved from https://www.thw.de

Camacho, A. (2002). Credo, necesidad y codicia: los alimentos de la guerra. *Análisis Político*, *46*, 137–150.

Carrión, F. (2016). La frontera colombo-ecuatoriana en el posconflicto. In A. Molano (Ed.), *Fronteras en Colombia como zonas estratégicas: Análisis y perspectivas* (pp. 181–194). Bogotá: Instituto de Ciencia Política Hernán Echavarría Olózaga.

Comisión Histórica del Conflicto y sus Víctimas. (2015, febrero). *Contribución al entendimiento del conflicto armado en Colombia*. Retrieved from http://www.altocomisionadoparalapaz.gov.co/mesadeconversaciones/PDF/Informe%20Comisi_n%20Hist_rica%20del%20Conflicto%20y%20sus%20V_ctimas.%20La%20Habana%2C%20Febrero%20de%202015.pdf

Dávila, A. (1999). Ejército regular, conflictos irregulares: la institución militar en los últimos 15 años. In M. Deas & M. V. Llorente (Eds.), *Reconocer la guerra para construir la paz* (pp. 283–345). Bogota: Ediciones Uniandes, Cerec, Norma.

Deas, M. (2003). Perspectiva Histórica de las Relaciones cívico-militares en Colombia. In F. Cepeda (Ed.), *Las relaciones cívico-militares en tiempos de conflicto armado* (pp. 77–85). Bogotá: Embajada de los Estados Unidos de América, Fundación Ideas para la Paz.

Defensoría del Pueblo. (2019). *Homicidios de líderes sociales y defensores de DDHH* [Dataset]. Retrieved from http://www.defensoria.gov.co

Departamento Nacional de Planeación (DNP). (2014). *Bases para el Plan Nacional de Desarrollo 2014–2018. Versión preliminar para discusión del Consejo Nacional de Planeación*. Retrieved from https://colaboracion.dnp.gov.co/CDT/Prensa/Bases%20Plan%20Nacional%20de%20Desarrollo%202014-2018.pdf

Departamento Nacional de Planeación (DNP). (2016, febrero 9). *Plan Colombia DNP 15 años*. Retrieved from https://www.dnp.gov.co

Dufort, P. (2017). A typology of military factions in the Colombian officer corps: Origins and evolution of Colombian counter-insurgency. *Canadian Journal of Latin American and Caribbean Studies*, *42*(3), 320–349.

Duncan, G. (2006). *Los Señores de la Guerra*. Bogotá: Editorial Planeta.

Duncan, G. (2009, marzo 9). Una visión alternativa del conflicto colombiano. *Razón Pública*. Retrieved from http://www.razonpublica.com

Fundación Ideas para la Paz (FIP). (2017). *La dejación de armas de las FARC y otros procesos de desarme en el mundo* [Infographic]. Retrieved from http://cdn.ideaspaz.org

Galtung, J. (1976). Three approaches to peace: Peacekeeping, peacemaking, and peacebuilding. In J. Galtung (Ed.), *Peace, war and defence: Essays in peace research* (Vol. 2, pp. 282–304). Copenhagen: Ejlers.

García Durán, M. (1992). *De la Uribe a Tlaxcala: Proceso de Paz*. Bogota: Cinep.

García, M., Montalvo, J., & Selligson, M. (Eds.). (2015). *Cultura política de la democracia en Colombia, 2015. Actitudes democráticas en zonas de consolidación territorial*. Bogotá: Observatorio de la Democracia, Universidad de Los Andes.

Gehring, H., & Cuervo, M. (2014). Colombia: From peace process to building a Country. *KAS International Reports*, *3*, 59–90. Retrieved from https://www.kas.de/c/document_library/get_file?uuid=e3d5351e-1246-df98-00b3-16ee48b1ddce&groupId=252038

Gehring, H., & Cuervo, M. (2016, octubre). Miedo al cambio: cómo un alemán reportó a sus paisanos lo que pasó el 2 de octubre en Colombia. *Konrad-Adenauer-Stiftung e. V*. Retrieved from https://www.kas.de

González, F., Bolívar, I., & Vázquez, T. (2003). *Violencia política en Colombia: de la nación fragmentada a la construcción del Estado*. Bogotá: Cinep.

Grupo de Memoria Histórica (GMH). (2013). *¡Basta ya! Colombia: Memorias de guerra y dignidad*. Bogotá: Imprenta Nacional. Retrieved from http://www.centrodememoriahistorica.gov.co/descargas/informes2013/bastaYa/basta-ya-memorias-guerra-dignidad-new-9-agosto.pdf

Gutiérrez, F., & Barón, M. (2006). Estado, control territorial y orden político en Colombia. Notas para una economía política del paramilitarismo, 1978–2004. In F. Gutiérrez, M. E. Wills, & G. Sánchez (Eds.), *Nuestra guerra sin nombre: transformaciones del conflicto en Colombia* (pp. 267–309). Bogotá: Editorial Norma.

Gutiérrez, F., & Sánchez, G. (2006). Prólogo. In F. Gutiérrez, G. Sánchez, & M. E. Wills (Eds.), *Nuestra guerra sin nombre. Transformaciones del conflicto en Colombia* (pp. 11–32). Bogotá: Norma, Instítuto de Estudios Politicos y Relaciones Internacionales.

Guzmán, G., Fals Borda, O., & Umaña, E. (1964). *La Violencia en Colombia. Estudio de un proceso social (Tomo II)*. Bogotá: Carlos Valencia Editores.

Hartlyn, J. (1984). Military governments and the transition to civilian rule: The Colombian experience of 1957–1958. *Journal of Interamerican Studies and World Affairs*, *26*(2), 245–281.

Hartlyn, J. (1988). *The politics of coalition rule in Colombia*. New York, NY: Cambridge University Press.

Huertas, J. (2019, enero 25). El Estatuto de la Oposición: más tilín que paletas, por ahora. *La Silla Vacía*. Retrieved from https://lasillavacia.com

Idler, A. (2012). Exploring arrangements of convenience among violent non-state actors. *Perspectives in Terrorism*, *6*(4–5), 63–84.

Jaramillo, S. (2013, mayo 9). La transición en Colombia. *Oficina del Alto Comisionado para la Paz [OACP]*. Retrieved from http://www.altocomisionadoparalapaz.gov.co

Jaramillo, S. (2014). *Todo lo que debería saber sobre el proceso de paz. Visión, realidades y avances en las conversaciones que adelanta el Gobierno Nacional en La Habana. Oficina del Alto Comisionado para la Paz [OACP]*. Bogotá: Imprenta Nacional.

Kriesberg, L. (2004). Transforming intractable conflicts. *Desafíos*, *10*, 188–199.

Kroc Institute for International Peace Studies. (2018, agosto). *Segundo informe sobre el estado efectivo de implementación del acuerdo de paz en Colombia, diciembre 2016 – mayo 2018*. Instituto Kroc de Estudios Internacionales de Paz, Escuela Keough de Asuntos Globales, Universidad de Notre Dame website. Retrieved from https://kroc.nd.edu/assets/284864/informe_2_instituto_kroc_final_with_logos.pdf

Leal, F. (2018). Militares y construcción de paz en la Colombia actual. *Nueva Sociedad*, *278*, 90–99. Retrieved from http://nuso.org/articulo/militares-y-construccion-de-paz-en-la-colombia-actual/

Legrand, C. (1986). Los antecedentes agrarios de la violencia: el conflicto social en la frontera colombiana, 1850–1936. In G. Sánchez & R. Peñaranda (Eds.), *Pasado y presente de la violencia en Colombia* (pp. 87–110). Bogotá: CEREC.

Lewin, J. E. (2014, noviembre 8). Las diez cosas que prueba la sentencia de Mancuso. *La Silla Vacía*. Retrieved from https://lasillavacia.com

Mason, A., & Tickner, A. (2010). Agentes de inseguridad en la región andina. Crimen transnacional y relaciones estratégicas. In A. Rettberg (Ed.), *Conflicto armado, seguridad y construcción de paz en Colombia* (pp. 351–372). Bogota: Ediciones Uniandes.

Misión de Observación Electoral (MOE). (2018a). *Mapas y factores de riesgo electoral. Elecciones nacionales Colombia 2018*. Reprieved from https://moe.org.co/wp-content/uploads/2018/02/Mapas_y_Factores_de_Riesgo_Electoral_MOE_Elecciones_en_Colombia_2018.pdf

Misión de Observación Electoral (MOE). (2018b). *Informe de la reincorporación política de las Farc-EP*. Bogotá: MOE. Retrieved from https://moe.org.co/wp-content/uploads/2018/11/Informe-de-Reincorporaci%C3%B3n-Pol%C3%ADtica-de-las-FARC_Digital.pdf

Misión de Observación Electoral (MOE). (2019, enero 11). *Resumen ejecutivo del informe de violencia contra líderes políticos, sociales y comunales*. Retrieved from https://moe.org.co/wp-content/uploads/2018/07/20190110_Informe_ViolPol.pdf

Molano, A., & Zarama, F. (2016). Fronteras: gobernanza, sensibilidad y vulnerabilidad. In A. Molano (Ed.), *Fronteras en Colombia como zonas estratégicas: Análisis y perspectivas* (pp. 17–46). Bogotá: Instituto de Ciencia Política Hernán Echavarría Olózaga.

Montenegro, A., & Posada, C. (2001). *La violencia en Colombia*. Bogotá: Alfaomega.

Murillo, G., & Valdivieso, Y. (2002). *El escalonamiento de la crisis política colombiana*. Working Papers N° 201. Institut de Ciències Polítiques i Socials website. Retrieved from https://www.icps.cat/archivos/WorkingPapers/wp201.pdf?noga=1

Nasi, C. (2007). *Cuando callan los fusiles. Impacto de la paz negociada en Colombia y en Centroamérica*. Bogotá: Grupo Editorial Norma-Universidad de los Andes.

Nasi, C. (2012). Instituciones políticas para el post-conflicto. In A. Rettberg (Ed.), *Construcción de paz en Colombia* (pp. 51–85). Bogotá: Ediciones Uniandes.

Observatorio de la Democracia [Democracy Observatory]. (2015). *Cultura política de la democracia en Colombia 2015. Actitudes democráticas en zonas de consolidación territorial*. Bogotá: Universidad de los Andes, Observatorio de la Democracia, Centro Nacional de Consultoría, LAPOP, Vanderbilt University. Retrieved from https://www.researchgate.net/publication/292155541

Observatorio de la Democracia [Democracy Observatory]. (2018a). *Colombia rural del posconflicto. Paz, posconflicto y reconciliatión 2017*. Bogotá: Observatorio de la Democracia, Universidad de los Andes, Ipsos, Vanderbuilt University. Retrieved from https://www.researchgate.net/publication/329402932_Colombia_Rural_Posconflicto_Paz_Posconflicto_y_Reconciliacion_2017

Observatorio de la Democracia [Democarcy Observatory]. (2018b). *Colombia rural del posconflicto. Democracia e Instituciones 2017*. Bogotá: Observatorio de la Democracia, Universidad de los Andes, Ipsos, Vanderbuilt University. Retrieved from https://www.researchgate.net/publication/329403800_Colombia_Rural_Posconflicto_Democracia_e_Instituciones_2017

Oficina del Alto Comisionado para la Paz (OACP). (2016). *Final Agreement to End the Armed Conflict and Build a Stable and Lasting Peace*. Retrieved from http://especiales.presidencia.gov.co/Documents/20170620-dejacion-armas/acuerdos/acuerdo-final-ingles.pdf

Palacios, M. (1999). Violencia y paz: sin Estado no habrá paz ni democracia. *Revista Credencial Historia, 119*. Retrieved from http://www.banrepcultural.org

Pizarro, E. (1991a). *Las FARC (1949-1966). De la autodefensa a la combinación de todas las formas de lucha*. Bogotá: Tercer Mundo Editores.

Pizarro, E. (1991b). Fuerzas Armadas y Asamblea Constituyente. *Revista Foro, 14*, 44–50.

Pizarro, E. (1996a). *Insurgencia sin revolución: la guerrilla en Colombia en una perspectiva comparada*. Texas: Universidad de Texas.

Pizarro, E. (1996b). Las fuerzas armadas en un contexto de insurgencia crónica. In J. M. Blanquer & C. Gros (Eds.), *Las dos Colombias* (pp. 81–116). Bogotá: Editorial Norma.

Pizarro, E. (2002). Colombia: ¿guerra civil, guerra contra la sociedad, guerra antiterrorista o guerra ambigua? *Análisis Político*, *46*(2), 164–179.

Pizarro, E. (2003). Colombia. El proyecto de seguridad democrática de Álvaro Uribe. *Nueva Sociedad, 186*, 4–17.

Pizarro, E. (2017). *Cambiar el futuro. Historia de los procesos de paz en Colombia (1981–2016)*. Bogotá: Penguin Random House.

Pizarro, E. (2018). *De la guerra a la paz. Las Fuerzas Militares entre 1996 y 2018*. Bogotá: Planeta.

Prem, M., Rivera, A., Romero, D., & Vargas, J. F. (2018). *Killing social leaders for territorial control: the unintended consequences of peace (Working Paper)*. Bogotá: Universidad del Rosario. Retrieved from https://ideas.repec.org/p/col/000092/016385.html

Ramírez, S. (2004). *Intervención en conflictos internos. El caso colombiano 1994–2003*. Bogotá: Universidad Nacional de Colombia.

Ramirez, S. (2017). Paz en Colombia: Miedos y riesgos. In W. Grabendorff & D. Gudiño (Eds.), *Proceso de paz y posacuerdo en Colombia: Efectos en la region* (pp. 49–73). Quito: Friedrich-Ebert-Stiftung.

Ramírez, S., & Restrepo, L. A. (1989). *Actores en conflicto por la paz*. Bogotá: Cinep, Siglo XXI.

Ramsbotham, O., Woodhouse, T., & Miall, H. (2015). *Contemporary Conflict Resolution. The prevention, management and transformation of deadly conflicts*. Cambridge: Polity.

Rettberg, A. (2002). *Preparar el futuro: Conflicto y post-conflicto en Colombia*. Bogotá: Libros de Cambio, Universidad de Los Andes, Fundación Ideas para la Paz.

Rettberg, A., & Quiroga, D. (2014). *Kolumbien: der Kongress und de Friedensverhandlungen. GIGA Focus 6*. Hamburg: German Institute Global and Area Studies.

Robinson, J. (2013, February). Colombia: Another 100 Years of Solitude? *Current History*, 43–48. Retrieved from http://scholar.harvard.edu/files/jrobinson/files/robinson-current_history.pdf

Rodríguez, R., & Ito, J. C. (2016). La frontera colombo-venezolana: dos visiones divergentes. In A. Molano (Ed.), *Fronteras en Colombia como zonas estratégicas: Análisis y perspectivas* (pp. 165–180). Bogotá: Instituto de Ciencia Política Hernán Echavarría Olózaga.

Romero, M. (2003). *Paramilitares y autodefensas, 1982–2003*. Bogotá: Editorial Planeta Colombiana.

Sánchez, G. (1987). *Colombia: Violencia y democracia*. Bogotá: Centro Editorial, Universidad Nacional de Colombia.

Sánchez, G. (2018). Líderes sociales, ¿víctimas de la paz? *Centro Nacional de Memoria Histórica*. Retrieved from http://www.centrodememoriahistorica.gov.co/micrositios/revista-conmemora_lideres-sociales/lideres-sociales-victimas-de-la-paz.html

Schultze-Kraft, M. (2010). La estrategia de resolución integral del conflicto armado y la construcción democrática del poder y del orden en Colombia. In A. Vargas & C. Medina (Ed.), *Colombia: escenarios posibles de guerra o paz* (pp. 287–302). Bogotá: Universidad Nacional de Colombia

Schultze-Kraft, M. (2012). La cuestión militar en Colombia: la fuerza pública y los retos de la construcción de paz. In A. Rettberg (Ed.), *Construcción de paz en Colombia* (pp. 405–433). Bogotá: Ediciones Uniandes.

UNHCR. (2018). Alto Comisionado de las Naciones Unidas para los Refugiados. *Colombia (Fact Sheet – Sept.* 2018*)*. Retrieved from https://www.UNHCR.org/5b97f3154.pdf

United Nations Development Programme (UNDP). (2011). *Colombia rural. Razones para la esperanza. Informe Nacional de Desarrollo Humano 2011*. Bogotá: INDH, Programa de las Naciones Unidas para el Desarrollo.

Vargas, A. (2000). Antecedentes del conflicto armado en Colombia. In R. González (Ed.), *Democracia y proceso de paz en Colombia: un debate desde la academia*. Barranquilla: Ediciones Uninorte.

Villarraga, A. (Ed.). (2015). *Biblioteca de la Paz*. Bogotá: Fundación Cultura Democrática.

Chapter 7

The Roads to Reinvigorate the Peace Agreements: Between Electoral and Justice Reforms in Guatemala

José Carlos Sanabria Arias

The challenge for Guatemalan society is to reinvigorate the Peace Agreements. After 20 years of the signing of the agreements, Guatemala faces the challenge of finding ways to strengthen peace and consolidate the democratic system. The following chapter seeks to describe the structural roots that motivated the internal armed conflict, the main aspects of the peace process, and the challenges that Guatemala faces in the consolidation of the democratic system, especially in electoral and justice reform. Relevant questions for some answers are: How and when did the democracy become part of the resolution process? What was the role of democracy in the resolution of civil conflict? The challenge of the reinvigoration the peace efforts is to identify the relationship between peace, development, and democratic consolidation. Peace in Guatemala has a name and a surname; these are democracy and development. The peace that must be built is directed at a very accurate diagnosis of our past, and to an expression of what we hope for it to be in the future.

Introduction

The peace accords were successful in closing the cycle of armed violence that lasted more than 30 years, with a balance at the end of the conflict, according to the Commission for Historical Clarification (CEH), it was 200,000 dead, 45,000 disappeared, and nearly 100,000 displaced. The parties fulfilled their commitments under the "operational Agenda," allowing critical goals of the peace process to be achieved. The demobilization, disarmament, and reintegration of the armed insurgents were successfully implemented. The insurgency became a political party, without any privileges, and former combatants participated in electoral politics at the local and national levels, obtaining the third place, with 12% of the votes.

International Perspectives on Democratization and Peace, 113–133

doi:10.1108/978-1-80043-067-920200007

The peace agreements are facing a historic moment. The implementation of the operative agreements was successful. Contrary to what happened with the substantive agreements in which there were delays and non-compliance, in the social imagination there are questions about the agreements as a country agenda. The lack of political will of the political actors, mainly the parties, and the general lack of interest contributed to the deterioration of the peace agreements. Therefore, this chapter seeks to be an academic contribution to review the peace process, the factors that motivated the conflict and analyze the relationship between the consolidation of democracy and the peace process. In this sense, I also describe the main processes of electoral and constitutional reform in the area of justice, both areas are the fundamental ones for the strengthening of democracy. The importance of institutional reforms raises the need to reinvigorate the peace agreements and take them as a starting point to strengthen democracy and institutions in the country. Efforts in electoral matters have allowed progress in some aspects, contrary to what has happened in the justice system, where they register, despite several attempts to reform the constitution, continuing challenges and important setbacks.

There is no peace without democracy, nor democracy without development, much less without institutional strengthening, there will be neither peace nor and democracy.

External Linkages

The armed conflict, like many in the region, was influenced by the geopolitical dynamics of the Cold War, where the geopolitical and economic interests of the world powers, the ideological conflict between capitalism and communism, involved a bloody confrontation between Guatemalans.

Since the colonial period, Guatemala has experienced different chapters of political instability in its history; the said instability had been created in significant part by the confrontation of the economic elites during several periods which ended in the cooptation of the state in favor of a privileged group of the population.

A clear example of this cooptation is what Guatemala's independence from Spain in 1821 represented as it was a result of creole elite's actions to preserve their status-quo over state institutions and to keep the socio-political order intact (Arévalo, 2017, p. 57). Even though the state's head changed regularly between liberal and conservative sides, no real change in the socio-political order was ever made until 1944, in which "La Revolución de Octubre"[1] produced the conditions that allowed the foundation of democracy for the first time in the country. The following 10 years, which are known as the "democratic spring"[2] saw the

[1]The revolution of October 20th in 1944 was a civil and military achievement that ended years of military dictatorship.

[2]"Democratic Spring" is the name of the period of the first democratic governments after the revolution in 1944 until the counter revolution in 1954. The governments of Juan José Arévalo (1945–1951) and Jacobo Árbenz (1951–1954) was characterized by the implementation of social reforms.

implementation of social, political, and economic reforms (Arévalo, 2017). These reforms[3] were intended to modernize the state and improve the living conditions of the population, especially of the indigenous people who had suffered oppression, even through legal mechanisms like the "law against vagrancy," which institutionalized forced labor.

Even though reforms carried out by president Jacobo Árbenz had the intention to benefit most of the population, it had repercussions with part of the economic elites and the United Fruit Company (UFCO) as the land reform[4] implemented in 1952 compromised most of the land owned by the company, which by the time was the most prominent landowner of arable land.[5] In those years, the Cold War and fight against communism was expanding throughout the world, and UFCO utilized this development in order to involve the Central Intelligence Agency of the United States, since a "communist threat" was emerging in Guatemala.

All of these developments led to the overthrow of Árbenz as president with the help of the US Government in 1954. Regarding this matter Bernardo Arévalo (2017, p. 5) notes:

> The victorious counter-revolutionary coalition – the landed elites that wanted to regain the control over the state, the U.S. Government whose interest in the internal politics of the tiny country was a function of its Cold War geo-political concerns, and the military elites that the U.S. coerced by fear into cooperation- established an authoritarian regime that, under a blanket definition of anti-communism, engaged in violent repression of political dissent and closed every possible electoral route for meaningful political reform.

The new regime reversed most of the changes implemented by Árbenz, beginning with land reform, and led the path for the beginning of 30 years of military governments which were characterized by political instability, the use of state institutions for personal enrichment, electoral fraud, and political violence through a democratic façade.

Conflict Stages

The overthrow of Árbenz in 1954 created the conditions for the first phase of the armed conflict. This phase represents the armed insurgency that emerged at the beginning of the sixties[6] and the response from the state, together with the

---

[3]The scope of the reforms included economic, labor, land, and civil rights issues.

[4]The land reform, known also as Act-900, was intended to end the feudal logic that prevailed in land possession.

[5]UFCO got to be the biggest land owner in the country due to its business with previous governments that made concessions of land in favor of the company. By that time, the company also owned the only railway in the country.

[6]The first insurgent group was the Rebel Armed Forces (FAR) that was founded in 1962. Then, in 1971 and 1972, the Revolutionary Organization of Armed People (ORPA) and the Guerilla Army of the Poor (EGP) emerged, respectively.

tutelage of the United States, the Guatemalan army became the first counterinsurgent army in Latin America (Jonas, 2000, p. 57). To Jonas (2000, p. 58), the second phase was the most violent phase of the war since in the eighties the counterinsurgent state managed to consolidate itself. This meant violent actions against guerillas and civilians as the strategy was intended to cut all support they could receive. Finally, a third phase of the armed conflict consists of the years when the conflict slowed down, and discussions between the guerrillas and the government began.

Since 1954, there were profound social changes that led to the emergence of new social movements (of workers, farmers, communities and indigenous people) who exercised continuous pressure on the state claiming better living and social conditions.[7] However, this pressure led to a level of repression without precedent in all of Latin America (Jonas, 2000, p. 58).

In the first phase of the armed conflict in the 1960s, the guerrillas focused on the western region, where the residents were ladinos and not Mayans. At this stage, even though the organization of the guerrillas was weak and without base amongst indigenous people, the insurgency could only be controlled with an effort organized, financed and run directly by the United States (Jonas, 2000, p. 57).

As Jonas (2000, p. 58) highlights, this was an essential moment for Guatemala as the American military advisers played an essential role in the professionalization of the Guatemalan army. The insurgents were not prepared for the counter-offensive of the army and suffered a temporal defeat in 1968. Nevertheless, they were able to reorganize by the 1970s around the indigenous plateau in the western region of the country, having the support of some Mayan communities.

With the arrival of Colonel Carlos Arana Osorio to the government after the presidential elections of 1970, the counterinsurgent state finalized its institutionalization. It is in this context that the State implemented mechanisms of counterinsurgency like death squads (whose base were the security forces) and the "disappearance" of people from the opposition as the objective was to eradicate all bases of civil support toward "la guerrilla" (Jonas, 2000, p. 58). All of this and the arrival of General Efraín Ríos Montt[8] through a military coup in 1982 lead to the most violent period of the conflict. Since then, in Guatemala more than forty thousand people went missing, representing more than 40% of the total disappearances in Latin America during those years (Jonas, 2000, p. 58).

Between 1981 and 1983, more than 400 villages were wiped out and approximately 100,000 civilians were murdered or disappeared. This is attributable in part to the new strategy of "scorched earth" that the army implemented.

---

[7]During those years, the region of Latin America experienced a growth in their economies. Guatemala was no exception, however inequality in the country rose instead of what happened in most of the region where poverty was reduced.

[8]Rios Montt was indicted for genocide in 2013. The sentenced was nullified by the CC of the country due to some procedural errors made during the trial. The process was resumed in 2015 and then in 2017 after legal resources by the defense. Ríos Montt died in April 1 of 2018.

The figures presented demonstrates the level of repression that the state was involved in during those years representing around 50% of the amount of people that died or disappeared during the entire conflict, that according to the Commission for Historical Clarification (CEH) is around 200,000 people.

All of these actions provoked the retirement of all four insurgent groups toward the mountains. As a consequence in 1982, the insurgency groups (Guerilla Army of the Poor [EGP], Revolutionary Organization of Armed People [ORPA], Rebel Armed Forces [FAR]) and the Guatemalan Workers Party (PGT) united as one organization called "Unidad Revolucionaria Nacional Guatemalteca" (URNG), ending years in which they acted separately due to their differences. Due to the damage, the army inflicted in the attacks mentioned above, the new group was debilitated and could only return at the end of the decade.

In 1983, the desire of Ríos Montt to perpetuate himself in power provoked a new *coup d'etat* that concluded with the election of a Constituent Assembly, the enactment of a new constitution and the call for the realization of new elections.

Coup d'etat's from 1982 and 1983 were the result of multiple causes, none of them referred to a willingness to democratize the country (Rivas & Aguilera, 1998 as cited in Blanco & Zapata, 2007). The most significant structural cause was the gradual decay of the democracy facade model that allowed the military and the economic, religious and political elites to govern the country for decades. At the same time, the national scenario started to show a profound economic crisis that turned the governmental administration unmanageable (Blanco & Zapata, 2007, pp. 297–298).

It is also important to highlight the international context of those years as Guatemala was isolated from the international community as a result of the different violations against human rights. Also, through Latin America the process of the third democratic wave was developing, a phenomenon that led the political elite to opt for the installation of democracy.

The first elections in the new democracy were won by Vinicio Cerezo of the Christian Democracy Party, and although the process only allowed participation from political parties from the center and the right, it allowed the start of a democratic process and with it the conditions for the solution of the conflict through political means.

Peace Efforts and Conflict Transformations

The conflict although it had some interruptions can be considered as a confrontation that was latent, with intense and light phases, throughout the 36 years. The conflict ended through political negotiations between the main parties that were involved in it. The peace process was not only aimed at ending the armed conflict but also, through spaces of discussion among different sectors of society, addressing the structural roots that led to the confrontation. The peace agenda, which is the result of the peace process, established agreements that addressed operative aspects, such as demobilization and disarmament, as well as the so-called substantive agreements, which address aspects of constitutional, electoral, and socioeconomic reform. The operative agreements were fulfilled, however, substantially they do not have positive results, partly due to the lack of political will to promote them.

The Negotiation Process (1987–1996)

The fall of the Berlin wall, the implosion of the Soviet Union and the end of the Cold War allowed for the emergence of a new context that favored regional efforts to solve and promote democracy in Central America. One of these efforts was "Grupo Contadora" which was constituted in 1983 by Colombia, México, Panamá, and Venezuela.

Derived from the work of this group, a first Central American president's meeting was called in May of 1986 and was known as Esquipulas I.[9] In this meeting, the presidents confirmed "Their will to sign the – Act of Contadora for Peace and Cooperation in Central America – assuming the complete fulfillment of the procedures and compromises in it" (Blanco & Zapata, 2007, p. 318). Following these advances, in 1987 the presidents of Central America reunited again and signed the Agreement of Esquipulas II in which the mechanisms to reach pacification and reconciliation of Central America through political means were established.

About this agreement, Blanco and Zapata (2007, p. 319) consider it important to remember the compromises required by the governments referred to "... initiate dialogue with all unarmed groups of political opposition and those who chose amnesty." The first attempt was to try to solve the conflict through a negotiation process. It is in this context that the first meeting between delegates from the government, Guatemalan army and URNG took place in Madrid in 1987. However, as soon as the meeting ended, the government and army of Guatemala announced that no following meeting would take place as URNG declined to dispose their weapons and be subjected to amnesty as a previous condition for the negotiation.

This event set the first moment in what would be the peace process negotiation, which according to Blanco and Zapata (2007) is divided into four phases, each one with different characteristics. The first phase covers from October of 1987 until the Oslo meeting that took place in March of 1990. The second phase covers the signing of the Oslo Agreements on March 29 of 1990 until the constitutional break that took place in 1993 that resulted in the removal of Jorge Serrano Elías as President. A third phase covers the time in which Ramiro De León Carpio took the presidency (1993–1996) and a fourth one covers the period since the beginning of Álvaro Arzú's government (January 1996) until the signing of the final peace agreement on December 29 in 1996.

The first phase was about the creation of the conditions to carry out the negotiation. A month before the meeting on Madrid in 1987 referenced before, a National Reconciliation Commission (CNR) was created through an executive order. This commission was considered in the agreement of Esquipulas II and was headed by a high-ranking member of the Catholic Church in the country,

[9]The agreement gets its name from the city of Esquipulas, in Guatemala.

Monsignor Rodolfo Quezada Toruño, and integrated by a representative of the government, a representative from political parties and a distinguished citizen with the objective to search for a political solution to the armed conflict. As part of its mandate, the commission established a "National Dialogue" with social groups and political parties of the opposition. However, there was no participation from URNG following the decision of the government to not have any further discussions after the meeting that took place in Madrid in October 1987 (Blanco & Zapata, 2007, p. 320).

The second phase of the process starts with the meeting of Oslo in 1990 with the participation of URNG and CNR. During this meeting, the parties reached an agreement, first of many to come, designating Monsignor Quezada Toruño as conciliator of the process and the United Nations (UN) as observer and guarantor of the fulfillment of the acquired compromises. At the same time, the parties agreed to start a round of meetings between URNG with different sectors of civil society like political parties, private sector (represented by CACIF[10]), religious groups, syndicates, and others.

The next year, Jorge Serrano Elías, who participated in these talks as a representative of the political parties, assumed the presidency. Shortly after that, he created the Peace Commission of the Government (COPAZ) which would become the entity in charge to negotiate directly with URNG.

At the beginning of the talks, two options were raised to be part of the negotiations. A traditional process of negotiation of the conflict matters (ceasefire, demobilization, disarmament) or to develop a process that focused on the roots of the conflict. In the end, they went for both options, and that, according to Blanco and Zapata (2007, p. 322), gave the negotiation process its *sui generis* characteristic.[11]

Months later the parties signed the "Queretaro Agreement" in which a reference frame about democratization was established. It identifies a vision of democracy beyond the procedural framework and sees it as part of the social, economic, political, and cultural rights (Blanco & Zapata, 2007, p. 323). Even though there were important advances, the negotiations were interrupted for two reasons. The first one was due to the impossibility to advance in the topic of human rights, and the second one was due to the constitutional break produced by the shutdown of the Congress made by President Jorge Serrano Elías in 1983 who at the end had to leave the government.

After this crisis, the then-ombudsman Ramiro de León Carpio was elected by Congress to be president, and after eight months the negotiation process was resumed with the "Framework Agreement for the Resume of the Negotiation Process between the Government of Guatemala and URNG" in Mexico on January 10 of 1994.

---

[10]Coordinating Committee of Agricultural, Commercial, Industrial, and Financial Associations of Guatemala.

[11]This ended up in the Agreement for the Search of Peace through Political Means, setting the topics and agenda for the negotiation process.

This (agreement) led to a substantial change in the negotiation format as the figure of National Conciliator was abandoned, and UN was assigned the function of moderator and verifier of the process. At the same time, a Civil Society Assembly (ASC) was constituted with the capability to propose suggestions, recommendations and to endorse the agreements that the government and URNG signed. Moreover, a new calendarization was established, and in parallel, it was created The Group of Countries Friendly with the Process[12] with the purpose to support the moderator in its tasks and give greater firmness to the reached agreements (Blanco & Zapata, 2007, p. 323).

These changes allowed civil society to be part of the negotiations, something URNG demanded. The assembly was integrated by different sectors like political parties, human rights, Mayan's and women's organizations, among others. The only sector that excluded itself from this assembly was CACIF, which represents the most influential actors of the private sector, and who ended up creating a peace commission of their own.

All of these developments allowed essential advances under challenging topics that ended in the signature of the next agreements about substantial themes: Global Agreement of Human Rights, Agreement for the resettlement of the uprooted populations by the Armed Conflict, Agreement on the establishment of the Commission for the Historical Enlightenment, and the Agreement about Identity and Rights of Indigenous People (Blanco & Zapata, 2007, p. 324).

The fourth and last phase goes through the first year of Alvaro Arzú's[13] presidency which was characterized by the quickness in which the negotiations were concluded. With the new presidency, new conditions came to the negotiation that led to more confidence between the parties. Following this, the commission of each party was reduced to only four members, an action that made the meetings more agile and evidenced the willingness of the parties to finalize the negotiations in the least time possible without affecting the contents of the agenda (Blanco & Zapata, 2007, p. 324).

The compromise of the parties allowed the negotiations to advance on the different themes considered in the agenda and led to the signature of the "Agreement on the chronology for the implementation, fulfillment, and verification of the Peace Accord" on December 29 of 1996, a date that symbolizes the signing of the peace (Tables 1 and 2).

The negotiation process of the Peace Accords resulted in the construction of a very hopeful country time horizon, where a path of action of public policies and institutional reforms is defined that seek to strengthen public institutions and promote integrated human development. Some of these aspects are contained in the substantive agreements that address the commitments of constitutional

---

[12]The countries that constituted this group were United States, Colombia, México, Spain, Norway, and Venezuela.

[13]Mayor of Guatemala City from 1986 to 1990 and 2004 to 2018 and president from 1996 to 2000.

Table 1. Negotiation Process.

Actor	About
Grupo Contadora	*Integrated by:* Colombia, México, Panamá, and Venezuela
Guatemalan Government	• President Vinicio Cerezo (1987–1991) • President Jorge Serrano (1991–1993) • President Ramiro de León Carpio (1993–1996) • President Álvaro Arzú (1996)
URNG	PGT *Insurgent groups:* • FAR • ORPA • EGP
CNR	Headed by a high-ranking member of the Catholic Church in the country, Monsignor Rodolfo Quezada Toruño *Integrated by:* • Representative of the government, • Representative from political parties, and • A distinguished citizen
United Nations	• Observer (1991–1992) • Mediator (1993–1995) • Verifier (1995–2004)
Civil Society	Political parties, private sector (represented by CACIF[14]), religious groups, syndicates, and, others
COPAZ	Institutional mechanism of the government in charge of the negotiation process (1993–1996)
ASC	Capability to propose suggestions, recommendations and to endorse the agreements that the government and URNG signed
Group of Countries Friendly with the Process	*Integrated by:* United States, Colombia, México, Spain, Norway and Venezuela

Data drawn and constructed from Blanco and Zapata (2007).

[14]Coordinating Committee of Agricultural, Commercial, Industrial, and Financial Associations of Guatemala.

Table 2. Peace Agreements Subscribed to During the Guatemalan Peace Process.

Place and Date of Subscription	Peace Agreements
Agreements that Establish Negotiation Procedures	
Oslo, Norway, March 29 of 1990	Oslo Agreement. Basic Agreement for the search for peace through political means
México DF, April 26 of 1991	México Agreement. Procedural agreement for the search of peace through political means and agreements of the general program
Querétaro, México, June 25 of 1991	Querétaro Agreement. Framework Agreement about democratization for the search of peace through political means
México DF, January 10 of 1994	Framework Agreement for the Resume of the Negotiation Process between the Government of Guatemala and URNG
México DF, March 29 of 1994	Calendar Agreement of the negotiations for long-lasting peace
Substantial Agreements	
México DF, March 29 of 1994	Global Agreement of Human Rights
Oslo, Norway, June 17 of 1994	Agreement for the resettlement of the uprooted populations by the Armed Conflict
Oslo, Norway, June 23 of 1994	Agreement on the establishment of the Commission for the Historical Clarification
México DF, March 31 of 1995	Agreement about Identity and Rights of indigenous people
México DF, May 6 of 1996	Agreement on socioeconomic aspects and land situation
México DF, September 19 of 1996	Agreement on the strengthening of the civil power and the function of the army in a democratic society
Operative Agreements	
Oslo, Norway, December 4 of 1996	Definitive Agreement on the cease of fire
Stockholm, Sweden, December 7 of 1996	Agreement on Constitutional reforms and electoral regime
Madrid, Spain, December 12 of 1996	Agreement on the bases for the incorporation of URNG to legality
Guatemala, December 29 of 1996	Agreement on the chronogram for the implementation, fulfillment, and verification of the Peace Accords

Adapted from Blanco and Zapata (2007).

reform and the electoral regime, such as those fundamental to strengthening the democratization process. The weak political support and the disinterest of the actors are the most important factors that influence the little progress in this matter. For this reason, it is necessary to generate processes to reinvigorate the peace agreements and resume the pending agenda.

Agenda for Institutional Reforms

The proposal of reforms included in the Electoral Reform Commission (CRE) considered the establishment of a fixed number of deputies and to eliminate indefinite re-election. It also considers actions for the strengthening of the judicial system through the promotion of judicial independence, the recognition of legal pluralism, the establishment of a judicial career, reforms to the Police, as well as the integration, organization and functions of the Army and the President of the Republic, among others.[15]

The few advances in these reforms and the unsuccessful processes are elements of analysis and reflection to contribute to the reinvigoration of the Peace Agreements, as an agenda to seek the development of the country. The relationship between the pending peace agenda and the consolidation of democracy in the institutionalization of it is strong and decisive.

The Peace Agreements allowed during the consolidation process of the democracy, meeting space between different sectors of society and established a minimal and strategic institutional reform route to promote peace, harmony, governability and democratic stability. The retardation in the fulfillment of the agreements has contributed to the deterioration and institutional weakening of the state, sharpening the fragility of the political system.

Therefore, given the substantive and symbolic relevance of these reforms, it is important to analyze the electoral and constitutional reform processes that have taken place within the framework of how these are still part of the pending peace agenda and how they can contribute to the reinvigoration of the *same* agreements and become an institutional route to strengthen democracy.

Electoral Reform

Currently, there is much dissatisfaction among Guatemalan citizens regarding the performance of political parties and the electoral system. This dynamic has a direct impact on the trust, credibility, legitimacy, and representativeness of the political system. The citizens do not feel represented by the political class; on the contrary, the dominant feeling is rejection and indignation. The peace agenda *contemplates* the importance of democratic institutional strengthening, measures that aim to correct the main problems of the electoral system and political parties.

[15]The proposal needs to reform the Constitution of the Republic of Guatemala and the LEPP.

In specific matters of the electoral regime, the CRE recognize on the one hand the role of the Supreme Electoral Tribunal (TSE) as the governing body in ensuring the custody and improvement of the democratic system, and on the other hand, mandates the integration of the CRE with coordination of the TSE and participation of political parties with parliamentary representation. This mechanism became the space for discussion among political actors to reach agreements on the reforms to be promoted, taking as reference and starting point, the Peace Agreements.

The reform agenda included aspects related to the identification document, the modernization and improving of the voter's registry, facilitation of access to the voting centers, public information campaigns to promote a democratic culture, regulation to campaign financing and the publicity and transparency in the processes of the nomination of candidates for public elections.

The CRE began its work in 1997 with the direction and organization of the TSE, active participation of the parties, and civil society organizations specialized in the matter. The commission prepared the report "Guatemala, Peace, and Democracy," which was presented by the electoral body to the Congress of the Republic. The report contained the discussion and proposals that were agreed upon by the actors involved in the commission.

The commission's work incorporated into the discussion both technical and political aspects, with the hope that the parties involved then in the approval phase in Congress would provide the support. This condition was not met since the proposal had many difficulties in Congress to move forward, reach agreements and be approved. It is contradictory but the same parties that participated in the CRE and agreed on the consensus were the parties that now complicate the approval process.

Blanco (2012) indicates that from 1998 to 2004 the process had advances, setbacks, stagnation and especially a profound modification of the reforms proposed in the report presented by the CRE. Finally, on April 21, 2004, the Congress of the Republic approved Act 10-04 containing 152 amendments to the Electoral Law and Political Parties (LEPP). On the other hand, Blanco (2012) states that after the approval of these so-called "first generation" reforms, weaknesses and inconsistencies were identified from various sectors and the omission of priority issues.

The accusations generated the conditions for the Congress to approve a new electoral reform with the purpose of addressing the problems identified. Thus, in 2006, a year before the electoral process, the second-generation reform or harmonization was approved, which corrected some incongruities and weaknesses of the 2004 reform, leaving out other important reforms that were requested by various actors and sectors in the country.

The elections of 2007, 2011, and 2015 showed the importance of reforming the electoral political system from an integrated perspective, especially after the deep crisis of legitimacy and representativeness which the political system entered in recent years. The crisis of the system became a window of opportunity for the political actors to resume the need to recover the aspects of the peace agreements that were related to the electoral regime.

The political crisis that the country experienced in 2015 was one of the most transcendental political moments in the country's political history (Duarte & Novales, 2017, p. 13) indicate that the general electoral process of 2015 was developed under a climate of citizen demonstrations against authorities of the three branches of government and rejection of the political class, as a result of the criminal cases for acts of corruption presented by the Public Prosecutor's Office (MP) and the International Commission Against Impunity in Guatemala (CICIG).[16]

Despite the political crisis, the citizens, in the midst of the rejection of the politicians, attended the polls to cast their votes. The electoral participation was the highest registered since the beginning of the democratic transition with a 70% participation of the electoral register (Tribunal Supremo Electoral, 2016). Duarte and Novales (2017, p. 13) argue that the high participation seems to indicate a high citizen expectation about the possibility of a change in the political leadership of the country; nevertheless, the electoral process was developed under the same set of rules as the previous ones, which did not allow the possibility of a significant change.

The electoral results and the political crisis left on stage the discussion of the initiative of reforms to the LEPP presented by the TSE in June 2015. The TSE in that context elaborated a proposal that contained contributions of discussion spaces promoted by the Congress and various proposals received from multiple organizations in society. The initiative was approved in the first and second readings in Congress during 2015 and awaited the ruling of the Constitutional Court (CC).[17] In 2016, the CC sent Congress its opinion on the reform initiative, with favorable and unfavorable comments, for the reading of articles and final approval.

Duarte and Novales (2017, p. 18) indicate that although the initiative to reform the LEPP, Decree 26 – 2016, was not approved in its entirety, it contains important advances in the matter of the control of party financing, as well as a new electoral propaganda regime based on the indirect financing of propaganda

[16]The United Nations and the Government of Guatemala signed the Agreement to establish the International Commission against Impunity in Guatemala (CICIG). CICIG was established as an independent, international body designed to support the MP, the National Civil Police (PNC) and other State institutions in the investigation of crimes committed by members of illegal security forces and clandestine security structures and, in a more general sense, help to disband such groups. To do so, CICIG assists with investigations and criminal prosecutions in a small number of complex cases, as well as implementing steps – in accordance with its mandate – aimed at strengthening the institutions of the justice system so that they can continue to tackle these illegal groups in the future. Available in: *https://www.cicig.org/*

[17]In Congress, the approval of laws requires three readings in the legislative chamber. In the case of the Electotal Law and Political Parties also, since it is a law of constitutional rank, the opinion of the CC that indicates the constitutionality of the reforms is required. The Congress must comply with the recommendations of the court and exclude the articles that, in the opinion of the court, are unfavorable and non-constitutional.

in the media. In addition, the Electoral Update Commission is created, chaired by the TSE and composed of the electoral body, political parties and civil society organizations, which will be responsible for conducting an evaluation of the elections and, derived from that analysis, propose reforms to the LEPP necessary to democratically consolidate the political system, after each electoral process.

The case of the last generation of reforms to the electoral and political parties law was not a reactionary proposal to the political crisis of 2015. This was just an opportunity to position the reform that since 2011 some organizations worked together with the TSE. Although the reform did not incorporate all the proposals worked with the TSE and the demands coming from the Plaza, none of the approved modifications represents a setback for the electoral system and political parties.

The approved reform includes aspects that strengthen and provide greater controls over the financing of political organizations, strengthens the TSE as the supreme organ in electoral matters and some aspects that drive the internal democratization of the parties.

Open Agenda

Currently, a large number of political parties lack strong ideologies and political platforms. The parties have not been able to generate roots within society, and therefore, they are vulnerable to disappearing very easily as they fail to institutionalize. The lack of democracy within the parties can, in turn, cause the lack of interest of the citizens toward the parties, as well as the lack of legitimacy and representativeness in the system (Lemus, 2012, p. 16).

These characteristics of the system have generated a consensus to promote reforms for internal democracy in political parties and representation in the Congress of the Republic. Both areas of reform are closely related to the peace agenda and current demands of citizenship. In this sense, the objectives of the next generation of reforms should be aimed at strengthening the rights of members of political parties and democratizing the mechanisms for nominating candidates and electing party authorities, as well as modifying the requirements for forming political parties. This is to be done with the purpose of democratically strengthening the party's institutions.

On the other hand, the most severe dissatisfaction is with the Congress, because the electoral system currently limits the voter in the free expression of his/her preference. The deputies are elected through a system of blocked and closed lists; this means that the citizen marks on the ballot the party of his/her preference. Moreover, that party has a previously defined list of candidates, with a specific order. Candidates enter Congress in the order proposed by the parties, regardless of how much confidence or popularity they have among voters. Given the centralization and exclusivity, they nominate lists of candidates that cannot be altered by citizens. There are candidates who, with the fact that they are in a large district party, have higher possibilities of being elected and virtually assure their deputation. This contributes to undesirable clientelist practices among financiers and party leaders.

Constitutional Reform

Since the signing of the Peace Accords in 1996 in the ACRE, the structural weaknesses of the justice system were identified, and as a result, the need to promote reforms and modernize this system was determined, with the objective of eliminating inefficiency, the eradication of corruption, to guarantee free access to justice and to promote judicial independence.

In this sense, it is important, as an exercise of analysis and reflection, to review the aspects that marked the reform processes. This is done with the purpose of contributing to identifying the elements that influenced their failure to materialize in order to identify lessons and good practices to take into account in future reform processes.

Since its creation in 1985, the constitution has only been reformed once. It was a political and democratic solution to the political crisis that occurred due to the constitutional breakdown, caused by President Jorge Serrano Elías, who tried to dissolve the Congress of the Republic and the Supreme Court of Justice. After that reform, there have been several attempts, among which we can highlight:

- Popular referendum in 1999
- Pro-Reform Group (2008–2009)[18]
- Consortium USAC – URL-ASIES (2011)[19]
- The government of President Otto Pérez Molina (2012)[20]

[18]The civic association ProReforma put together by citizens presented a constitutional reform proposal to modify the Guatemalan political system. The proposal presented contains aspects to reform the judicial, legislative, and executive bodies, as well as the control and oversight institutions contemplated in the Constitution of the Republic. This proposal obtained an unfavorable opinion in the Congress Legislation and Constitutional Organisms.

[19]The Rectors Lic. Estuardo Gálvez Barrios, from the USAC, Father Rolando Enrique Alvarado López. S.J., of the URL and the Executive Secretary of the Association of Social Studies (ASIES), Licda. Raquel Zelaya Rosales, delivered to the President of the Congress of the Republic and the Instance of Chiefs of Block, a proposal for a legal initiative to reform the Political Constitution of the Republic, exclusively in security and justice in five aspects: Supreme Court of Justice, judicial career, free legal assistance, MP and national civil police. Available in: *http://brujula.com.gt/usac-url-y-asies-proponen-reformas-constitucionales-en-seguridad-y-justicia/*

[20]The President of the Republic, Otto Pérez Molina (2012–2015), presented the Initiative to reform the Political Constitution of the Republic that contains modifications to the justice system, public and citizen security, representative democracy, recognition of diversity within the national unity, as well as transparency and accountability. Available in: *https://www.congreso.gob.gt/2012/08/27/CONGRESO-RECIBE-PROYECTO-DE-REFORMAS-CONSTITUCIONALES-PLANTEADAS-POR-EL-EJECUTIVO/*

- Three State bodies (Executive, Legislative and Judicial) proposal supported by CICIG, MP, PDH, and OACNUDH.[21]

Mack (2017)

Constitutional Reform of 1999

The first attempt at constitutional reform was developed as a result of the intense work carried out by the government of President Alvaro Arzú. As a signatory of the Peace Accords, he reflected a strong willingness and political will to comply with the commitments assumed in them.

To facilitate the execution of this objective, President Álvaro Arzú Irigoyen, in the Council of Ministers, presented to the Legislative Body the proposal for the constitutional reform of 13 articles that included changes in the State Organisms, as well as the redefinition of the Army in a society in peace. The Congress, after a process of discussion and debate, extended the scope of the reform to 50 articles. This aspect weakened significantly the viability of this effort as a referendum was needed.

In this context, the TSE summoned the population to the Popular Consultation on March 1, 1999, defining the ballots where the reforms to be consulted were divided. The referendum was a process marked by disinformation, discrimination, and racism that was coupled with apathy and indifference influencing a high abstention rate of the people since this rose to 81% of the people registered to vote (Galicia, 2015).

The consultation was carried out on four ballots where the citizens were asked whether or not they agreed with the reforms, which were grouped into four categories. On all the ballots, he did not win foreclosing the possibility of approving the reforms and modifying their institutionalization.

This constitutes the first defeat of the Peace Accords. The political context was marked by the proximity of the elections, the deterioration of the government, and the repositioning of new political actors that were articulated as adversaries to advance the substantive agreements of peace. This same dynamic is evident in

---

[21]The presidents of the Executive, Legislative and Judicial Organisms presented in the Congress of the Republic, the project of reforms to the Political Constitution of the Republic in the aspects of: (a) The express recognition of the legal system of the indigenous peoples and their constitutional control; (b) Guarantees and guiding principles for the administration of justice system; (c) Separation of administrative and jurisdictional functions of the Supreme Court of Justice; (d) Creation of professional careers; (e) The strengthening of the republican mechanisms of exercise of power through the adoption of an inter-organic control system for the selection of the highest judicial authorities, among them, the election of the Attorney General of the Republic and Head of the Public Prosecutor's Office. Available in: *https://www.congreso.gob.gt/2016/10/06/PRESIDENTES-DE-LOS-TRES-PODERES-DEL-ESTADO-PRESENTAN-REFORMAS-AL-SECTOR-JUSTICIA/*

other processes where the lack of political will and disinterestedness dominated and imposed themselves in front of the peace agenda.

However, the obstacles identified in 1996, which were intended to be overcome in the 1999 referendum, rejected by the people, remain valid. Despite the achievements made with the democratic opening, the cessation of the armed conflict and some changes in the legal framework made in the following years, as indicated in the Report "A new justice for peace" of the Commission for Strengthening Justice, as well as different studies, investigations and reports, both national and international. These reiterate the persistence of the obstacles registered years ago; and identify new challenges for security and justice systems, such as the transnationalization of crime and its complex ways of operating, organized crime and drug trafficking, among others.

With the aim of overcoming the obstacles mentioned above, different social and political actors with legal initiatives have promoted modifications to the Constitution. Each of the constitutional reform proposals has unique characteristics, origins and different scope, with different delimitations that require different entities and processes.

However, all these initiatives from their perspectives and conceptions propose modifications to the constitution as an indispensable mechanism to achieve the balance between the needs of constitutional stability and the demands of the social, political and economic changes demanded by the Guatemalan State.

The Last Three Reform Processes

These initiatives emphasize aspects related to security and justice. There have been efforts promoted by the Executive, universities and research centers. The three reform proposals that have advanced the most in the legislative process are: (1) the one submitted by the Consortium formed by the University of San Carlos of Guatemala (USAC), Rafael Landívar University (URL) and the Association for Research and Social Studies (ASIES), which was approved by ten deputies in 2011, and which sought to reform aspects related to security and justice; (2) the proposal by President of the Republic in the Council of Ministers in 2012; and (3) the one presented by the three State powers (Executive, Legislative and Judicial) supported by the Public Ministry (MP), Office of the Human Rights (PDH), the International Commission against Impunity in Guatemala (CICIG) and the Office of the United Nations High Commissioner for Human Rights (OACNUDH) – placed on the table a proposal for constitutional reform in the area of justice.

It should be noted that in the absence of a suitable regulation that includes all aspects necessary for a process of constitutional reform by Congress, as well as mandatory provisions that establish a participatory democratic process of reflection, discussion and debate prior to its approval or rejection of the full measure, a situation subject to the discretion of the Legislative Body itself is generated.

The reform proposals had as starting point the Peace Agreement for the strengthening of the civil power and function of the Army, in a democratic society, the CRE, the recommendations of the National Commission for Monitoring and Supporting the Strengthening of Justice, as well as the suggestions made in the studies on progress and weaknesses in the justice system made by several research centers in the country.

In general terms, constitutional reform efforts have been aimed at solving the problems of a weak justice system to strengthen the rule of law. In one way or another, in each of the proposals there is a need to promote these reforms in order to provide the justice system with greater independence, transparency and guarantee better access to justice; also guarantee the suitability, capacity and honesty of the officials of the judicial system; on the other hand, depoliticizing justice, especially in the process of nominating officials; and finally, the importance of having an adequate mechanism to face impunity and corruption. All this is to stop the galloping impunity and corruption that reigns in the country. The heart of the justice reform is to promote judicial careers.

Without a doubt, we need better judges to fight against injustice, to end corruption and impunity. Judges who are subjected to real performance evaluations, who manage to climb the judicial career by merit and ability, and not by political favors, and who can answer for the mistakes they make. We have already lost more than 20 years since the signing of the Peace Accords. Justice cannot wait any longer.

Conclusion

The process of peace was negotiated with the insurgency for 10 whole years, and by 4 separate governments holding different ideologies. Guatemala always had the support of the international community, so that these changes of government did not mean stalling the negotiations. The role of the group known as Countries Friends to the Guatemalan Peace Process was relevant, as was the support of the United Nations, which through its representatives acted at the beginning as facilitators, then as mediators, and finally as verifiers of compliance to the subscribed peace commitments.

It is relevant to emphasize that the peace efforts came from an authentic and very worried regional and political forces. We did not want more war in the region. The economic, political, and social cost was too high for our societies. We were in a scenario where the Cold War played itself out viciously. Both the army and the insurgency received support from the countries involved in the Cold War.

The socioeconomic roots that motivated the internal armed conflict have not been addressed. The Peace Agreements are an agenda that seek to establish actions in various areas to transform and solve poverty, inequality, exclusion, discrimination and promote integrated human development.

In the same way, the peace agenda draws a path of institutional strengthening and the democratic system. The substantive agreements tried to frame actions that would lead not only to the end of the armed confrontation, but also the foundations for the solution of the country's structural problems.

We could not talk about a peace process without democracy and democracy without a peace process. This is because democracy needed a process of maturation to not only stay as a legal and political process but to create a real culture in the society. The peace accords signed by the government and URNG considered this and set the framework so the democratization process could be carried out.

Democracy played an important role in the peace process, and in turn, peace agreements assume a deep commitment to consolidate democracy in the country. This is the starting point, a bidirectional relationship that seeks to consolidate peace, strengthen democratic institutions and promote integrated human development.

On the other hand, democracy allowed the consolidation of efforts and fora for encounter, dialog and agreement among different political, social, economic, and institutional actors throughout the peace process. The meeting point between democracy and peace processes is the agenda of institutional reforms in the area of justice and the electoral system and political parties.

These reforms are intimately related to the strengthening of democracy and governance. Although the process of the signing of peace and the Peace Agreements contribute to discuss and reach minimum agreements in these areas, then the political actors waste the processes and opportunities to seek to concretize them and in this way prevent the consolidation and strengthening of democracy.

Regrettably, the political actors who signed the Peace Accords lost power and political relevance in the national scenario. This caused that the commitments assumed in the agreements to remain, if in the symbolic plane and public agenda, but without the support and commitment of the new political actors. The Peace Agreements remained orphaned and the lack of interest in retaking them and being able to comply with the substantive aspects that were agreed upon each day increases.

Therefore, to promote analysis, discussion, and reflection on the progress of the Peace Accords is a fundamental task, considering the recent political context of the country, the crisis of legitimacy and governability that the system faces. To some extent, in recent years, "new" institutional reforms have been promoted that take up the objectives and the spirit embodied in the Peace Accords, evidencing their validity and the need to reinvigorate them, so that new political actors can appropriate them, promote and approve these reforms.

The discussion on the need to reinvigorate or revise the Peace Agreements starts from the premise of giving legitimacy to the agreements as a minimum agenda of actions and reforms with a state vision, and on the other, in view of the need to address the structural issues that motivated the conflict and they are not resolved yet.

The challenge is not to define the minimum agenda to seek consensus among political, social, economic and institutional actors in the country, the biggest challenge is that these new actors assume a political commitment to retake ownership of the Peace Accords, reinvigorate them, and promote with political will the actions, agreements, and reforms agreed upon.

In this context, one of the variables that have most affected the possibilities, conditions and institutional political feasibility of respecting and assuming real commitments with political agreements is the deinstitutionalized system of political parties. It is a system that creates and reproduces weak political organizations, without ideological foundation that have become part of the electoral machinery.

Under these conditions, it is impossible to reach agreements and manage them within the present politico-institutional framework.

References

Acción C. (2011). *¿Cuánto costó la campaña electoral?: Análisis del gasto y la rendición de cuentas de los partidos políticos en el proceso electoral*. Guatemala, Magna Terra Editores.

Arévalo, B. (2017). *Challenging the Conventional: Can Post-Violence Reconciliation Succeed? A Guatemalan Case Study*. Kofi Annan Foundation.

Asociación de Investigación y Estudios Sociales (ASIES). (2008, febrero). *Guatemala: informe analítico del proceso electoral 2007*. Retrieved from https://s3.amazonaws.com/asies-books/books/200802_guatemala_informe_analitico_del_proceso_electoral_2007.pdf

Azpuru, D., Blanco, L., Córdova, R., Loya, N., Ramos, C., & Zapata, A. (2007). *Construyendo la democracia en sociedades posconlficto. Un enfoque comparado entre Guatemala y El Salvador*. Guatemala: ASIES.

Blanco, L. (2012, febrero 27). *Reformas electorales: un callejón sin salida*. Retrieved from https://www.plazapublica.com.gt/node/2490/backlinks

Blanco, L., & Zapata, A. (2007). Contribucion del proceso de paz a la constuccion de la democracia en Guatemala. In D. Azpuru, L. Blanco, R. Córdova, N. Loya, C. Ramos, & A. Zapata (Eds.), *Construyendo la democracia en sociedades posconlficto. Un enfoque comparado entre Guatemala y El Salvador* (pp. 291–511). Guatemala: ASIES.

Brett, R., & Delgado, A. (2005). *The role of constitution-building processes in democratization*. Stockholm: Institute for Democracy and Electoral Assistance (IDEA).

Brolo, J. (2012). Evolución del sistema de partidos políticos guatemalteco de 1985 a 2012. In Asociación de Investigación y Estudios Sociales (ASIES) (Ed.), *Partidos políticos guatemaltecos: Dinámicas internas y desempeño* (pp. 41–53). Guatemala: ASIES.

Brolo, J. (2013, octubre). *El Tamaño importa: Variaciones por distrito en elecciones legislativas de Guatemala (1984–2011)*. Guatemala: ASIES.

Duarte, G., & Novales, H. (2017, febrero). 2016: entre el desencanto ciudadano y las reformas institucionales. *Actualidad Política*, *13*, 13–34.

Galicia, N. (2015, mayo 15). 1999: rechazo a reformas constitucionales. *Prensa Libre*. Retrieved from https://www.prensalibre.com

Jonas, S. (2000). *De Centauros y Palomas. El proceso de paz guatemalteco*. Guatemala: FLACSO.

Lemus, J. (2012). Democracia interna en los partidos guatemaltecos: un desafío pendiente. In Asociación de Investigación y Estudios Sociales (ASIES) (Ed.), *Partidos políticos guatemaltecos: Dinámicas internas y desempeño* (pp. 1–30). Guatemala: ASIES.

López, S. (2016, octubre). Reforma electoral 2016: positiva y necesaria. *Actualidad Política*, *12*, 23–26.

Mack, L. F. (2017, febrero 3). La reforma constitucional, en perspectiva histórica. *Diálogo – Revisita Electrónica*. Retrieved from http://www.flacso.edu.gt/dialogo

Presidentes de los tres poderes del estado presentan reformas al sector justicia. (2016, octubre 6). *Congreso de la República de Guatemala*. Retrieved from https://www.congreso.gob.gt/2016/10/06/PRESIDENTES-DE-LOS-TRES-PODERES-DEL-ESTADO-PRESENTAN-REFORMAS-AL-SECTOR-JUSTICIA/

Proyecto de reformas constitucionales planteadas por el Ejecutivo. (Agosto, 2012). Retrieved from https://www.congreso.gob.gt/2012/08/27/CONGRESO-RECIBE-PROYECTO-DE-REFORMAS-CONSTITUCIONALES-PLANTEADAS-POR-EL-EJECUTIVO/

Tribunal Supremo Electoral. (2016). *Memoria de elecciones generales y de Diputados al Parlamento Centroamericano 2015*. Retrieved from https://www.tse.org.gt/images/memoriaselec/me2015.pdf

USAC, URL y ASIES proponen reformas constitucionales en seguridad y justiciar. (2011, mayo 2). *BRÚJULA*. Retrieved from http://brujula.com.gt/usac-url-y-asies-proponen-reformas-constitucionales-en-seguridad-y-justicia/

Electronic reference:

https://www.cicig.org/

https://muso.ufm.edu/wp-content/uploads/2017/11/Pro_reforma.pdf

http://brujula.com.gt/usac-url-y-asies-proponen-reformas-constitucionales-en-seguridad-y-justicia/

https://www.congreso.gob.gt/2012/08/27/CONGRESO-RECIBE-PROYECTO-DE-REFORMAS-CONSTITUCIONALES-PLANTEADAS-POR-EL-EJECUTIVO/

https://www.congreso.gob.gt/2016/10/06/PRESIDENTES-DE-LOS-TRES-PODERES-DEL-ESTADO-PRESENTAN-REFORMAS-AL-SECTOR-JUSTICIA/

Chapter 8

The Angolan Process of Peace and Democratization: A Case Study

Raul Tati

Introduction

Angola became independent in 1975 in the context of war between the three liberation movements: National Liberation Front of Angola (FNLA), People's Movement for the Liberation of Angola (MPLA), and National Union for the Total Independence of Angola (UNITA). Unlike other Portuguese colonies in Africa, where the anti-colonial struggle was led by a single movement, Angola had a political triumvirate in the leadership of the struggle for independence. The major leaders and the parties that they represented were Holden Roberto (FNLA), Agostinho Neto (MPLA), and Jonas Savimbi (UNITA). Each of these parties envisioned a different route for Angola both in terms of foreign interests and in terms of its own interests. The process of decolonization was clouded by the Cold War incidents in southern Africa in general and Angola in particular. Since then, Angola has been the scene of a fierce battle for the consolidation of power, where the contenders had the external support of the Cold War powers (USSR and the United States) and states aligned with them (Cuba, Zaire, South Africa, among others).

With the collapse of the Alvor Agreement of January 1975, a state of civil war became inevitable and the resulting hostilities were enough to make the country the scene of southern Africa's biggest battles in the Cold War context. However, the end of the Cold War provided a favorable environment for resolving the conflict with the withdrawal of Cuban and South African troops from Angola under the New York Agreement of December 1988. The Bicesse Agreement of May 1991 restored the hope of peace with a ceasefire. However, once the disarming was settled, the political problem had to be tackled. And this came in the form of the democratization of the country. This was the great innovation of the Agreement that opened the doors for the reform of the Constitutional Law of Angola. This reform allowed for the transition from one-party rule to a multiparty situation and the holding of general elections in September 1992. However, post-electoral

International Perspectives on Democratization and Peace, 135–148

doi:10.1108/978-1-80043-067-920200008

conflict once again plunged Angola into a bloody and ferocious war for another 10 years from 1992 to 2002, having known its epilogue only with the death of insurgent leader Jonas Savimbi. These facts are the main concern of this chapter which hopes to answer the question whether democratization can offer an effective way for peaceful resolution of conflicts.

Democracy in the African Context

Most of the African countries have been constituted as authoritarian or autocratic states after the achievement of independence. In some of my previous research about democracy in Africa, I discussed about

> one of the characteristics of the new independent states of Africa, despite their different economic, social, cultural and ideological nuances, is that they all have almost similar political regimes. Authoritarianism is roughly the common denominator, where all power is concentrated in the hands of a super-citizen or of a small clan circle. (Tati, 1998, p. 80)

This statement is based on the assumption that in Africa the modern state does not exactly correspond to an already existing nation. Rather it is under construction where here are several sociological communities grouped in the same space by force of colonization. Consequently, the state in Africa, in the absence of a homogeneous sociological support, is intrinsically imbued with some structural fragility. Hence, the idea of Monique Lions who discusses about this issue,

> the political regime that logically imposes on newly independent Africa must be of authoritarian and centrist inspiration for a dual goal of edification and education. It is nothing more than building the state, educating the masses and raising their standard of living, suppressing the tribal milieu and engendered micro-nations, eliminating regional rivalries and realizing national unity; in short, it is a question of transforming the whole tribe into a set of modern states. (Lions, 1964, p. 58)

Generally, these states compensated for their fragility with strong leaders, charismatics, demagogues, dictators, populists, and like-minded elites. They ignored republican values such as human rights, fundamental freedom of the citizens, freedom of the press and freedom of expression, participatory citizenship, political and economic rights. Many of these states have known bloody dictatorships for many years. Coups and tribal conflicts have long been the milieu of the new states in Africa. Such contestation and conflict is the norm rather than the exception.

Political violence was the constitutive element of power during the first decades of the establishment of the post-colonial state in Africa. In most of these cases, there was also an interest from external powers who in their lust for Africa's natural resources actively encouraged the violence of the state and the insurgent groups. From the point of view of the geopolitics of natural resources, Africa, between 1980 and 1982, contributed to world production with the following proportions: 63 per cent of cobalt, 54 per cent of diamonds, and 24 per cent of phosphate. In this context, colonial countries did not have a favorable terrain to install democracy. In fact, most of these new states was an expression of the centrist and authoritarian paradigm of post-colonial states. These were not exactly democracies, though, as Professor Adriano Moreira explains in an interview, all colonial empires claimed for themselves the prerogative of democrats; even the Portuguese regime was a corporate democracy, just as the Russians were a popular democracy. The word democracy covered everything (Moreira, 2017).

In any case, the democratic requirements that the United Nations Charter implies constitutive fundamental principles, such as the separation of powers between the executive, legislative and judicial arms and supervision of such diffusion among others. Considering the post-colonial prototype based on an extractive type of administration, the new regimes in Africa was not expected to be politically and socially inclusive. According to Emmanuel Terray, the colonial period cannot be seen only as a kind of parenthesis that independence was near. The political and administrative institutions imported by the Europeans are not mere facades under which political play would continue according to the rules inherited from the past. From this perspective, the author also argues:

> the ruling groups appropriated external inputs and handled them according to their projects and interests, but they had to accept their rules at the same time and the result is a *sui generis* reality for which we will have to invent new categories. (Terray, 1987, p. 10)

Democratic Transitions in Sub-Saharan Africa

It was only in the late 1980s that the "Third Wave" of the democratization advocated by Samuel Huntington began to permeate into the African continent. Most of these countries had undertaken a process of transformation through political reforms. In 1991, after the Berlin Wall came crashing down, at least 91 new democratic regimes have come into being worldwide. In this context, nearly 37 per cent of sub-Saharan African countries became liberal democracies and 20 per cent became electoral democracies. In the last two decades, these rates have been significantly increasing. In fact, with the exception of a few countries, democracy was adopted just like the Coca-Cola soft drink. Both the word and the idea are extremely in vogue now. In the political speeches of African politicians, this word is frequently used notwithstanding a basic disregard for the fundamental meaning of democracy and the moral values that such governance is meant to encapsulate. Democracy is purely a popular term for most of them with little linkage to procedural requirements and core values. This is the reason that the reality is so far different from the ideal of democracy. Therefore, we still have in these countries authoritarian regimes hidden under a mask of electoral democracy. Some people used to call them "zombie democracy." Of course, winning elections is enough for them to gain and to legitimate their power. After that they feel free to govern their people as they choose with autocratic tendencies.

In addition to the endogenous factors of African states themselves, there have been external factors influencing the democratic transition in Africa. The end of the Cold War, the collapse of the USSR, the fall of the Berlin Wall are all events that inspired Francis Fukuyama to consecrate the apocalyptic triumph of liberal democracies with his book *The End of History and the Last Man* (1992). We can witness the impact of this ideology in Africa as well. The "triumph" of liberal democracy brought out a militant proselytism inspired by the missionary morality of the West with a view of bringing to all corners of the world the best political model ever discovered by these people: the democracy *prêt-à-porter*. Some developed Western states and the international financial institutions like the World Bank and the International Monetary Fund have made cooperation and financial assistance conditional on African states to their political and economic reforms. In this way, democracy will be born in Africa with "congenital malformation." I will briefly explain the reasons. Why Western democracies came from a certain time and space. They have gone through centuries of reflection and maturation both in Europe and North America. We have a whole slew of thinkers who contributed with their theories to shaping these political systems. Furthermore, we must consider the contribution of Christian civilization to the humanization of politics. These are in my view "the foundations" that brought to light democratic experiences in the Western context.

None of this has happened to Africa. We have not had a mature reflection on democracy and its political and anthropological implications. Because of international pressures, African leaders have implanted democratic regimes *sui generis*, since they are nothing more than "electoral democracies" or in some cases even "autocratic democracies," however paradoxical they may seem. Notwithstanding this reality, some data available in the Afrobarometer (June 14, 2018) indicate that Africans increasingly accept multiparty democracy, but party trust remains low. It is estimated that 63 per cent of the population support multiparty democracy and 56 per cent feel close to a political party in their country (in the 36 countries studied). However, less than half believe in political parties. The truth is that some fundamental presuppositions of the democratic state are non-existent: the rule of law or constitutionalism, popular legitimacy, pluralism, participatory and inclusive citizenship, alternating power, separation of powers, good governance practices and accountability, among others, did not find fertile ground to grow.

Another problem is the African context of poverty. According to Samuel Huntington,

> Poverty is a principal and probably the principal obstacle to the democratic development. The future of democracy depends on the future of economic development. Obstacles to economic developments are obstacles to the expansion of democracy. (Huntington, 1991, p. 311)

I agree with Huntington in the sense that there are some significant implications of the impact of poverty that bear on the prospects for democracy and its entrenchment. Nevertheless, I do not mean that it is an excuse to avoid democratic reforms in poor countries such as those from sub-Saharan Africa. In fact, the problem of poverty could be a reason to justify the *status quo* where there is not a strong will for democratic changes. In my opinion corruption is generally rife in countries with high rates of poverty. Thus, there is not a good preexisting environment to build democratic institutions. In this sense, some people argue that those countries "are not ready for democracy" because they "care about the material rather than democracy" (*primum vivere, deinde philosofare*). However, as we have noted above, most of the sub-Saharan countries have become democratic regimes. Perhaps that the economic conditions are not so favorable to democratization should be thought about in relative terms. It should not be allowed to make a kind of dark list of some countries where the introduction of democracy is regarded as impossible. It is purely a myth that must be overcome in the context of political studies. Thus, how can an impoverished and weak political system still help to solve political and armed conflicts? This question is addressed in relation to the Angolan case.

Peace and Democratization in Angola: Roots of the Conflict

The roots of the conflict in Angola are to be found in the contemporary history of the country (Weeler & Pelissier, 2013, pp. 355–375). A political science approach suggests the same starting point (Guimaraes, 1992, pp. 31–59). Angola became independent in November 1975. The new State was born as a single-party state with a Marxist Leninist tendency. The MPLA took over as a party of the vanguard of the Angolan people and exclusive representative of the interests of Angolans of all social classes (proletarians, peasants, intellectuals, etc.). A monophasic regime was being created that gave no place or space for other political and ideological expressions. However, the government installed by the MPLA in Angola did not have a minute of tranquility for more than a decade from 1975 to 1991 because of the armed rebellion carried out by UNITA with US support (Wright, 1997). UNITA was able to exploit skillfully the weaknesses of the MPLA's autocrat and pro-communist regime by launching the message to the Western world that Jonas Savimbi and his movement were "freedom fighters." They were described as resisting the implantation of communism in Angola. They in turn were heralded as proponents of democracy and Western values. This message was good for the United States and other Western countries that were close to UNITA. This bifurcation of power and support was Angola's Cold War context. The situation in turn led to the country becoming the largest battlefield of the so-called "proxy wars" in southern Africa.

However, a quiet analysis can effectively demonstrate the essential reason for the civil war in Angola. The main reason was the power dispute. The UNITA intended to take power through armed violence, radically altering the existing political situation. This movement was inspired by a kind of "messianic mission" that was to be carried out by the freedom and political, economic and cultural emancipation of the natives of so-called "Angola profunda." The MPLA regime did not take kindly to the rebels, doing everything to conserve power and annihilate the rebels with all the resources at their disposal. Officially, the government legitimized the struggle as a defensive war against the aggressions of the external enemy axis (the United States – South Africa) to its sovereignty and territorial integrity. It also legitimized the presence of Cuban troops in Angola under international law. Regarding the external intervention in the Angolan conflict, I agree with William Minter when he concludes: "although external intervention did not cause the conflict in Angola, it lengthened and deepened it" (Minter, 1994, p. 271). In the same sense Justin Pearce notes:

> Cold war involvement in Angola received fresh attention in the early 2000s as newly available materials from both Western- and Eastern-bloc archives stimulated historical research into the impact of the superpower rivalry on state formation and political contestation in developing countries. (Pearce, 2015, p. 3)

The Angolan civil war is a conflict that resulted from a twinning of internal and external factors. The war fought in the period from 1975 to 1976 between the MPLA and the FNLA–UNITA coalition to succeed Portuguese colonialism in Angola, involved the intervention of external powers on behalf of both sides. "In the case of superpowers intervention in third states became part of the very structure of international politics which their rivalry had established in the post-war period" (Guimaraes, 1992, p. 14). In this sense, the internal actors (MPLA and its rivals)

> expressed their differences in ideological and political terms that served to establish their war as part of the wider global conflict between East and West [...]. The ideological and political competition between East and West was one of the battlefields on which the Angolan adversaries sought to fight each other. (Guimaraes, 1992, pp. 11–12)

Previous Attempts to Resolve the Conflict

However, the reality on the ground required some pragmatism. It was clear that the conflict would not find a solution through violence. The experience of the battles of Mavinga (between 1985 and 1988) and the tragedy of the Cuito Cuanavale battle had opened the door of diplomacy for conflict resolution. Moreover, curiously, diplomacy and war cohabited throughout the conflict, for as the war continued on the ground where the contenders sought military advantages to negotiate from a position of strength, diplomatic contacts multiplied among the main internal and external actors. Perhaps we can bring here *en passant* the strange concept of "coercive diplomacy" by Magalhães (2005, p. 18) or "plumbing of violence" 'by Thomas Schelling (1973, p. 75) where ceding or intransigence depends on not only negotiating skills or political technics, but specially the position of strength or weakness in the war "the power to hurt is bargaining power. To exploit it is diplomacy – vicious diplomacy, but diplomacy" (Schelling, 1973, p. 75; Apud Magalhães, 2005, p. 18). Even in the form of contacts, the use of direct strategy was always underway either from the perspective of coercion through predominantly military means, or by making the same coercion directly on the opponent (Correia, 2010, p. 42). It is not surprising, however, that the war actors were the same actors for diplomacy. This is one of the paradoxes of the Angolan situation.

The New York Agreement between Angola, Cuba, and South Africa (December 13, 1988) brought a very important deal that completely changed the situation in Angola: the withdrawal of the Cuban contingent and the South African forces from the Angolan territory. American diplomacy, by Chester Crocker, and later Herman Cohen, skillfully seized this environment to persuade the Angolan government to enter into direct contacts with UNITA for an internal reconciliation. The logic was that with the departure of external forces the conditions had been created for the inevitable understanding among Angolans that a historic opportunity had presented itself for conflict resolution. The Bicesse Agreement (May 31, 1991) was the culmination of many meetings and negotiations between the government and the UNITA rebels. The focal points of the Bicesse Agreement are the following: (a) the end of the war and the opening of the peacebuilding process with the solemn signing of the ceasefire; (b) the creation of a republican army and the dismantling of FALA (Forças Armadas de Libertação de Angola) and FAPLA (Forças Armadas Populares de Libertação de Angola); (c) recognition of UNITA as a legal party under the revision of the constitutional law that opened the doors to a multiparty system; (d) the end of one-party regime and the timing of the elections. When speaking of democratization in this context, the main reference will be the organization of multiparty elections in the country for the first time. From this logic, it can be inferred that the election served only as an instrumental protocol and not intrinsic value. In other words, the electoral act was more like a game rule to solve the issue of power in Angola. Both internal and external actors believed that democracy would definitely solve the conflict and preempt the return to war. Unfortunately, that assumption was wrong. Failure was drawn on the horizon, because the peace process and the process of democratization were formally reduced to the electoral act as an instrument for "adjusting accounts left by the Cold War" (Messiant, 2004, p. 18).

This failure will quickly bring to light several fracturing aspects that undermined the process in the phase of its implementation. The key observation is that the two main actors in the process were not so interested in reconciliation and democratization. According to Christine Messiant, a researcher on the political and social history of Lusophone African countries,

> Neither the MPLA nor UNITA were interested in reconciliation or democratization. Above all, the MPLA wanted to avoid defeat and accepted certain conditions reluctantly and under pressure. UNITA only wanted peace because it was certain – like almost everyone at the time, including the MPLA – that it would win the elections, and achieve its goal of achieving state power. (Messiant, 2004, p. 18)

The electoral act would be just a pretext to impose the winner takes all logic instead of the "power sharing" logic: whoever wins, wins everything and whoever loses, loses everything. A question of hegemony (or supremacy) was at stake.

As the transition process was practically delivered to the two-armed parties, at that time both the Troika (Portugal, Russia, the United States) and the United Nations ended up playing a less persuasive role than expected in the peacekeeping process. With regard to the United Nations, the Charter itself restricts, in some way, the taking of initiatives by reason of the principle of non-interference in the internal affairs of its members:

> Nothing in this Charter shall authorize the United Nations to intervene in matters which depend essentially one of the internal jurisdiction of any State, or compel the members to submit such matters to a solution under the present Charter. (Charter of the United Nations chapter 1 (Purposes and Principles), art 2, para 7)

This provision, in the case of the Angolan peace process, not only entrusted ownership of the process to the Angolans themselves but also left the power of decisions in their hands. The United Nations and the Troika played a less intervening and more peripheral role in the process. As Paulo Pinheiro wrote in an article on the Angolan peace process,

> the ownership of the process is by the Angolans who chair the supervisory body, the CCPM (Joint Political-Military Commission), monitor the ceasefire (CCVF – Joint Commission of Verification and Monitoring of the ceasefire), form the single army (CCFA – Joint Commission for the Armed Forces), and prepare elections. The mediation ends and Troika and the UN observe and assist the parties. (Pinheiro, 2006, p. 142)

For his part, Luis Castelo Branco points to this limitation as a reason for the failure of the Bicesse agreements.

Following the agreements, the Angolan government requested the participation of the United Nations to verify compliance with the ceasefire and to supervise the actions of the police. With the adoption of Security Council Resolution 696, on May 30, 1991, a peacekeeping mission (UN peacekeeping mission) was established and became known as UNAVEM II (United Nations Verification Mission for Angola). In the light of the complexity of the situation on the ground, however, the initial mandate of UNAVEM II was extended by the adoption, on March 27, 1992 of the Resolution 747 of the Security Council to include the process of observation of the September 1992 elections (Branco, 2003, p. 91). In this sense, while recognizing the fundamental role of the UN presence in Angola, the author also recognizes that the UN in many aspects was confronted with consummate facts, merely acting in scenarios that did not consider the ideas. In his opinion, this marginalization of the UN from the center of the Angolan transition process "was due to the combination of the following factors"

(Branco, 2003, p. 92). The MPLA government made it clear from the outset that the elections should be organized only by itself. Still imbued with the spirit of bipolar confession,

> the MPLA feared that a UN, heavily influenced by the Americans, was in favor of UNITA. That being so [...] the UN was not able to follow all the stages of the preparation of the electoral act.

UNITA also did not look favorably upon a UN mission with strong means on the ground, "which would make it difficult to conceal troops, or heavy weapons, situations in clear violation of the peace agreement signed" (Branco, 2003, p. 92). For the international society, a small mission in Angola was also of interest. (...) there was a widespread desire for savings. This desire was made clear by

> the inability of the UN Secretary-General's Special Representative, Englishwoman Margaret Anstee, to obtain the number of blue helmets she considered necessary to carry out the mission of UNAVEM II, including cease-fire, demobilization and the cantonment of troops. (Branco, 2003, p. 92)

In fact, within the Troika, there were also some important interests. The United States, for example, expected UNITA to become the power in Angola, as Christine Messiant states:

> In fact, for the United States, peace was not the first and only goal. The peace process was seen more as a way for UNITA to come to power. This almost guaranteed outcome could be achieved with minimal political and financial costs, thanks to the central role assigned to the Troika. (Messiant, 2004)

Entry and Impact of Democratization on the Conflict

It is quite clear that in the Angolan context none of the actors was prepared to take the electoral results to their detriment. The elementary assumptions of democracy, such as respect for people wills expressed at the ballot box, transparency and fairness of the process, fair play after publication of results, and so on, were still lacking at this time. Following the logic of the conflict resolution in the case of Angola, it was a mistake to seek a solution throughout the elections. What happened, in my view, is just the attempt to organize elections in a post-war context where was no democracy. I think that the elections should have been the result of a process of pacification and democratization, more or less consolidated. Elections should not kick-start democratization. The more consolidated the process of democratization, the more peaceful and fair the elections will be. Today, it is a fact shared by the scholars of the matter that there was precipitation. It was only about 18 months after the end of war for the election preparation.

Many new political parties created in this period practically did not have time enough to implant themselves in the national territory.

In my opinion, after a long conflict, the transition might be perhaps at least for three years. Then, a provisional or transitional government of national unity with democratic institutions, freedom of the press and freedom of expression, separation of powers, a strong civil society, and the like could have been introduced and institutionalized. For the general population, this time could be useful for a kind of social *catharsis* to heal the wounds of war, especially psychological ones, and create a more propitious environment for true reconciliation between children of the same homeland. This period could be also useful for the resettlement of displaced populations because of the conflict and the organized repatriation of the refugees. However, some opinions point to the weak engagement of the international community, particularly the UN, as one of the main causes of the failure of the peace process in Angola. Although it has highlighted missions to verify the implementation of the peace agreement by blue helmets, the United Nations has never lived up to the scale of the involvement required after conflict in Angola. The engagement was weak in terms of both staff numbers, logistics and financial availability. Justino da Glória Ramos refers to the testimony of Margaret Anstee herself. She expressed her disappointment at the

> lack of interest of the international community in Angola and, at a round table held in Portugal on October 27, 1993, expressly stated that, for the United Nations, Angola was a matter of low priority, that the international community underestimated the Angolan process and that the cheap project was expensive. (Ramos, 2018, pp. 627–628).

Conflict Transformation from Democratization

There is another fundamental aspect that must be highlighted among the reasons for the failure of the process: the whole peace architecture was designed to the interests of both contenders and never had as its main horizon the general interest of the Angolan nation. After all, it was necessary to solve the problem of power and this is the main subject that was present in all the rounds of negotiations. The whole peace process in Angola after the Bicesse Agreement was always in the logic of a political, ideological, and military duel between the two signatory parties to the Agreement. Even political speeches on both sides revealed this observation to be true. This logic was so radical that it eventually determined the end of the conflict through a military victory of the government forces against the UNITA rebels. There was a deep belief among the parties that the conflict would be solved militarily. That is why there was greater investments in war than in diplomacy. Contrary to what the Angolan diplomat Mário Augusto thinks, it was not the broad movement for peace and national reconciliation or the dialog that brought the war to an end (Messiant, 2004). It was the end of the war that finally opened the door to a new phase of national dialog and reconciliation.

The tragic death of the leader of UNITA had a direct and immediate outcome, the total surrender of his forces. This act paved the way for reintegration of the rebels into state institutions. The death of Jonas Savimbi (February 22, 2002) became an opportunity to attempt to renegotiate a peace deal with UNITA's surviving leaders (the Luena Agreements):

> When Jonas Savimbi died in battle in 2002 after a long war of attrition, the Angolan government took the opportunity to persuade UNITA's surviving leaders to accept peace on the MPLA's terms. The ensuing settlement served to dismantle what remained of UNITA's structures in rural Angola. (Pearce, 2015, p. 159)

The ceremony of April 4, 2002, with the signing of the Luena *Memorandum of Understanding*, was not exactly the result of negotiations between the parties. Given that one of the parties was deeply fragile and unable to impose demands, one cannot speak of negotiations. According to negotiation theory, the best agreement is one that is based on the win-win principle and not a win-lose scenario. What happened in reality were punctual "punts" aimed at avoiding the futile continuation of the slaughter, since the main target was already off the stage. Moreover, both the Bicesse Agreement (May 31, 1991) and the Lusaka Protocol (November 20, 1994), despite the resumption of the war, maintained their validity as important instruments of pacification and reconciliation through the "power sharing" paradigm by the institutionalization of the Government of Unity and National Reconciliation (GURN).

> The failure of Bicesse and Lusaka ensured that by the end of the 1990s, Angolan political elites deeply distrusted international mediation as a way of bringing the war to an end. This distrust towards the international community was shared by the MPLA and by religious and civil society leaders, who by the end of the decade were beginning to constitute an independent and coherent voice in Angolan politics. (Pearce, 2015, p. 160)

Therefore, considering the total situation of the Angolan peace process, I think that the attempt to solve the conflict from democratization was not so strong but it allowed building new sustainable ways to look for peace. The conflict transformation from democracy has become for both the Angolan government and the UNITA a great opportunity but also a big challenge because nobody was ready for the democratic rules that were to subsequently obtain.

Contributions from the Angolan Case Study

It was from these facts that some people came out to extol the experience of Angola in the resolution of conflicts turning it into a model paradigm for the conflicts in the African continent. As if that were not enough, both the official discourse and some with pro-regime tendencies argue that Angola was able to resolve the conflict by itself without the support of the international community. I do not agree with this assessment of the situation. There were international factors and conditions that influenced the outcome of the war in Angola. Moreover, the first major factor was the loss of legitimacy of UNITA in the new post-Cold War context of the international political landscape. On the one hand, the refusal of the election results and the restarting of the war, for which responsibility – in my opinion – was never exclusive to UNITA, became the big mistake that the international community accused the UNITA of. On the other hand, the ruling MPLA government came to have greater international recognition and legitimacy. The Angolan foreign policy elites knew that a re-alignment would culminate in the establishment of diplomatic relations with the United States. UNITA lost its best partner and its leader was subjected under the international pressure to disarm. The Security Council has repeatedly condemned UNITA by imposing the following sanctions on the organization and its leaders: suspension of financial assets in foreign banks, the *embargo* on the sale of diamonds, preventing the supply of arms and military products by all member countries, restriction of the movement of leaders, etc. (UN Resolution 864 adopted by Security Council at its 3277th meeting on 15 September 1993 about the deterioration of the political and military situation in Angola.).

The Angolan government made also diplomatic contacts with the aim of declaring UNITA as a terrorist group. Although it failed to achieve this intention, the Angolan government started to cultivate support from several countries to defeat UNITA. Without external support, their own resources could not have trapped UNITA forces. The regime had these elements and knew that the final tragedy was only a question of time, since it had become irreversible. It was in the sense that former President José Eduardo dos Santos declared the three possible scenarios for Jonas Savimbi, before traveling to the United States a few days before the murderer of his rival: (a) surrender; (b) catch; and (c) death in combat.

Therefore, the idea that Angola solved the internal conflict without the support of the international community is not at all sustainable. Even without the official presence of a United Nations mission in Angola, the international community played an active and decisive role in defeating UNITA forces. José Eduardo dos Santos bet on the war and had the necessary support (and international legitimacy!) to take to the extreme his will to annihilate his enemy. It is no wonder that any international body has not condemned the murder of Dr Jonas Savimbi. It seems to be a "complicity" or, in other words, a tacit approval of the act.

Given these facts, strictly speaking in terms of conflict resolution and in terms of peace process and democratization, the Angolan paradigm does not serve as a paradigm for the other African countries. We cannot agree with the statement according Augusto that the Angolan paradigm of conflict resolution must be followed by others African countries (2018, pp. 93–121). The Angolan experience is *sui generis*. Peace and democratization in Angola resulted from a long and tragic fratricidal war. Paradoxical as it may seem, the war brought peace and the conflict brought democracy. But it is a peace of the silence of weapons, a peace of winners and losers; a peace that cemented even more the supremacy of the winners; the democracy made in Angola is also a formal democracy marked by the supremacy of the MPLA. The state, although officially confirmed by the constitutional presuppositions of a democratic state of law, is an overly partisan state that is not representative of the peoples of the entire country.

Concluding Remarks

Peace and democratization processes can be viable for conflict resolution. However, post-war contexts, such as Angola's, can make such outcomes difficult to achieve. This means that democratization alone is not is not a sufficient condition. It needs to set in motion other important tasks like the processes of peacebuilding and peacekeeping. These tasks failed in Angola and the process of democratization collapsed giving way to another 10 years of war. Curiously, the current democratic experience in Angola that is taking its steps is still timid and is the product of war; the logic is that it is necessary to make war for democratic transformation. Therefore, in Angola we have a democracy with scars from the civil war that was not brought to a fair close. Winning the war, the MPLA consolidated its power by controlling all state organs and established a skewed democracy where the alternation of power is far from being a reality, considering the rigid control it maintains over all electoral processes and their organs. Like all processes, consolidating democracy will take time hence some patience may be required. I do not share the Afro-pessimistic views and analyses that question the convenience and ability of Africans to construct democratic regimes by suggesting other forms of political organization more attuned to the cultural nature of Africans and their ancestral values. The values of democracy are based on an axiological foundation that is human dignity and the labor and fulfillment of the common good. If human dignity is placed at the center of democratic systems, Africa cannot stay out by claiming particularities. There are no perfect democracies or peoples better suited to the realization of the democratic ideal than others. I believe that the economics and cultural conditions supportive of democratization is emerging in the last two decades in sub-Saharan countries like Angola. People are gradually convinced that democratic regimes are so much better than dictatorial or authoritarian regimes. It is an important view to hold for making the necessary changes to institutionalize democracy. Democracy in Africa is a challenge, not a myth. We can defeat challenges but the myth is something that we cannot control at all. Democracy appears to the only political regime type that is overwhelmingly increasing its reach throughout the world and based on that development Africa can seek solace in the future.

References

Afrobarometer. (2018, June 14). *Afrobarometer's data on African's Views on Democracy*. Retrieved from www.afrobarometer.org

Augusto, M. (2018). *Conflictos em África*. Lisboa: Guerra e Paz.

Branco, L. C. (2003). As Missões da ONU na África Austral: sucessos e fracassos. *Nação e Defesa*, *105*(2), 81–102.

Correia, P. P. (2010). *Manual de Geopolítica e Geostratégia, Vol I. Conceitos, Teorias, Doutrinas*. Coimbra: Edições Almedina, S.A.
de Magalhaes, J. C. (2005). *A Diplomacia Pura*. Lisboa: BIZANCIO.
Fukuyama, F. (1992). *The end of history and the last man*. New York, NY: The Free Press.
Guimaraes, A. (1992). *The Origins of the Angolan Civil war. International politics and domestic political conflict (1961–1976)*. Doctoral dissertation, University of London. Retrieved from http://etheses.lse.ac.uk/2414/
Huntington, S. (1991). *The Third Wave. Democratization in the twentieth century*. Norman, OK: University of Oklahoma Press.
Lions, M. (1964). *Constitucionalismo y Democracia en el África recién independizada*. Mexico: Universidad Nacional Autonoma.
Messiant, C. (2004). As Causas do fracasso de Bicesse e Lusaka. *Uma análise crítica. Accord, 15*, 16–23.
Minter, W. (1994). *Apartheid's Contras: An inquiry into the Roots of war in Angola and Mozambique*. London: Zed Books Ltd.
Moreira, A. (2017). Interview with Adriano Moreira, Entrevista, Lisboa, 15 de Fevereiro de 2017.
Pearce, J. (2015). *Political identity and conflict in Central Angola, 1975–2002*. New York, NY: Cambridge University Press.
Pinheiro, P. V. (2006). Angola de Bicesse a Lusaka. In M. Franco (Ed.), *Portugal, Estados Unidos e África Austral* (pp. 137–149). Lisboa: Fundação Luso-Americana.
Ramos, J. G. (Ed.). (2018). *Angola pelos Caminhos da Paz. Guerra e Diplomacia (1975–2002)*. Luanda, Angola: Mayamba Editora.
Schelling, T. (1973). Diplomacy of Violence. In C. Beitz, & T. Herman (Eds.), *Peace and War*. San Francisco, CA: W.H. Freeman and Company.
Tati, R. (1998). *Crise Africana e o Processo de Democratização em África. Implicações ético-antropológicas*. Doctoral dissertation, Accademia Alfonsiana, Roma.
Terray, E. (1987). *L'Etat Contemporain en Afrique*. Paris: Editions L'Harmattan.
Weeler, D., & Pelissier, R. (2013). *História de Angola*. Lisboa: Edições Tinta-da-China.
Wright, G. (1997). *The destruction of a nation: United States' Policy Toward Angola since 1945*. London: Pluto Pr.

Chapter 9

Peace and Conflict in Mozambique: A Long Road to Democracy?

António L. Fontes Ramos

In the history of Mozambique, several influences have conditioned to a great extent the current society and its problems. In this text, we will follow a long path in which several relevant historical events will be emphasized, whose social and political impact will have to be taken into account when trying to understand the current context. From an approach to the circumstances that shaped the country in colonial times, we will move on to the Frelimo-led independence struggle for which power was transferred without limitations or constraints, after the Revolution of April 25, 1975 in Portugal. Then the chapter will analyze the implementation of a single party regime in Mozambique whose policies led to a long and very violent conflict that only ended with the implementation of a multiparty system and the 1992 General Peace Agreement. It follows a period of peace, but not of equity, nor of power-sharing that has led to a new conflict context and finally to a constitutional change that may pave the way for a better political accommodation.

Historic Roots of Conflict

Portugal Reaches India

Many features of present-day Mozambique are deeply embedded in its history, but three periods highlight the complex and frequent swings between peace and war: the presence of Portugal in the Indian Ocean; the demarcation of Mozambique's western borders in a confrontational context; and the violent independence process leading to the transference of power to Frelimo.[1]

[1]FRELIMO (Frente de Libertação Nacional de Moçambique) is the acronym in Portuguese for Mozambique Liberation Front.

International Perspectives on Democratization and Peace, 149–170

doi:10.1108/978-1-80043-067-920200009

After turning the Cape of Good Hope, Vasco da Gama's fleet arrived on January 25, 1498 at the River of "Bons Sinais"[2] to repair the ships, mend the sails and attempt to gain information about the route to India. It was an historic event with meaningful geopolitical consequences. The negative effect on the traditional commerce using the routes to Europe through the Arabian Peninsula and Egypt caused a strong reaction from local traders to impede access of the newcomers to the local markets. This led to the deployment to the Indian Ocean of a strong Portuguese naval presence supported in three bases spanning from Ormuz at the entrance of the Persian Gulf, to Malacca in Southeast Asia, with the central position in Goa in the west coast of India. It was under this "maritime empire," headed by a Portuguese Vice-King,[3] that Portuguese sailors reached the Southeast Asian Islands, Australia, China, and Japan in 1543.

For centuries, the Portuguese presence and interests were centered in India. The eastern coast of Africa played a supporting role, offering indispensable harbors to support the movement of ships that started making this long journey.[4] The first permanent Portuguese presence in the littoral was in the port of Melinde (in today's Kenya), and then further to the south in the Island of Mozambique, Sofala and latter Lourenço Marques, today's Maputo (Costa, José, & Oliveira, 2014, p. 107). Other countries followed Portugal. Inland the Dutch settled in the strategic geographical position of Cape that controlled the access to the Indian Ocean. From there they could supply the ships sailing and returning from the West Indies (Fage, 2014, p. 365). Their local descendants, the Boers, would build a long history in Africa. After being replaced in the Cape area by the United Kingdom, most of them moved away constituting the Boer Republics in today's north and east of South Africa, one of the most resource-rich African regions, maintaining contacts and interests in Mozambique primarily to guarantee access to the sea through the Lourenço Marques harbor.

The movement of the Portuguese from the littoral to the interior of Mozambique started in the second part of the sixteenth century[5] mostly along the rivers and primarily along the Zambezi valley. It was a slow and discrete penetration negotiated with local populations that allowed the establishment of some settlements in the area like in Sena and Tete. The presence of the Dominicans in the valley from 1580, and the signature of the 1607 and 1629 treaties with the king of Monomotapa[6] helped to achieve a general peaceful presence in the region (Costa et al., 2014, p. 214).

---

[2]It was named "Bons Sinais" (Good Signals) because they received important indications from the locals about the route to India and even found a pilot to guide them along the coast.

[3]Francisco de Almeida (1505–1509) was the first "viceroy" of India.

[4]Like the "Carreira da India," a commercial fleet that started to make annual trips to the region.

[5]As it happened with the occupation of the Atlantic Islands, Brazil, and Angola.

[6]Mutapa Empire (Monomotapa in Portuguese) was a powerful kingdom with the capital in today's Zimbabwe extending from the Eastern part of Angola to Zambia, Zimbabwe and in Mozambique between the Limpopo and Zambezi Rivers.

The consolidation of the luso presence in the Zambezi valley led the King to issue letters of donation known as the "prazos of Zambézia."[7] Portuguese and mainly Portuguese-Asians could receive land for three generations to promote local occupation and development (Costa et al., 2014, p. 182). In July 1752, the king separated the government of Mozambique from India-Goa. The new governor under direct dependency from Lisbon fixed the Captaincy in the island of Mozambique and received a territorial jurisdiction from Lourenço Marques Bay to Cabo Delgado but with a less well-defined interior.

Opposing Plans for Mozambique

In the nineteenth century, Africa was at the center of the European imagination and interest. A cycle of journeys along the rivers had led several explorers to the center of the continent, discovering the sources of the Nile, the great Lakes and the passage from the Atlantic to the Indian Ocean through the rivers Cuanza and Zambezi or the Congo River basin. The "Scramble for Africa" was eminent. European countries not only had an unprecedented level of power, they also had acquired the "moral conviction" that European civilization should be at the center of peoples' development (Fage & Tordoff, 2014, p. 342).

The 1894–1895 Berlin Conference mostly dealt with the freedom of navigation and trade on the Niger River and the Congo Basin. However, its Chapter VI, Article XXXIV, also defined the conditions for new occupations on the African Coasts that should assume the form of a Protectorate and its respective act be "addressed to the other Signatory Powers"[8] (implicitly meaning that new occupations should be undertaken by one of them). Article XXXV of the same Chapter completed the norm expressing the obligation of the Signatory Powers "to insure the establishment of authority in the regions occupied by them on the coasts of the African continent…" (General Act, art. XXXIV, XXXV).

The occupation of the hinterland was not agreed upon, but the same principles started to be applied. This led to the formulation of the need of "effective occupation" to demarcate new areas of influence in Africa (Costa et al., 2014, p. 397). Portugal felt the intromission of the colonial powers and made another approach to the region. In 1889, exploiting the opportunity of signing the treaty to delineate the borders of Guinea with France and Angola and Mozambique with Germany,[9] it added to these treaties a clause in which the two countries would recognize the constitution of a continuous entity between Angola and Mozambique.

The need for "effective occupation" of the territory in line with the new post-Berlin prescription in an environment of Anglo-Portuguese contestation among

---

[7]"Prazo" is a Portuguese word for: "amount of time." The Portuguese or luso-asiatics that settled in the inland received territory for three generations.

[8]Signatory Powers were: Austria, Belgium, Denmark, France, Germany, Great Britain, Italy, the Netherlands, Portugal, Russia, Spain, Sweden and Norway, Turkey, and the United States (General Act).

[9]Germany had established the German South West Africa colony (today Namibia) at the south of Angola.

the loyalties of the local people, altered the Portuguese stance in Mozambique and led to a series of military campaigns of occupation beginning in 1895 that lasted until 1912.

The borders of Mozambique were then established amidst the emergence of new powers in the region. Germany, which established the German East African colony (later Tanganyika, now Tanzania) north of the Rovuma River, and England, which through the British South Africa Company seized areas that traditionally had established ties with Portugal and established the colonies of North and South Rhodesia.

This process resulted in a long (2,000 km in length) but narrow country, which reduces in the center to a width of 250 km. This represents a geographical fragility, since in this area it is possible to cut off the north–south links, as it happened for instance with the positioning and performance of Renamo in the region of Gorongoza. Due to the artificial definition of boundaries, the ethnic groups living in the north were separated in different countries, such as the Makonde. Some of these were incorporated into the German colony of East Africa, while others remained in Mozambique. The Maravi (or Nyanja) were separated between the provinces of Cabo Delgado, Tete in Mozambique, and some incorporated in Malawi. Most of the southern peoples were separated between Mozambique and the Boer Republics (currently South Africa) or Northern and Southern Rhodesia (now Zimbabwe).

On the other hand, Mozambique's location close to resource-rich countries such as Zambia, Zimbabwe or Malawi, but without access to the sea, has led the Mozambican communications system to be developed horizontally. Routes and rail roads were primarily designed to support the linkage between these hinterland countries and the coastal ports. The narrowing in the center of the country has repeatedly paralyzed the circulation between North and South during conflictual perturbations, causing a disproportionate impact on the economic, social, and political life.

Ethnic diversity is yet a relevant issue for Mozambique because prolonged wars and instability have resulted in a tendentially lower sense of national unity. And most Mozambicans can see themselves primarily as members of their ethnic group and only later as members of the nation and in general.

External Links to the Renamo-Frelimo Conflict

The Independence Struggle

The decolonization movement after the Second World War was followed with apprehension by the Portuguese autocratic regime of Salazar. Denouncing the support provided by USSR and China to most of the African independence movements, Salazar maintained a stubborn defense of a multiracial and multicontinental nation from "Minho to Timor"[10] presented as a contribution against the communist threat to the West. The ferocious attacks in the north of Angola

[10]Minho is located in the Northwest of Continental Portugal, and Timor was the farthest eastern colonial possession.

launched in March 1961 by the União dos Povos de Angola (UPA)[11] against white settlers and local populations, caused general consternation in Portugal and were used to justify a substantial deployment of military forces overseas. A prolonged conflict developed in Angola, and later in Guinea-Bissau and Mozambique that lasted for 15 years and ended only with the so called "Carnation Revolution" of 1974.

In Mozambique, there were some nationalist or anticolonial organizations before 1961 but the local government was able to minimize or restrain their activities. It was therefore among the half million Mozambicans working in the neighboring countries that the first organizations for social contacts, mutual aid and later political affirmation developed. In 1960, the first nationalist organization, União Democrática Nacional de Moçambique (UDENAMO),[12] was created in South Rhodesia. Over time it incorporated students and middle-level cadres from the South and Center of Mozambique. Two other movements also emerged. Mozambique African National Union (MANU), in Tanzania, mostly formed of Makonde people living on the two sides of the common northern border and União Nacional Africana de Moçambique Independente (UNAMI),[13] in Malawi, with migrants mostly from Tete and Central Mozambique. These movements stimulated by Tanzania's President Julius Nyerere, united and on June 25, 1992 constituted Frelimo[14] as a single front, with Edward Mondlane as President and Urias Simango as Vice-President (Cabrita, 2000, p. 5; Cann, 1998, p. 53; Chissano, 2010, p. 343). Many separations, evictions, return to the former political entities or the constitution of others happened over time, but Frelimo had the major role in the struggle for independence.

During the first years, Mondlane supported by the Kennedy administration (Cabrita, 2000, p. 18) tried to reach a negotiated agreement with Portugal, but this led to criticism in some Frelimo ranks and even to accusations of cooperation with Portugal. Therefore, after a preparation of some forces in Algeria, in September 1964, Frelimo launched the first armed attack in the Makonde's region, against the administrative post of Chai in Cabo Delgado (Cabrita, 2000, p. 29). In the following years, Frelimo tried to expand its military activity southwards. It was able to open another front in Niassa that was expanded eastwards in the direction of Cabo Delgado. Progress to the South through the Zambezian province was not achieved, however, due to the lack of support of the ethnic Makua group that represented about one-third of the Mozambican population. Plans to start guerilla activities in other areas were not successful, like in the Tete Province due to the opposition of the Rhodesian Ian Smith regime. Only in 1968, and through Zambia, was it possible to initiate some activity in the region.

[11]UPA is the acronym in Portuguese of Union of the Peoples of Angola.

[12]UDENAMO is the acronym in Portuguese of National Democratic Union of Mozambique.

[13]UNAMI is the acronym in Portuguese for African National Union for an Independent Mozambique.

[14]FRELIMO (Frente de Libertação Nacional de Moçambique) is the acronym in Portuguese for Mozambique Liberation Front.

The Tete front was reactivated in the 1970s, when the Cahora Bassa Dam began to be built, but Frelimo did not have the capacity to affect or prevent its construction. However, it developed a more substantial action in the region and managed to make some prolonged albeit weak penetrations toward the village of Vila Pery, now Chimoio, alarming the population in central Mozambique at the beginning of 1974. In April of that year, the Portuguese government was overthrown by a coup d'état and the political and military situation changed radically.

Portugal had prepared since the late 1950s to fight a long and complex war in the three different and separated territories of Guinea, Angola, and Mozambique. The general approach toward the colonies, considered Provinces of Portugal and later a form of administrative States, was substantially based on development and industrialization. This policy had a significant effect and in Mozambique where the

> number of enterprises increased from 150 in 1947, two years after the Second World War, to 1,025 in 1961. Capita stock expanded from 796 million escudos in 1947 to 4,610 million escudos in 1961. This implied a steady production expansion. From 1955 to 1961, the production index, in fact, doubled. (Cruz, Guambe, Marrengula, & Ubisse, 2014, p. 4)

> In 1975, Mozambique was considered the 8th largest industrial producer in Sub-Saharan Africa. Manufacturing value added was above 10 per cent of the GDP. The manufacturing sector had diversified within a context of high effective protection. Mozambique also had one of the largest hydro power plants in Africa: The Cahora Bassa Dam. (Cruz et al., 2014, p. 8)

Before independence, there was a constant growth of Mozambique GNP[15] and GNP per capita. That situation was followed by a constant fall after independence in both indices, the trend being reverted after the Rome Peace Agreement of 1992. Only in 1997 did Mozambique's GNP reached the value it had had in 1973 (Cruz et al., 2014, pp. 11–12).

The Portuguese military response was mostly based on the progressive increase of small military units living close to rural populations. In the guerrilla affected areas, they were gathered in *aldeamentos*[16] with better living conditions, subtracting them from the influence of Frelimo. The military often supplemented local needs by maintaining schools, health posts and various services such as electric lighting, drinking water, and transportation. Agriculture became more secure even in areas affected by the guerrillas (Ramos, 2016, pp. 400–401).

Frelimo's action was therefore contained in two pockets, one in Cabo Delgado and another in Niassa, and progressively limited to the Northeast and Northwest of Mozambique. There were Frelimo military actions in these areas,

---

[15]Gross National Product.

[16]Small villages with better accommodation, mostly with a local self-defense structure.

but they had no political-strategic significance in terms of Mozambique, and it was therefore possible to maintain a situation of general peace and progress in the territory and even to launch the construction of a major dam 400 km inland without the hindrance of Frelimo.

Over time and with the development of guerilla warfare in Mozambique, two different group dynamics developed in Frelimo. The "civilians" constituting the political leadership installed in the Tanzania capital Dar es Salaam. Meanwhile the rank and file "military" living in training bases, like Nachingwea, close to the border, with direct contact with the grass roots inside the country developed as a somewhat parallel and competing structure, criticizing the softness of the politicians (Cabrita, 2000, p. 46). Superimposed on this tension was a permanent ethnic issue between the ones doing the fighting, originating mostly form the north Makonde provenience and the leaders mostly from the south (like Mondlane, Urias Simango, Samora Machel, Joaquim Chissano and other). This fracture become apparent in 1965 and developed into a "faction" led by Vice-President Urias Simango which included the Makua Frelimo defense chief Filipe Magaia (later murdered) and Lazaro Kavandame provincial secretary for Cabo Delgado and himself a known Makonde (Cabrita, 2000, p. 47).

The assassination of Magaia, an ethnic Makua, was considered by some a conspiracy from the southerners as his replacement by Machel was made without the knowledge of Frelimo vice-president Urias Simango. To guarantee a political leadership Frelimo was reorganized. This was followed by a wave of removals of those loyal to Magaia and their replacement by men trusted by Samora mostly form the south. During 1967 and 1968, the situation worsened with judgments, public trials and executions followed by a "witch-hunt" of those accused of being opposed to the Frelimo leadership (Cabrita, 2000, p. 49). The assassination of Mondlane on February 3, 1969 led to a major change in the leadership. Frelimo's Central Committee decided to replace Mondlane with a three-man Presidential Council including Urias Simango, Samora Machel and Marcelino dos Santos. The purges continued however and on November 3, 1969 Simango apparently considering himself to be under attack released the often-quoted paper "Gloomy Situation in Frelimo." It denounced the internal upheaval and ethnic cleavages that had affected the organization from its origin leading to the execution of fighters, civilians and leaders. He also distanced himself from those who wanted to "steer Frelimo ideologically toward the Eastern bloc" and "rejected the notion that the movement was establishing a socialist system in the country," warning against antagonizing the domestic bourgeoisie, which should instead be accepted into Frelimo so as to contribute to the independence struggle" (Cabrita, 2000, p. 64). This led to the deportation and then the expulsion of Simango from Frelimo, and later after Mozambique's independence to his assassination when he was detained with his wife in a Re-education Camp in Niassa.

In May 1970, Samora Machel was designated Frelimo's President and Marcelino dos Santos his vice-president. The Marxist faction had achieved power. "Frelimo made its realignment with the Eastern bloc countries communist countries even more obvious," "strengthening its ties with the Moscow-aligned Portuguese Communist Party" (Cabrita, 2000, pp. 66–67).

Portugal Transfers All Powers to Frelimo

The April 25 coup in Portugal brought a unique opportunity for Frelimo. The cadres of the Portuguese armed forces were exhausted after 15 years of conflict in Angola, Guinea and Mozambique. The political immobility of the Portuguese government had lost the opportunity for a peaceful and progressive autonomy of overseas possessions, or to a negotiated settlement with the local populations and pro-independence movements.

Development, democratization, and decolonization were the fundamental objectives of the "Movement of the Armed Forces" that brought about the 25 April "Carnation Revolution." Yet, there were substantially different views about the decolonization processes from António de Spínula's defense of a Lusophone Community of Nations[17] through a political process where all the communities should have a say and a vote, to those that simply wanted to transfer power to the revolutionary and independence movements with whom they were ideologically aligned

The Portuguese Movement of the Armed Forces (MFA)[18] heavily influenced the decolonization process in Mozambique. The first exploratory contacts with Frelimo in Zambia to achieve a ceasefire only led to an increase of its operations. Frelimo felt the opportunity to increase the demand to receive full power without limitations. Delegates of the Portuguese Movement of the Armed Forces in Mozambique pressed to limit the operation of Portuguese forces on the ground, threatening to end its supply if an agreement was not reached in a month (Cabrita, 2000, p. 72).

In Mozambique immediately after the 1974 coup in Portugal, there was a heavy political mobilization from the white population to the constitution of diverse political movements. Among them, Grupo Unido de Moçambique (GUMO)[19] aiming to protect the rights of ethnic minorities to Partido de Coligação Nacional (PCN)[20] mostly constituted by Frelimo dissidents like Joana Semião or Uria Simango and many other aiming to a multiracial society respecting tradition and the culture of the various races and ethnic groups (Cabrita, 2000, p. 74). They were surprised and circumvented, however, by the signing of the September 5–7, 1974 Lusaka Agreement which transferred sovereignty rights to Frelimo.

The Portuguese "President Spínula had been effectively outmaneuvered by the MFA faction committed to an unconditional transfer of power to Frelimo" (Cabrita, 2000, p. 74). His aim to include a "clause stating that the Mozambican people would 'freely and democratically choose the country's political and social regime' was turned down during the 5–7 September talks in the Zambian capital" (Cabrita, 2000, p. 74). No arrangements were made to allow "a democratic basis for the future countries" (Cabrita, 2000, p. 4), to negotiate national compensations, or to protect private property or interests. Decolonization had profound strategic consequences opening the South Atlantic to Soviet naval power (Moreira, 1976, p. 11).

---

[17]Spínula's Portugal and the Future book published some weeks before the coup looked like his Political Program to achieve that.

[18]MFA is the Portuguese acronym for Movimento das Forças Armadas.

[19]GUMO is the acronym in Portuguese of Mozambique United Group.

[20]PCN is the acronym in Portuguese of National Coalition Party.

Power was transferred to the independence movements and Frelimo was considered as the sole representative of Mozambique's population. Frelimo (and the interim government) reacted harshly against old and recently formed political movements so as to suppress all internal and external opposition. Following a "meticulous" plan old and new opponents and dissidents were arrested.[21]

A Totalitarian State Builds a Long Civil Conflict

Mozambique merely shifted from one autocratic structure to another. Instead of promoting the separation of its original political components and respecting other old and recent political organization, thereby allowing all to fulfill their dreams in an open society, Frelimo promoted an absolute centralization of power to implement a Marxist–Leninist state excluding all opposition.

The June 20, 1975 Constitution drafted and approved by Frelimo's Central Committee was designed to implement a "State of popular democracy" where "power belongs to workers and peasants united and directed by Frelimo..." (Constitution 1975, art. 2). The President of Frelimo accumulated all power. He was the President of the Mozambique "People's Republic," the Commander-in-Chief of the Armed Forces, the Speaker of the People's Assembly and the President of the Council of Ministers. The Constitution nationalized land and natural resources and (art. 9) entrusted the state with the duty to promote the planification of the economy. Article 22 guided foreign relations: "Mozambique People's Republic consolidates and develops solidarity with the socialist countries, their natural allies, solidarity forged in the struggle for national independence."

The 1975 Constitution marked the start of a hard process to implement popular democracy in Mozambique. "Unity of Thought" become the guiding principle for society at large (Cabrita, 2000, p. 86). The youth, women, journalists, writers, students and workers in fact people from all walks of life, were grouped into the so-called mass democratic organizations (Cabrita, 2000, p. 87). Party cells were established in all strata of activity from workplaces, political, administrative, and economic structures to residential areas. Some months after the independence a net of informants was developed under the control of the *Serviço Nacional de Segurança Popular*,[22] known as SNASP "with sweeping authority to detain suspected of anti-state activites." Suspects, opponents, "unproductive" even vagrants were sent to newly established re-education camps continuing a process that was implemented early during the fight for independence. Reports of torture and mistreatment are well known. All religions were attacked, but the Roman Catholic church was particularly targeted, and some 10,000 Jehovah's Witnesses were sent to re-education camps (Cabrita, 2000, p. 90; Rupiya, 1999, p. 12).

A month after independence all private schools, hospitals and legal services, missions and even private houses were confiscated, and the private exercise of

---

[21]Hundreds of dissidents were arrested including Urias Simango and his wife, Joana Simeão, Paulo Gumane, Judas Honwana, or the priest Gwengere.

[22]National Popular Security Service, in English.

education, medicine or law become a criminal offense. This increased the exodus of white people and deprived the country of much needed experts, artisans, teachers, and so on. Those residents that did not opt for acquiring the new Mozambican citizenship were expelled and their properties confiscated (Cabrita, 2000, p. 110). Frelimo did make however an effort to increase the number of children in primary schools and the number of health clinics to international acclaim for the new government (Rupiya, 1999, p. 12).

It was in rural areas that the impact of measures to produce a "new man" was harshest. Frelimo considered agriculture as the foundation of Mozambique's economy and made substantial efforts to introduce large state enterprises in some of the best agricultural land. Angonia and the Limpopo valley close to Maputo were conceived to be the show-cases of the new communitarian, mechanized agriculture. Large amounts of money were invested to buy eastern bloc countries equipment, only to discover the indispensable need of skilled manpower to operate and maintain them. In the end, it all came as a "fiasco" and production steadily decreased to less than half of the previous local commercial production (Cabrita, 2000, p. 112). There was a lack of investment in peasant farmers, who previously produced about 70 per cent of domestically consumed agricultural products. Additionally, the replacement of the net of small *cantineiros*[23] scattered over the country by inefficient "People's Shops" and the centrally determined pricing of products by Agricom the state marketing company further eroded the activity of peasant farming leading to a worsening shortage of foodstuffs in the country.

Two more fundamental issues are worth mentioning, due to their future implications in the conflict situation. These are the dislocations of hundred of thousands of peasants to "communal villages" and the effort to eradicate traditional authorities so as to extend the centralized form of government to rural areas. At independence, the government announced that the rural population was to be resettled to communal villages. This was considered necessary to promote the economic and social development of the country, on the basis that a net of very small villages made it impossible. Communal villages were conceived to "combat obscurantism" and radically transform the way of living of rural society, but they interfered with old customs, traditions and beliefs and the program was resisted everywhere particularly in the central and northern regions. However, six years after it was initiated more than 1.8 million people or about 20 per cent of the rural population had been forcibly displaced to 1,360 communal villages and this figure was expected to reach 10 million in 10 years (Cabrita, 2000, p. 118). This immense resettlement program instead of creating a "new man" had however the opposite effect of appealing to old traditions and led to a strong hostility toward Frelimo.

"The strong state economic intervention turned out to be unsustainable, leading to costly distortions in the allocation of resources and badly disrupted private sector production." "By the second quarter of the 1980s the productive sector was operating at 10 per cent to 30 per cent of its capacity." "The agricultural sector

[23]Network of small commercial establishments spread over the country constituting the first contact with the rural communities.

was reduced to subsistence level. Exports, in particular tea, cashew nuts, cotton and sugar declined to one-third of pre-independence levels." In the middle of the 1980s, the country was close to economic collapse (Cruz et al., 2014, pp. 10–11).

If Frelimo's domestic policies created an environment conducive to an internal reaction, its external relations would develop new oppositions. In the middle 1970s, when Mozambique achieved independence, colonialism had practically disappeared from the region leaving only two albeit significant cases, in the immediate vicinity of Mozambique: South Africa under the apartheid regime and Rhodesia dominated by the Ian Smith white minority regime. Vesting its revolutionary alignment with the eastern bloc, Frelimo declared its support to the movements fighting against those regimes in both countries, and also to the opponents of Kamuzu Banda in Malawi. This posture represented two challenges for them however: the possible installation of the African National Congress (ANC) and Zimbabwe African National Liberation Army forces within a protective Mozambique from where they could conduct operations into their own territories; and the possible threat of Mozambique to limit their vital access to the seashore by the Lourenço Marques (now Maputo), Beira and Nacala (now Pemba) ports. That led not only to their incursions in Mozambique to pursue opponents but also to support Frelimo defeaters and opposition forces that were displaced in their countries. It was in this context that *Partido Revolucionário de Mozambique*[24] led by Amós Sumane was born in Malawi and *Resistência Nacional de Moçambique*[25] (RNM later RENAMO) led by André Matsangaice and then by Afonso Dhlakama, all Frelimo defeaters, was created in Rhodesia (Coelho, 2009, p. 90; Cabrita, 2000, pp. 127–128). As more Mozambicans sought refuge in these countries, they gained more potential to operate against Frelimo. In 1976, Renamo started a campaign inside Mozambique that over time spread to most of the territory.

The conflict turned ever more violent and in the next decade led to the destruction of most infrastructure, along with a severe limitation on circulation, the disruption of health and education services, and to a substantial decrease of exports leading to an ever-increasing foreign debt and to Mozambique's demand to its rescheduling in 1984. When Malawi achieved independence in 1978, Frelimo understood that Renamo was now only dependent on South Africa and therefore easier to isolate. It thus approached this country and in 1984 negotiated a "Non-aggression and good neighborhood accord," the so-called Nkomati Accord, to end the mutual assistance of forces opposed to each other (Renamo and ANC) (Rupiya, 1999, p. 13). But the resistance in Mozambique only increased and in the final years of the decade, the insurgency reached not only Maputo the capital city but also the northern provinces of Cabo Delgado and Niassa.

The Church raised its voice once more and in "A Calling for Peace," Bishops Dinis Sengulane and Jaime Pedro Gonçalves (one of the mediators of the 1990 Rome Peace process) strongly manifested the need for dialog between Renamo and the Government to achieve a peaceful situation in Mozambique (Armon, Hendrickson, &

[24]Mozambique Revolutionary Party, in English.

[25]Mozambique National Resistance, in English.

Vines, 1998, p. 6). Finally, Frelimo (even if with dissenting views within its ranks) agreed to hold some talks in Pretoria involving Renamo and South Africa, the Tripartite Talks. These talks however bore no results since there was a world of differences between the Renamo proposal of a transitional government to prepare the way to implement a democratic regime, the reorganization of Mozambique armed forces and the return of traditional authorities and the Frelimo demand of the cessation of hostilities and offer of some posts for Renamo leaders in commercial and industrial companies and some funding to help their subordinates to settling outside Mozambique (Cabrita, 2000, pp. 228–229).

It took another five years and a complete economic and military deterioration, and a growing international reluctance to provide the necessary financial support, so that Frelimo would accept bilateral talks with Renamo to find a political solution. On June 12, 1989, exploratory talks were held in Nairobi and later in Rome, under the auspices of the Sant'Egidio Community, including Jaime Gonçalves, Bishop of Beira and Mario Raffaeli, representing the Italian government, who coordinated the overall mediation.

The Long Road to Democracy

Rome General Peace Agreement

The first round of negotiations started in Rome on July 8, 1990 with final declarations of mutual commitment to end the war and to create the conditions to achieve a lasting peace. However, as the second round was under way Frelimo announced that it had introduced a multiparty system in Mozambique (Cabrita, 2000, p. 270). In the meanwhile, it had approved and enacted the November 1990 Constitution of Mozambique. This can be considered as the most essential result of the overall context, but in was done as a preemptive move to avoid the inclusion of the constitutional theme in the negotiation process. Frelimo had again produced a Constitution by itself without the contribution of different national views and avoided its discussion during the negotiations in Rome, maintaining the political profile of Renamo as low as possible.

The Constitution accommodated some of Renamo's public requests such as a multiparty system, the end of a centrally planned economy, and another designation for the country (now Republic of Mozambique) and for the People's Assembly (now Assembly of Republic) but it failed to address other fundamental issues such as an independent judiciary (Cabrita, 2000, p. 270). The new Constitution maintained state ownership of the land and showed no sign of decentralization. The Provincial Governments had the duty of implementing, "at the provincial level, the centrally defined government policies," and the Head and Members of the Provincial Governments continued to be "appointed centrally" (Constitution of Mozambique, 1990). The lack of access of the political parties to a political and administrative role through local and regional structures maintained the spirit of centralization and of the "winner takes it all" situation that has thus far prevailed in Mozambique.

The General Peace Agreement (GPA) signed in Rome on October 4, 1992 represented more than two years of negotiation and led the way to the first democratic elections in the Mozambique's history. The GPA had however two important limitations, that are somewhat repetitive in peace agreements. First, it was the short timespan available to fulfill the different tasks and to hold elections. Protocol III, Chapter V, Number 1 (c) determines that "elections should take place one year after the signing of the General Peace Agreement." It should be remembered that after 15 years of fighting, a million casualties and 5 million of refugees, the tasks that needed to be fulfilled involved the ceasefire process, the return the refugees, the cantonment of combatants in assembly areas, their disarmament, demobilization and reintegration into society, the constitution and legalization of the political parties, the creation of the new armed forces, the electoral political campaign and voting. In fact, it took much more time and the first elections were held only on October 27–28, 1994. The delay resulted in severe complications mainly with soldiers waiting (in bad conditions) in the Assembly Areas reducing their interest to participate in the new armed forces (Rupiya, 1999, p. 16) that did not reach the expected levels. This issue has been a permanent cause of friction with Renamo claiming that their forces were not well integrated, and that the Mozambican National Armed Forces did not consist of a 50 per cent division of mutual participation.

Fast processes in those conditions normally offer more possibilities to some entities such as existing organized political parties, as it was the case of Frelimo. If there is no proviso for power-sharing namely by the participation in a temporary government of national unity,[26] or on local or regional political structures through elections (which the 1990 Constitution did not consider), then the result is a "winner takes it all" scenario under imbalanced circumstances.

The second limitation relates to guarantees. There is a moment in a negotiated process when the parties that took most of their power from the use of weapons turn them in, hoping to participate in a clean political process. It is a very sensitive tradeoff and therefore it is essential to create conditions to guarantee a free, fair, and transparent process. Otherwise what may happen is that the parties conceal some elements of their forces and do not demobilize them. To avoid this, there are some conditions that should be respected. In my opinion, two of them can be highlighted in Mozambique's peace process.

The first is the assurance that irregularities and electoral fraud can be impartially investigated and corrected. Within the GPA was created a National Elections Commission, by Protocol III, Chapter V, Number 3. Its role was to "monitor the electoral process and insure compliance with the laws" and "to receive, consider and settle complains with respect to the validity of elections." Yet its composition was not even and only "[o]ne third of the members to be appointed to the Commission shall be nominated by Renamo." Although there was a recent reorganization, until today Renamo had always felt and claimed to be a minority impaired voice in this structure. The results of every election since then have been contested but neither the National Elections Commission, nor the Supreme Court to which alleged irregularities were referred gave much consideration although it was felt

---

[26]During the implementation of the GPA asked by Dlhakama made however "strident demands for a bipartisan 'government of national unity'" rejected by Chissano (Rupiya, 1999, p. 16).

by the society at large that it should have done (Cabrita, 2000, pp. 271–272). This is probably one of the reasons that can explain the decrease of Mozambicans participation in the electoral processes afterwards.

The second guarantee for a fair and just process can be provided by external interveners, like countries supporting the establishment of the Peace Accord (like Australia in East Timor in the 1990s) or, more commonly, international organizations like the UN.

One week after the signing of the GPA, the United Nations Security Council established the 6.800-strong United Nations Operation in Mozambique. The UN assumed the Chair of the Supervisory and Monitoring Commission responsible for guaranteeing the "implementation" of the General Peace Agreement, the "authentic interpretation" of the Agreement, "settle any disputes" between the Parties and "guide and co-ordinate" the activities of the "subsidiary commissions." These included the Joint Commission for the Formation of the Mozambican Defense Forces, the Cease-fire Commission, and the Reintegration Commission. But under the proviso of Protocol V, Chapter 2, Number 6, it "shall cease to function when the new Government takes office." That meant one year later and almost immediately after the elections. Post-conflict peace building is a complex, long, and difficult process and it is well known that in a significant number of cases there is a return to violence some years later. Mozambique had been in a state of conflict for more than 30 years, it was devastated, and it simply did not look achievable to reach positive peace after one round of democratic elections.

Ramsbothan and others have called our attention to the complexity of "post War Reconstruction" particularly with regards to the different sectors that should be involved and to the timing of the withdrawal of "external interveners." He produced a matrix combining in one axis three temporal phases (Intervention, Stabilization and Normalization) and in the other axis the type of actions (Peacemaking/Peacekeeping, Structural peacebuilding, and Cultural peacebuilding) with the activities in each type of action detailed in five sectors (security, law and order, political, economic, and social cultural) (Ramsbothan, Woodhouse, & Miall, 2011, pp. 209–213).

Ramsbothan's argument was that that the withdrawal of the external interveners must be linked to the transference of their assumed responsibilities to adequate national structures able to fulfill them. And that the first partial withdrawal should only be made during the Stabilization Phase after the accomplishment of significant Structural peacebuilding:

> National armed forces under home government control are stronger then challengers; adequate indigenous capacity to maintain basic order impartially under law; sufficient governmental legitimacy, which may include democratic credentials of elected government with system seen to remain open to those dissatisfied with the initial results; a reasonable stable relationship between center and regions;...adequate success in managing conflict priorities of peace and justice, protecting minorities rights and fostering a reasonable independent yet responsible media. (Ramsbothan et al., 2011, p. 217)

The final withdrawal should be done even later, after the accomplishment of the Cultural Peacebuilding type of actions has taken place. Some relevant aspects such as Law and Order were not even included in the GPA, nor were they formally addressed during its implementation. The United Nations Operations in Mozambique (ONUMOZ) ended in December 1994, just two months after the elections. It faced and overcame difficult obstacles during the mission and made an indispensable contribution to lead the country for the first free and peaceful multiparty elections. It helped the return of more than 5 million refugees, disarmed more than 70,000 combatants and coordinated the preparation of some 10,000 soldiers of the new Mozambican Armed Forces (FADM), even if it was well below the expected number. Yet, its withdrawal seems to have been early and, in fact, the overall process leading to a formal democratic multiparty regime has contributed to legitimize a system in which the party in power – Frelimo – has benefited from advantages acquired in the past mainly by its insertion in all levels and economic and social structures of the country. Some of the fundamental tasks of constituting the new armed forces, namely the mutual participation of Frelimo and Renamo combatants have been a permanent complaint by Renamo since then.

The Democratic Experiment

The first elections in Mozambique were held in an atmosphere of great hope with 88 per cent voter turnout. Frelimo's presidential candidate was elected. In Parliament, the opposition parties Renamo and Democratic Union (UD) obtained the majority of votes but due to the use of the d 'Hondt method Frelimo retained the majority of deputies (Cabrita, 2000, p. 271).

The results though marked by some irregularities were accepted opening the way to a long period of peace and development with a gross domestic product increase of more than 7 per cent a year. Renamo's transformation into a political party and its electoral success were surprising. Nonetheless its political activity was reduced to the parliament, where an experienced and better organized Frelimo continued to lead, maintaining its cells in all administrative, economic, and social organizations. This effectively allowed what has been called a "party-state" to remain in power.

Over the time some trends, expressed in the following Chart, are worth mentioning:

The most visible, is the constant increase of Frelimo votes during the three first elections until 2014 when it had a marked decrease returning to results close to those of the 1990s. Almost symmetrically, Renamo consistently lost votes, until 2014 when the trend was reversed. Small political parties are almost without representation although there are some 15 in all. Only the Democratic Movement of Mozambique (MDM) has a significant share, namely at the municipal level.

The change in the 2014 election results marks also a change in the social context in Mozambique. Renamo expressing its discontent with the monopolization of the country by Frelimo (da Silva, 2016, p. 34) have returned in 2012 to a conflictual posture marked by the departure of its leader to an unknown location in the Gorongoza area. It was the start of a military confrontation that in fact

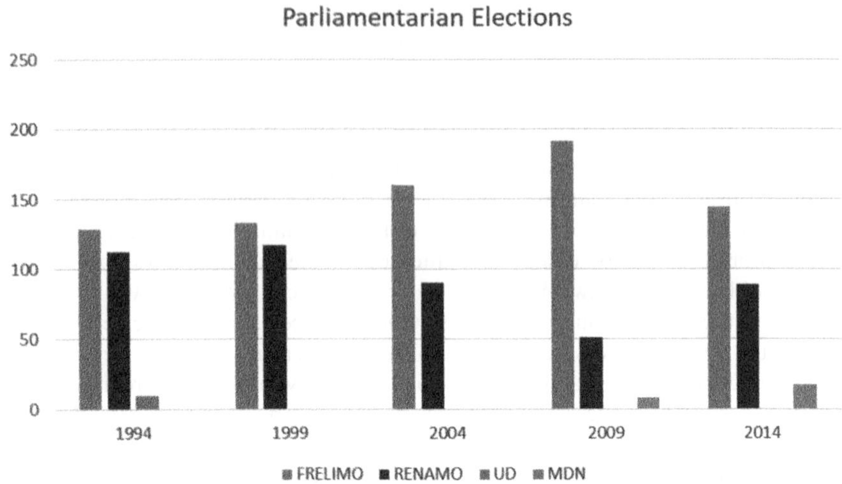

Source: Illustrated by author from results announced by the National Election Commission.

affected the economy in the central regions and the movement by land of people and goods between the south and the north of the country.

The democratic enchantment had begun to fade, and the electoral processes began to experience a high abstention rate. Suspicion and violence in the more recent elections indicate a serious democratic crisis. "The most important indicator of democratic legitimacy of a country – the share of the population in electoral processes – fell exponentially" (da Silva, 2016, p. 34). The record turnout of 88 per cent in 1994 and 74 per cent in 1999, came down to 43 per cent in 2004, 45 per cent in 2009 to slightly increase to 49 per cent in 2014[27] (Hanlon, 2014, pp. 1–2) "The official abstention rate was 13 percent in 1994, 30 percent in 1999, 63 percent in 2004 and 56 percent in 2009" (Brito, 2010, p. 4).

Finally, it should be noted that Renamo has maintained a strong share of the vote in the country's provinces of Niassa, Nampula, Zambézia, Tete, Manica, and Sofala (Hanlon, 2014, pp. 2–39) regions from where Renamo had conducted most of its military operations before, and presently some of the poorest regions of the country. This probably explains why regionalization and the direct election of Provincial and Administrative leaders and respective structures was the Renamo condition to return to peace that finally led to a change in the Mozambican Constitution in 2018 opening the way to a new settlement.

There are probably different reasons to justify this "growing disengagement" from the political process. One may be the fact that political parties have failed to respond to citizens' expectations. Another is the pervasive sense that, whatever the election outcome, Frelimo would win and Renamo will lose (da Silva, 2016, p. 34). The massive

[27]It should be mentioned that are some variations in these numbers, but the overall trend is similar.

turnout in the first election may have represented a deeply shared national will to contribute to the end of a destructive war and be in effect a "vote for peace." This reason may well be the basis for the general increasing of voters in a new confrontational situation in 2014 and particularly in support of Renamo (da Silva, 2016, p. 35).

In fact, according to the Afrobarometer survey in Mozambique, responses suggest a problematic deterioration in the public perception of elections and democracy. "More and more citizens see the elections as less free and fair and doubt the guarantee of representation of the opinions of the voters in elections" (Isbell, 2017, p. 12).

Azevedo-Harman argues that Mozambique may be considered a "hybrid regime" where

> procedural rules of democracy exist, there is a relatively strong and free media, but there is still control of the state and economy by the ruling party – or rather by party members – which makes it difficult for the opposition to establish itself.

It lacks the "political rotation" or at least the "fear of uncertainty" by the ruling party for the possible accountability of the electorate in elections. Azevedo considers that opposition also bars a considerable responsibility on this political process. "Division within the opposition and difficulty [of Renamo] to adapt from a rebellion movement to a political party made the main opposition party increasingly fragile" (Azevedo-Harman, 2014, p. 1; Darch, 2018, p. 10).

Another relevant issue marks this period of peace from 1992 to 2012. According to the International Monetary Fund, inclusive growth is a key problem in Mozambique because "while the poverty rate declined in Mozambique from 69 percent in 1997 to 54 percent in 2003, it seems to have remained stagnant since then."

> As a result, few countries offer such a stark contrast as Mozambique: one of the highest rates of economic growth in the world (average of 7.5 percent over two decades), coupled with an extremely low elasticity of poverty with respect to growth (about 0.1 percent). This suggests that a large share of the Mozambican population is not benefiting enough from these high levels of growth. (IMF, 2016, p. 16; Vines, Thompson, Jensen, & Azevedo-Harman, 2015, p. 1)
>
> In Mozambique, income inequality has increased despite high rates of economic growth. Both market-income inequality and the net Gini coefficient[28] are worse in the 2000s than in the 1990s. Income inequality in Mozambique also has a spatial dimension. Most of the country's wealth is located in the southern area, and especially around the capital Maputo. Similarly, higher rates of poverty appear to be highly concentrated in the central and northern regions, particularly in rural areas. (IMF, 2016, pp. 17–18)

---

[28]Quoting IMF: Net Gini coefficient measures inequality after taxes and transfers.

The Democracy Index 2018 of the Economist Intelligence Unit considers the country living under an "Authoritarian Regime" where "political pluralism is absent or heavily circumscribed" in which the Democracy Index has constantly decreased form 5.28 (out of 10) in 2006 to 3.85 in 2018 (Economist Intelligence Unit (EIU), 2019, p. 45). In the Human Development Report Rank, of 188 countries, Mozambique ranks 180 (United Nations Development Programme (UNDP), 2018, p. 25).

Conflict Transformation: The Return to a Conflict or to a More Democratic Settlement?

This is the section that should be dedicated to the transformation of the conflict as the result of the introduction of a democratic process. However, as we have seen, democracy brought peace, some would say negative peace, to Mozambique for 10 years, but not fairness, political rotation, or at least the fear of the voters' accountability in elections. The decrease in poverty is stagnant, inequalities have increased particularly in the central and rural regions of the country and several cases of corruption were reported. Mozambique's political regime is now considered from Hybrid to Authoritarian.

The confrontational stance developed by Renamo from 2012 onwards demonstrated the support it still has and its capacity to significantly affect the normality of the country, disrupt the circulation along the main north–south route and impede economic and industrial activities particularly at the center of the country (Dzinesa & Motsamai, 2013, p. 2). The choice to revert again to a military confrontation resulted from several circumstances, but among them some can be highlighted.

A major factor was probably the continuous degradation of Renamo representation in Parliament and its reduction to little more than a pressure group with neither national expression nor meaningful regional presence which was blocked by a Constitution that did not permit elections to the provincial and regional structures, that may have been more accessible to Renamo in some regions of the country. Another was the reiterated Renamo's accusation that the Frelimo elites had monopolized the state and illegitimately appropriated the resources of the nation without instituting an equitable distribution (Bowker, Kamm, & Sambo, 2016; Darch, 2018, p. 10)

Also to be noted are the circumstance that at a time of increased expectations due to the news of the development of several megaprojects since the 2000s, and of a constant and significant growth of the national GDP, not only the reduction of poverty had stopped but the inequalities had increased particularly in the central and northern areas. Finally, there is an accumulation of long held issues such as the parity integration of Renamo personnel in Mozambique's armed forces and its adequate participation in the police and security organs as determined by the Rome Peace Accords, complaints dragging on since the early 1990s.

The return to arms can therefore be seen as the only possible way to force a political and administrative decentralization that could allow a more reasonable sharing of power, in a moment of Frelimo vulnerability. To this end, Dlakama threatened to control six central and northern provinces in which he had, according to him, reached a majority vote (Darch, 2018, p. 9).

In February 7, 2018 following lengthy negotiations, a set of proposals was submitted to the Assembly of the Republic that approved the punctual amendment to the Constitution in June 2018 and new Autarchic Electoral Law in August of the same year. The Constitutional amendment introduced the election of provincial governors and district administrators, as well as their respective assemblies. The provincial governors and districts administrators will be allocated by the "list head" method (Brochura Informativa, 2018). However, it took two conflicts and one million casualties before there is some hope of power-sharing in Mozambique.

It is also relevant to mention that during these last years of confrontation (from 2012 to 2018) negotiations between the parties have always been present. Renamo parliamentarians continued to operate and it was possible to agree to the elections in 2014. Most importantly, President Filipe Nyusi elected by Frelimo and Afonso Dhlakama, Renamo leader were able to agree on the most "transformative" change in the Mozambican Constitution. This is certainly one of the results of living in a democracy even if not a perfect one.

Conclusions

Mozambique is a case study because its history overlaps several layers of deforming and conflicting particularisms. First and foremost, it is a country that has resulted from an eccentric colonization mainly focused on India. It may even be said that Mozambique was a colony of India-Goa until the creation in 1752 of a captaincy in Mozambique directly dependent on the Portuguese Crown, which explains the strong community of Indians and their influence in the country. On the other hand, in its western part was the powerful neighborhood of the Boers Republics and the British Colonies and Protectorates of Rhodesia that resulted from the British expansion into the region, all leading to an artificial border dividing several communities and the design of a long country, narrow in the center, whose most important regional function is to connect the inland countries to the sea. This brought advantages yet also frequent external interference.

Despite the independence movement in Africa after the Second World War, Portugal maintained a long colonial presence in Mozambique based on the affirmation of a multicontinental and multicultural homeland, without promoting a progressive and peaceful autonomy. Decolonization as a result of the coup d'état of April 25, 1974 strongly influenced by "progressive" forces in Portugal led to an unconditionally transfer of power to Frelimo, at the time dominated by the Marxist line allied with the Communist countries of the Eastern bloc. In power, Frelimo radically nationalized private property, forced the white community to leave, extinguished all rival political entities, and founded a one-party totalitarian state. This state's internal and external policies led to a violent response from a substantial part of the population driven by Renamo, and to a fierce fighting lasting a dozen years, causing about 1 million deaths and 4 to 5 million refugees.

Frelimo has become a kind of "party-state" with a strong sense of organization and strategy, maintaining an effective insertion in all the political, administrative, economic, and social structures of the country which lasts to this day. Forced by the circumstances to engage in bilateral negotiations with Renamo, Frelimo unilaterally conceived and approved a Multiparty Constitution during the 1992 Rome negotiations without submitting the discussion of this constitutional change to these talks. The resulting 1992 Rome General Peace Agreement in practice, has served as a democratic legitimization for Frelimo's maintenance of state control, without allowing an effective power-sharing or access to regional political representation.

GDP growth in the years of peace was about 7.5 per cent a year being unanimously considered a remarkable achievement. However, as of 2013, poverty reduction has stagnated, and inequality has increased in what is considered an anomalous case, in the face of such substantial GDP growth. Besides, this it is happening at a time of high expectations of the population in view of the large foreign investments made in the exploitation of coal, natural gas, and other natural resources.

It also worth noting that inequality has a geographical distribution. The richest areas are located in the south close to Maputo, the capital, while the most disadvantaged areas are located in the center and north of the country, the Renamo bastion. That may explain why Renamo could so easily return to a stance of military violence in 2012 after returning to the Gorongosa area as it had done in the 1980s.

It was in this context that Renamo threatened to forcibly seize power in the areas of the country in which it had a majority of votes. In 2016, finally there was a new negotiated agreement that led to a fundamental change in the Constitution. This change will permit the direct election of the leaderships and structures at the Provincial, Administrative and Municipal level. This agreement and Constitutional Change already approved, represent a great source of hope for Mozambican society in general. To live in democracy requires much will and effort. Mozambique faces a complex challenge ahead, in which both Frelimo, Renamo and the other existing parties must perceive themselves as part of the same system, with a responsibility for mutual aid as well as healthy competition. This must happen for the sake of freedom, respect for the inalienable rights of people and a better future for all.

References

Adedokun, A. (2017). Emerging challenges to long-term peace and security in Mozambique. *The Journal of Social Encounters*, *1*(1), 37–53. Retrieved from https://digitalcommons.csbsju.edu/cgi/viewcontent.cgi?article=1003&context=social_encounters

Armon, J., Hendrickson, D., & Vines, A. (1998). Preface. In J. Armon, D, Hendrickson, & A. Vines (Eds.), *The Mozambican peace process in perspective* (pp. 5–8). London: Conciliation Resources.

Azevedo-Harman, E. (2014). Dominance of the ruling party and the turmoil of the opposition in Mozambique. *Revista Electrónica de Investigação e Desenvolvimento*, *2*. Retrieved from http://reid.ucm.ac.mz/index.php/reid/issue/view/4

Bowker, T., Kamm, S., & Sambo, A. (2016, May 6). Mozambique's invisible civil war. *Foreign Policy*. Retrieved from https://foreignpolicy.com

Brito, L. (2010, April). A challenge for democracy: low turnout in Mozambique, Lesotho and Zâmbia. Paper presented at Conference on Electoral Processes, Liberation Movements and Democratic Change in África, Maputo, Mozambique.

Brochura Informativa. (2018). *A Reforma Constitucional e da Legislação Eleitoral Autárquica em Moçambique*. Available at https://www.eisa.org.za/pdf/moz2018brochura.pdf

Cabrita, J. (2000). *Mozambique: The tortuous road to democracy*. New York, NY: Palgrave Macmillan.

Cann, J. P. (1998). *Contra-insurreição em África: O modo português de fazer a guerra, 1961–1974*. S. Pedro do Estoril: Atena.

Chissano, J. (2010). *Vidas, Lugares e Tempos*. Portugal: Texto Editores, Lda.

Coelho, J. P. B. (2009). 'Quantitative Literature' and the interpretation of the armed conflict in Mozambique (1976–1992). In C. R. Udelsmann & A. B. da Costa (Eds.), *Poverty and peace in the portuguese speaking African countries* (pp. 88–106). Lisboa: Centro de Estudos Internacionais

Constitution of Mozambique. (1990). Approved and enacted in November 1990. Retrieved from http://confinder.richmond.edu/admin/docs/moz.pdf

Costa, J. P., José, D. R., & Oliveira, P. A. (2014). *História da Expansão e do Império Português*. Lisboa: A Esfera dos Livros.

Cruz, A. S., Guambe, D., Marrengula, C. P., & Ubisse, A. F. (2014). *Mozambique's Industrialization*. WIDER Working Paper: 2014/059. UNU-WIDER website. Retrieved from https://www.wider.unu.edu/sites/default/files/wp2014-059.pdf

da Silva, C. R. (2016). As eleições e a democracia moçambicana. Janus 2015–2016. Retrieved from http://janusonline.pt/images/anuario2015/1.13_CarolinaSilva_DemocraciaMocambique.pdf

Darch, C. (2018). *A Success Story Gone Wrong? The Mozambican Conflict and the Peace Process in Historical Perspective*. FES Peace and Security Series No. 30. Friedrich-Ebert-Stiftung Mozambique website. Retrieved from https://library.fes.de/pdf-files/bueros/fes-pscc/14344.pdf

Dzinesa, G., & Motsamai, D. (2013). *Renamo's War Talk and Mozambique's Peace Prospects*. ISS Policy Brief 50. Institute for Security Studies website. Retrieved from https://www.files.ethz.ch/isn/175323/PolBrief50.pdf

Economist Intelligence Unit (EIU). (2019). Democracy Index 2018: Me too? Political participation, protest and democracy. Latvijas Pilsoniskā alianse website. Retrieved from http://www.nvo.lv/site/attachments/10/01/2019/demokr%C4%81tijas__indekss.pdf

Electoral Institute for Sustainable Democracy in Africa (EISA). (2018). *A Reforma Constitucional e da Legislação Eleitoral Autárquica em Moçambique 2018 – Brochura Informativa*. Retrieved from https://www.eisa.org.za/pdf/moz2018brochura.pdf

Fage, J. D. (2014). *Biblioteca Nacional de Portugal – Catalogação na publicação, 1921–2002*. História de África (História Narrativa).

Fage, J. D., & Tordoff, W. (2014). *História da África*. Lisboa: Edições 70.

Forquilha, S. (2017). Descentralização e Conflito em Moçambique: Os desafios da construção do Estado. In L. de Brito, C. N. Castel-Branco, S. Chichava, S. Froquilha, & A. Francisco (Eds.), *Desafios para Moçambique 2017* (pp. 35–59). Mozambique: Instituto de Estudos Sociais e Económicos [IESE]. Retrieved from http://www.iese.ac.mz/wp-content/uploads/2018/05/part1-2sf.pdf

General Act of the Berlin Conference on West Africa. (1885, 26 February). Retrieved from: https://loveman.sdsu.edu/docs/1885GeneralActBerlinConference.pdf

Hanlon, J. (2014, November 28). Frelimo wins another tainted election. *Mozambique Political Process Bulletin, 56*. Retrieved from http://www.open.ac.uk/technology/mozambique/sites/www.open.ac.uk.technology.mozambique/files/files/Mozambique_Bulletin_56_Election_results_2014%281%29.pdf

Hanlon, J. (2016, February 15). Mozambique: Nyusi grapples with Guebuza's toxic legacy one year on. *African Arguments*. Retrieved from https://africanarguments.org/2016/02/15/mozambique-nyusi-grapples-with-guebuzas-toxic-legacy-one-year-on/

Hanlon, J. (Ed.). (2018, June 26). Mozambique News reports & clippings. *Open University*. Retrieved from http://www.open.ac.uk/technology/mozambique/sites/www.open.ac.

uk.technology.mozambique/files/files/Mozambique_416-26June2018_Frelimo-ambush_Cabo-Delgado-articles.pdf

International Monetary Fund (IMF) African Department. (2016, January 08). *Republic of Mozambique. Selected Issues* (Country Report No. 16/10). Retrieved from https://www.imf.org/external/pubs/ft/scr/2016/cr1610.pdf

Isbell, T. (2017, abril 20). Um voto de desconfiança? Os Moçambicanos ainda votam, mas a fé na democracia está a diminuir. *Afrobarómetro: Boletim, 139*. Retrieved from http://afrobarometer.org/sites/default/files/publications/Dispatches/ab_r6_dispatchno139_eleicoes_e_demoracia_em_mocambique.pdf

Moreira, A. (1976). *Saneamento Nacional*. Lisboa: Torres e Abreu.

Ramos, F. (2016). O Comando e a Opinião. Pública - Moçambique 1970. In S. Torres (Ed.), *O Jornalismo Português na Guerra Colonial*. Lisboa: Autores e Guerra e Paz Editores, S.A.

Ramsbothan, O., Woodhouse, T., & Miall, H. (2011). *Contemporary conflict resolution* (3rd ed.). Cambridge: Polity Press.

Republic of Mozambique. (1975). *Constituição da República Popular de Moçambique de 20 de junho de 1975*. Retrieved from http://cedis.fd.unl.pt/wp-content/uploads/2016/02/CONST-MOC-75.pdf

Ross, D. (Ed.). (2014). *Mozambique rising: building a new tomorrow*. International Monetary Fund [IMF] website. Retrieved from https://www.imf.org/external/pubs/ft/dp/2014/afr1404.pdf

Rupiya, M. (1999). Historical context: War and peace in Mozambique. In J. Armon, D. Hendrickson, & A. Vines (Eds.), *The Mozambican peace process in perspective* (pp. 10–17). London: Conciliation Resources.

Sociedade de Geografia de Lisboa (SGL). (2015). *Boletim da Sociedade de Geografia de Lisboa, 133*(1). Retrieved from http://www.socgeografialisboa.pt/wp/wp-content/uploads/2017/11/SGL-Boletim-133-Ano-2015.pdf

The Rome Process: General Peace Agreement for Mozambique. (1998). In J. Armon, D., Hendrickson, & A. Vines (Eds.), *The Mozambican peace process in perspective* (Issue 3, p. 40). London: Conciliation Resources. Retrieved from https://rc-services-assets.s3.eu-west-1.amazonaws.com/s3fs-public/The_Mozambican_Peace_Process_in_Perspective_Accord_Issue_3.pdf

United Nations Development Programme (UNDP). (2018). *Human Development. Indices and Indicators. 2018 Statistical Update*. UNDP website. Retrieved from http://hdr.undp.org/sites/default/files/2018_human_development_statistical_update.pdf

Vines, A., Thompson, H., Jensen, S. K., & Azevedo-Harman, E. (2015). Mozambique to 2018 managers, mediators and magnates. *Chatham House Report*. Retrieved from https://www.chathamhouse.org/publication/mozambique-2018

Chapter 10

Comparative Analysis of the Regional Security System of Europe and Asia: Dilemmas of the Asian Security System

Gen Kikkawa

Introduction

In his book entitled *The Better Angels of our Nature*, Steven Pinker discusses the causal factors of the "long peace" in the Euro-Atlantic region in the second half of the twentieth century. Long peace was sustained by the following:

- War friendly mindsets such as nationalism, territorial ambition, popular acceptance of war, and indifference to its human costs, went out of fashion.
- International norms such as territorial integrity, non-intervention in internal affairs, and respect for sovereignty were observed.
- Peace and security based on the concept of democratic peace and liberal peace became institutionalized. (Pinker, 2011)

However, the Asia-Pacific region has contrasted the Euro-Atlantic one in many respects. Since the end of World War II, Asia has witnessed wars and violence of all sorts – de-colonization wars such as the Indochina War and Indonesian Civil War; international wars such as the Korean War, Indo-Pakistan War, and Sino-Vietnamese War; international intervention wars such as Vietnam War and Afghan War (by the Soviet Union). Besides, it is "democide" (mass murder by governments)[1] that occurred in Asia – Great Leap Forward and Cultural

[1]"Democide" is a term coined by R. J. Rummel. In his definition, democide is any action by government (1) designed to kill or cause the death of people (1.1) because of their religion, race, language, ethnicity, national origin, class, politics, speech, actions construed as opposing the government or wrecking social policy, or by virtue of their relationship to such people; (1.2) in order to fulfill a quota or requisition system; (1.3) in furtherance of a system of forced labour or enslavement; (1.4) by

International Perspectives on Democratization and Peace, 171–188

doi:10.1108/978-1-80043-067-920200010

Revolution in China, 30th of September Movement in Indonesia, mass murder under the Pol Pot regime of Cambodia, and perpetual politicide in North Korea.

The contrast between the Euro-Atlantic and the Asia-Pacific regions is the inevitable corollary of their different approaches to security issues. A community-based security order in the Euro-Atlantic region was one where multilateral security institutions are in place and shared political interests and common values existed to shape and limit how power can be exercised. The security order in Europe was shaped by two developments. There is the evolution of international security institutions during the Cold War period: the European Community/European Union, as a tool for international integration, the North Atlantic Treaty Organisation (NATO), as a tool for collective self-defense, the Council of Europe as a tool for protecting human rights and rule of law, and the Conference on Security Cooperation in Europe (CSCE), as a tool for multilateral security cooperation in the Euro-Atlantic region.

It is noteworthy that the CSCE, and the multilateral process of security cooperation (CSCE Process/Helsinki Process) originated in the Helsinki Final Act of the CSCE signed in 1975, made a substantial contribution to building regional security order in a deeply polarized world in which an atmosphere of hostility and mistrust prevailed. The evolution of the CSCE process consequently led to the demise of the Soviet bloc from within and overcame the division of Europe, leading to the convergence of liberal and democratic values across the region (Kikkawa, 1994). In November 1990, the CSCE Summit declared the Charter of Paris celebrating the victory of democracy, gave post-Cold War substance for the Helsinki Final Act, turning the CSCE from a community of security into a community of values based on common principles and values. The CSCE has developed into the Organization for Security Cooperation in Europe (OSCE), making its move from a more political forum and cooperation process to a formal international organization, and started to grapple with the building of a security community, a community of states and societies whose values, social orders, and identities converge to such a degree that wars among them become unthinkable through the Euro-Atlantic region (Adler, 1998). This has been necessary because the security agenda in Europe is now dominated by concerns over actual and potential internal threats.

In contrast, the Asia-Pacific region was originally severely under-institutionalized, and regional security order during the Cold War was defined by the

massacre; (1.5) through imposition of lethal living conditions; or (1.6) by directly targeting non-combatants during a war or violent conflict, or (2) that causes death by virtue of an intentionally or knowingly reckless and depraved disregard for life, as in (2.1) deadly prison, concentration camp, forced labor, prisoner of war, or recruit camp conditions; (2.2) murderous medical or scientific experiments on humans; (2.3) torture or beatings; (2.4) encouraged or condoned murder, or rape, looting, and pillage during which people are killed; (2.5) a famine or epidemic during which government authorities withhold aid, or knowingly act in a way to make it more deadly; or (2.6) forced deportations and expulsions causing deaths (Rummel, 1994, pp. 36–37).

United States and Soviet-led bilateral alliance system. Although the building of security institutions is of particular relevance to the region, the security institutions that are available to manage the international conflicts were scattered, weak or non-existent (Williams, 2008, pp. 313–314). Only South East Asia had any track record of regional organization prior to the 1990s – namely, the Association of Southeast Asian Nations (ASEAN), created in 1967. Institution-building is largely a post-Cold War phenomenon (Karns & Mingst, 2010, pp. 188–203). After the collapse of the international bipolar system of the Cold War, the parameters of security domains gave rise to a new wave of regionalism and new institutions were formed in the Asia-Pacific region and in the former Soviet areas of control. Although we see a rapid process of institution-building such as ASEAN Plus Three, East Asian Summit (EAS), and the Trilateral Cooperation Secretariat, Shanghai Cooperation Organization (SCO) forum, most of the institutions are functional or weak organizations (Yeo, 2018). Instead, regional states have embarked on a far-reaching military build-up in the name of military modernization after the end of the Cold War. As a result, Asia and East Asia in particular, have been extensively militarized, and have been in a state of crisis.

This chapter explores the security order in Asia today through three perspectives. First, I briefly survey the security environment in Asia today, and the structure of the security order that underpinned the region. I then elaborate why there is no meaningful multilateral security institution in Asia, exploring the reasons for Asia's regional security architecture that is defined by bipolar security alliances. Second, I explore how the end of the Cold War affected the changes to the bipolar system of the Cold War. I discuss then causes and factors that were in the way to post-conflict peacebuilding, and also discuss the emerging new hierarchical security systems in Asia. Third, I identify the reasons why the United States and China are not active in building a regional security institution in the region. I also discuss Japan's disinterest in the regional security institution and Japan's dilemma in pursuing a policy of multilateralism.

Changing International Order

Militarized Asia

Asia encompasses a diverse mixture of rival great powers, thorny territorial disputes, unresolved historical memories, competing political ideologies, competing national and sub-regional identities, and divergent cultures. Uncertainty and military tensions are core features of the contemporary Asian security environment. Bilateral military alliances and arms races may also be prominent features in the region. Militarized conflicts are frequent, and militarized capabilities are targeted toward specified enemies, usually neighboring states.

The Asia-Pacific is a highly militarized region in the world today. Four of the top 15 military spenders in the world are found in the Asia-Pacific region: China (ranked 2nd), Japan (8th), South Korea (10th), and Australia (13th). Additionally, there are two major non-Asian military powers, the United States (1st) and

Russia (3rd), which have strong strategic commitments in the region. Noteworthy is the increasing military spending in the Asia-Pacific region. Military spending in the region has increased by 59 per cent between 2008 and 2017. This overall increase is heavily driven by an increase in China, which accounted for 48 per cent of the region's total arms spending in 2017 (SIPRI, 2018, p. 156).

This upward trend in military spending is a reflection of the security environment in the region. The regional security environment in Asia today is perceived to have undergone considerable deterioration. China's rise both in the economic and military realms, North Korean's nuclear development, and maritime security issues have accelerated the uncertainty in the region. China's rise and growing assertiveness in the South China Sea in particular has placed maritime security issues at the top of regional security concerns (Pan & Kavalski, 2018). Maritime security is being threatened by territorial disputes that have been escalating recently, such as the South China Sea conflicts (Spratly Islands and Paracel Islands), and building of a Chinese naval base in the Indian Ocean.

Maritime security issues in general is a critical regional one due to the heavy reliance of the region on important sea lanes of communication, with over 50 per cent of world shipping by tonnage passing through the South China Sea, via the Strait of Malacca between Indonesia and Malaysia (SIPRI, 2014, p. 189). Military spending levels and priorities in the region are also affected by a range of other issues, notably the perennial conflict on the Korean peninsula.

Despite the accelerating crisis, international relations in Asia and East Asia in particular are least institutionalized in the world and institutional commitments are almost absent in Asia. There is no overarching regional security institution in the sense that they conceive themselves to be bound by a common set of principles in their relations with one another. There is no international security institution in the sense that states should honor agreements into which they enter, and they should be subject to certain limitations in exercising force against one another.

Although the security discourse began in the late 1980s starting with M. Gorbachev's Vladivostok proposal, several ideas concerning security institutions in Asia have been proposed so far (Mack & Kerr, 1995). Yet, there is no effective security institution in Asia. In fact, the Asia-Pacific region is only in the early stages of organizing its security order. However, Southeast Asia and Northeast Asia are themselves at quite different points in the security community building process. Since 2000, in Southeast Asia, multilateral approaches have been taking shape, attempting to develop a multilateral security community based on the European model. In Northeast Asia, on the other hand, Western approaches to multilateral security are not widely accepted (Ba, 2014, p. 667).

Hub-and-Spokes Alliance System

What stands in the way of regional security institutions? Before looking into this problem, we need to take a glance at the global security order of the bipolar system during the Cold War.

States previously tied themselves to the United States or the Soviet Union for their security protection based on a hub-and-spokes relationship.

The hub-and-spokes relationship, which both the United States and the Soviet Union pursued during the Cold War, is in essence a patron-client partnership based on a set of consensual political bargains. The patron states provided security protection to bolster client regimes with a strategic aid policy providing them with arms, military training, economic aid, and at times troops. For example, the United States and the Soviet Union long maintained an extensive network of patron-client partnerships, which guaranteed the security of anti-communist regimes through military, economic and political aid and through deploying its forces in these client states and established a system of extended deterrence. At the same time, the United States as patron provided client states with open markets, and client states in return agreed to affiliate themselves with the patron state providing it with logistical, economic, and diplomatic support within the broader United States-led international system (Ikenberry, 2011, pp. 29–30). Through this patron-client partnership, the United States tied these client states down to an American-centered security system.

The Soviet Union, on the other hand, cultivated clients such as Castro's Cuba, North Korea, Nasser's Egypt, Somalia and a unified Vietnam, backing the communist regimes through the same strategic aid. China to a certain extent supported some African communist states with economic aid, although on a rather small scale. Because the Asian international system was (and has been so to date) a balance of power system, this alliance structure served as an instrument for balancing clearly against the designated rival patron-client partner system.

Through the bilateral security alliance patron states were bound to the region, establishing fixed commitments and mechanisms that have increased certainty and predictability about the expectations of the patron states. The patron-and-client alliance system thus provided the political foundation for the projection of superpower influence into the region.

The Asian security order as part of the broader global arrangements was also a bipolar and hierarchical one that relied on balancing against Soviet communism on the one hand, and against the United States allied countries on the other hand. Notably, the United States has been the most critical factor in shaping the Asia-Pacific region's security order. In the decades after World War II, the United States played a different hegemonic role in Asia than it did in Western Europe. The United States policymakers saw in their Western European allies relatively equal members of a shared community, willing to create a range of multilateral institutions. In Asia, on the other hand, the United States was unambiguously the dominant partner in each bilateral alliance, and therefore preferred bilateral relationships over multilateral ones. What the United States created was a network of deep, asymmetric bilateral alliances, formed around a hub-and-spokes relationship with the United States as a hub, and Japan, South Korea, the Philippines, Taiwan, Thailand, and Australia as spokes in this set of relationships.

Why did the United States prefer a hub-and-spokes relationship? The United States faced a different array of states – less developed and few being democratic – while it pursued bilateral security pacts that provided more control. In fact, the United States had an experience in Europe where it was locked into a multilateral security relationship. The United States did not need to give up policy autonomy to secure its objectives in Asia because the United States had much more unchallenged hegemonic power in Asia than in Western Europe, consequently it had fewer incentives to secure its dominant position within international institutions.

Relying on bilateral relations in Asia, the United States opposed an "Asian Helsinki" because of justifiable fears that the Soviet Union would try to manipulate a regional security institution because it was vulnerable to collective opposition from its alliance on specific issues. The United States power in Asia being much greater than in Europe, it was not in the interest of the United States to form security institutions in Asia that would constrain the power of the United States to make independent decisions (Katzenstein, 2005, p. 51).

Security Protection of Weak States

It should be stressed that most Asian states have been receptive to the patron–client partnership on their own accord. Newly independent states in Asia were most apt to seek protection when they faced both serious external and internal security threats. Traditionally, the international community has attempted to secure "political independence" and "territorial integrity" from "external threats" (Article 10 of the Covenants of the League of Nations and article 2 para.4 of the Charter of the United Nations). However, during the Cold War, the protection of the security of client states in fact came to mean the protection of incumbent regimes and the threat was perceived not only as an external threat but also an internal one such as insurgency which was usually supported from outside through ideologically rival states, and separatism which threatened territorial integrity from within the state.

It might do well to take note of the fact that the internal threat generally originates from the governance structure of the "weak states." According to Barry Buzan, "weak or strong powers" will refer to the traditional distinction among states in respect to their military and economic capability in relation to each other. "Weak or strong states," however, will refer to the degree of socio-political cohesion. Where the state is strong, national security can be viewed primarily in terms of protecting the political independence and territorial integrity from an outside threat. Newly independent post-colonial states, however, are basically weak states in terms of domestic governance (authority to rule) and/or in terms of social and territorial integrity (Buzan, 1990, pp. 97–98).

Using the concept of the weak state thesis, Kelevi Holsti argues that the critical variables in the assessment of weakness of the state is legitimacy, conceived in two dimensions: vertical legitimacy which establishes the connection between society and political institutions and regimes, and horizontal legitimacy, which defines the limits of and criteria for membership in the political community which is ruled (Holsti, 1996, p. 97). The state must be strong enough to build more unity within the society, to help construct national identities. Yet, post-colonial Asian states do not have the resources to accomplish these tasks (Holsti, 1996, p. 116).

Consequently, weak states in general are apt to be caught in a state-strength dilemma and be caught in a vicious circle even with the external material support from patron states. To be a strong state, governments resort to predatory and unlawful practices, which only exacerbate social tensions and erode loyalties of the people. Everything it does to become a strong state actually perpetuates its weakness. Attempts to increase state strength generate resistance that weakens the state. In attempts to overcome resistance, governments rely on coercive measures against local power centers of various types, as well as against communal, religious, and ethnic groups. The exclusion of important groups by denial of access to power or resources consequently helps destroy horizontal legitimacy and exacerbate social tensions (Holsti, 1996, p. 117).

Strategic Aid and Democide

Many recipient governments of aid were guilty of significant human rights violations against their own people, but superpower competition for influence in the Third World was a major cause of civil conflicts and democide. Noteworthy as well is that the patron-and-client partnership was an indirect yet important cause of democide and domestic violence in non-democratic states in Asia. As discussed earlier, newly independent post-colonial states were weak states in terms of domestic governance and territorial integrity. When the weak states faced an internal threat and the governments addressed the internal threat in a coercive way, causing humanitarian crises, the patron states usually connived at the atrocities, or even indirectly supported them through aid to the incumbent regimes.

The practice of giving aid to those suffering the impacts of war has long been based on humanitarian concerns. However, the international state system had changed by the time when newly independent Asian states joined the system. Before World War II, sovereign states were assumed to be self-reliant. But as colonialism ended, the moral and legal framework was established that underdeveloped states were to be supported externally regardless of their level of economic statehood. International norms were also informed that it was the responsibility for the developed states to extend their welfare beyond their borders to support the underdeveloped states through material and economic support.

The aid from external patrons during the Cold War was seen more as a tool to pursue foreign policy concerns rather than the alleviation of human suffering or the promotion of development. The United States, the Soviet Union, China, and some other big/middle powers belonging to either hierarchy used bilateral aid selectively to reward weak state regimes that supported their positions, and even to bolster-related counterinsurgency strategies. In other words, the regimes of weak states were underpinned by strategic aid diplomacy of the patron states.

State support or sponsorship of an insurgency in a state that belonged to the rival group was common during the Cold War. The United States supported insurgent movements such as the Afghan mujahidin, Tibetan Buddhist fighters as a part of its policy to contain and even roll back communism. The Soviet Union and China backed communist guerrillas in Angola, Greece, and other parts of the world to step up their influence (Byman, Chalk, Hoffman, Rosenau & Brannan, 2001, p. 1).

The international community, let alone the patron states would not intervene to stop the atrocities within the client state. For example, what did the patron state do when more than half a million people were hunted down and killed during the September 30th Movement in the Indonesian massacres from 1965 to 1968? What did the patron states do when Pol Pot's regime killed 1.5 million of its own citizens from 1975 to 1978? They usually overtly or tacitly supported the atrocities. Domestic violence after all was not put on the security agenda of the United Nations. The main international norms, non-intervention in internal affairs, prevented the United Nations, let alone the rival group, to commit to the violation of human rights and atrocities arising from bad governance.

Democracy and Peace

The End of the Cold War

Strategic aid lost its rationale as the Cold War ended, and consequently the superpowers reduced their largesse. In fact, the end of strategic aid to beleaguered governments weakened many authoritarian regimes since 1989 (Byman & Van Evera, 1998, p. 38), and this caused a marked decline in the strength of superpowers' influence on client states.

After the collapse of the Soviet Union and Yugoslavia, the regimes that relied on the Soviet Union as a model for their economies and politics suffered a blow to their legitimacy. Indeed, the collapse of communism discredited authoritarian regimes of all stripes, leading them to be "failed states" or "failing states" throughout the Third World (Rotberg, 2004). At the same time, the end of the Cold War led to the drastic reduction of insurgencies and many of the insurgencies driven largely by Marxist ideology in Africa and Latin America collapsed. This decline in both the number of insurgencies and government sponsorship may reflect the end of the patron–client partnership which was prevalent during the Cold War. While ideologically oriented insurgencies decreased drastically on the one hand, those more religious or ethnic in nature have often survived on the other. The new form of civil war, or "new wars" to quote Mary Kaldor (Kaldor, 2006) ensued from the loss of government legitimacy.

The priorities and modalities of bilateral aid policy changed drastically too. The aid from Western states was now often conditioned on democratic or market reforms. Accordingly, the international community came to address new agendas for international peace and security. While Western states started to globalize "good governance" based on democracy, rule of law and respect for human rights, the CSCE/OSCE embarked on attempts to assist post-conflict peacebuilding, and to assist democratization of transitional states of former communist regimes in Eastern Europe and former Soviet and Yugoslavian regions.

Contrary to popular expectations democratic backsliding has been witnessed in all regions of the world. Democracy is in crisis. In the recent annual report of Freedom House, political rights and civil rights around the world deteriorated to their lowest point in more than a decade in 2017. Since the global slide began in 2006, 113 states have seen a net decline, and only 62 have experienced a net improvement.[2] Repressive regimes in Asia and Central Asia continued to consolidate their power.

In the established democracies in the Euro-Atlantic region, democratic structures are being put under pressure by social and economic disparities, partisan fragmentation, terrorist attacks, and an influx of refugees. Besides the retreat of democracies in all the regions in the world, worthy of note is the fact that China has risen in power to provide diplomatic and material support to the repressive governments from Southeast Asia to Africa.

Thwarted Peacebuilding

It is interesting that the resurgence of ethnic conflicts brought the United Nations to focus increasingly on conflict prevention and post-conflict peacebuilding. The United Nations adopted four ways of strengthening and making more efficient its capacity of preventive diplomacy, peace-making, peace keeping and post-conflict peacebuilding in the report "An Agenda for Peace" prepared by Boutros Boutros-Ghali, then General Secretary of the United Nations

These ambitious projects were seen as effective formulae for transition from war to peace. Large-scale international intervention, often in the form of support for electoral assistance, was designed to bring peace and economic progress to countries that had been wracked by violence. The United Nations established special political missions in a number of post-conflict states, including Afghanistan, Bosnia-Herzegovina, Cambodia, El Salvador, Guatemala, Iraq, Liberia, Libya, Mozambique, and Sierra Leone.

However, the international community's efforts to promote stability in war-torn states by encouraging democratization and marketization in the 1990s had created not a liberal peace but, instead, renewed competition and violence resulting in a stalemate. This is partly because peace builders had not made sufficient efforts to build the basic institutional structures that both democracy and market economics required to function well. This reform pressure, in turn, often precipitated conflicts. Bosnia, Rwanda, and Cambodia were stark illustrations of the limitations of utilizing aid to promote peace or deal with the consequences of violent conflicts. For example, analyzing more than 20 major multilateral peacebuilding missions deployed to post-conflict societies, conducted from Namibia in 1889 to Darfur in 2007, with the goal of preventing the resumption of violence, Roland Paris and Timothy D. Sisk conclude that one of the lessons from the preceding experiences of peacebuilding was that peacebuilding operations tended to rely on quick fixes, such as rapid elections and bursts of economic privatization, while paying too little attention to constructing the institutional foundations for functioning post-war governments and markets (Paris & Sisk 2009, pp. 2 and 10). Another lesson from the preceding peacebuilding experience is that efforts to democratize were predisposed to lead to a growing governability crisis, which in turn leads the regime to hunker down and abort its democratization experiment.

---

[2]Retrieved from https://freedomhoU.S.e.org/report/freedom-world/freedom-world-2018.

This "reform trap" generates further dissent and leads to civil war (Byman & Van Evera, 1998, p. 36).

Noteworthy as well is a new and serious impediment to the promotion of democratization: emerging China's strategic aid diplomacy. China's aid policy is distinctive in that the norms and conditions attached to Chinese aid are less intrusive than the Western model, guaranteeing a relatively high degree of autonomy in exchange for deference to Chinese authority (Ciorciari, 2015, p. 249). As a matter of fact, for centuries existed the so-called "tribute system" with China as a hegemon in Asia, and this international system helped obtain deference from weaker neighboring states in exchange for recognition and other cultural, economic, and security benefits. The tribute system has been revived in a way as China has risen to economic and military superpower status.

China does have ample resources to use for patronage, including military and economic power. Now the recent model of China's patron-and-client partnership, seeking policy support from clients, relies heavily on economic inducement. Using its considerable economic power, China has cultivated many clients of developing states in Africa and Asia by providing substantial benefits to incumbent government leaders without requiring democratization. It should be noted that China's aid policy without preconditions is particularly appealing to internationally ostracized states such as North Korea, and transitional post-conflict states such as Cambodia and Sri Lanka. For example, after a few decades of terrifying internal conflict and mass murder that took place under the Khmer Rouge regime, the United Nations deployed the United Nations Transitional Authority in Cambodia (UNTAC), and Japan and France proactively assisted in peacebuilding of the state after UNTAC withdrew, supporting democratization and implanting good governance in Cambodia. In fact, the peacebuilding process supported by Japan and France was seen as a successful blueprint for further instances of Japanese diplomacy (Kikkawa, 2009). In the years that followed, however, as China rose to become Cambodia's largest donor of economic and military aid (Saudi Arabia, second), Prime Minister Hun Sen's administration came to be inclined toward China in order to have political and economic breathing space (Ciorciari, 2015, pp. 251–252). Through this rearrangement, the peacebuilding process of Cambodia was thwarted leaning instead toward an authoritarian state.

The Emergence of New Hierarchies

The Cold War's end destabilized the United States -centric hegemonic system across the world, and the Soviet-dominated hegemonic system collapsed totally. With the demise of the Soviet Union, alliance theorists predicted that the United States -led alliance system would be dissolved because its primary rationale was no longer operative (Nye, 2001, p. 95). Since the end of the Cold War, Asia's institutional landscape has changed dramatically, and ASEAN played an important role in forming regional institutions such as the ASEAN Regional Forum (ARF) and the Asia–Pacific Economic Cooperation (APEC) forum. Nonetheless, the building of security institutions which started in Southeast Asia does not seem to expand as far as Northeast Asia. Unlike Europe, post-Cold War East Asia still lacks a dense web of international institutions (Williams, 2008, pp. 316–318). East Asia in particular remains hostage to the legacy of the Cold War – the strained relations between mainland China and Taiwan, and between North and South Korea – remain a threat to peace and stability.

While there have been some modest multilateral efforts to improve dialogue between these governments, their fragile bilateral relationships dominate the security politics of East Asia in general. Besides, the US-centered security alliances in the region such as the United States–South Korean alliance, and the United States–Japan alliance remain intact. Then questions arise. Why do certain alliances survive the structural change following the reduction or elimination of the mutually perceived threat? A number of factors that have exerted negative influence on the underdevelopment of Asian regional security order include China's opposition to the institutionalization of security and the United States preference for bilateralism.

The most significant structural challenge to peace and stability in Asia are two distinct hierarchies. One is a security hierarchy dominated by the United States and the other is an economic hierarchy dominated by China. China is the dominant economic power in the region, and the economic fortunes of states across Asia are being increasingly tied to China, while the United States continues to be the dominant security provider. However, neither the United States nor China has been especially interested in forming new institutional mechanisms (Ba, 2014, pp. 669–670).

Disinterest in Multilateral Security System

China's Challenge

Domestic politics has been a factor influencing the evolution of regional security order. Because most states in Asia have authoritarian governments, concern for political legitimacy explains their reluctance to create strong regional institutions. China's motivations for its security policies are twofold: first, China wants the United States out of East Asia, and second, China wants to expand its power around its dramatically rising economic power. China has been relatively ambivalent about a regional multilateral security system, but its case is slightly more complicated. For many years, China has been suspicious of the United States dominated alliance system in Asia. China has also been traditionally wary of any security organization because China fears that other states – most of which were the United States Cold War partners – would use new mechanisms to interfere in China's internal affairs including the Taiwan issue and territorial disputes (Karns & Mingst, 2010, p. 198).

China's fears are well reflected in its conceptualization of preventive diplomacy in the document "ARF Concept and Principles of Preventive Diplomacy," adopted at the 8th ARF, 25 July 2001. Because of strong opposition by China, the definition of conflict was eventually limited to "conflicts between states." As a result, it defines the aim of preventive diplomacy as being to "prevent disputes/conflicts between states from emerging, to prevent such disputes/conflicts from escalating into armed confrontation, and to prevent such disputes and conflicts from spreading" (para 8). This stands in stark contrast to the UN's preferred definition, which asserts that conflicts are to be prevented between "parties" and not "states."[3]

Behind this negative approach to preventive diplomacy is the fact that China faced dire threats both external and internal after the end of the Cold War: an external threat of the wave of globalization of good governance, and the internal threat of separatism. Viewing the rise of democracy as a threat to its own regime, China set out to discredit it globally and to defend the security of neighboring states collectively. It is against this background that the Shanghai Cooperation Organisation (SCO) was formed in 2001. The SCO emerged out of the disintegration of the former Soviet Union and China's concerns about security along the border it shares with Russia, Kazakhstan, Tajikistan, and Kirgizstan. The leaders of these states shared security concerns of border conflicts and separatist movements of Islamic fundamentalism. Gradually they expanded their agenda of security issues to address the triple threats of the SCO to address extremism, separatism, and terrorism.

Although the SCO's creation marked a broad shift in Chinese regional foreign policy from bilateralism to multilateralism, the SCO differs from other security organizations in that it is not a security organization based on the concept of common and comprehensive security concept like the OSCE, but it is an organization to provide national security protection to member states and to counter the wave of democratization and good governance from the Euro-Atlantic region (Xuetang, 2006, p. 121).

China has long been suspicious of the United States dominated alliance system in Asia. With a number of its own initiatives, such as the SCO and the ASEAN–China Free Trade Area, and more recently the Asian Infrastructure Investment Bank, China has sought to lure Asian states away from the US-centered security architecture and toward one that is more regional, within which it would potentially exert greater influence. Consequently, many Asian states today face a complicated strategic situation. They increasingly look to China for their economic future. But they are also wary of increasing Chinese dominance and are consequently eager to see the United States remain a provider of regional security protection.

The United States Opposition

Despite some evidence of embryonic multilateralism in the Asia-Pacific region as mentioned earlier, East Asia still depends heavily upon the military presence of the United States. The United States may be able to reduce the costs and reap more gains from providing security in Asia through developing new regional

[3]The UN's definition of preventive diplomacy is as follows: preventive diplomacy is action to prevent disputes from arising between parties, to prevent existing disputes from escalating into conflicts and to limit the spread of the latter when they occur (An Agenda for Peace, paragraph 20).

security institutions. However, the United States shows no signs of wanting to transform the bilateral hegemonic order in East Asia into a fully functioning multilateral security community because the United States views new institutional mechanisms as direct challenges to United States interests and arrangements. In fact, for nearly half a century the United States – as the hub in the network – did not encourage connections among the spokes into larger multilateral groupings such as a "Pacific NATO" (Cha, 2009/2010, p. 738).

Besides, the key bilateral allies of the United States in Asia, including Japan, have not been uniformly enthusiastic about developing region-wide security architecture. Japan particularly shows no interest in multilateralism. Japan's disinterest in multilateral security stemmed from both structural and historical factors. Structurally, the bilateral alliance provided all that Japan needed. The United States support of Japan in Asia effectively removed any motivation for Japan to explore the opportunities of building security institutions in the region. The ambivalence toward regional integration also stemmed from an acute sensitivity to the region's lingering historic suspicions. Any multilateral security arrangements would by definition require a larger Japanese leadership role than would be deemed unacceptable by many in the region because colonialism and Japanese imperialism prior to World War II left a legacy of wariness of regional cooperation that might involve new forms of Japanese domination (Cha, 2009/2010, pp. 731–737; Midford, 2000, p. 374).

In this regard, the United States bears partial responsibility for the gap between Japan's disinterest in building regional security institutions and the region's distrust of Japan's leadership role in such an effort. It is thought that the legitimacy of the United States military role involves not only deterrence of nuclear threats from Russia and China, but also reassures Japan's neighbors that it will remain "a benign power" and that there is no need for an arms race in the region (Nye, 1992–1993, p. 100). Ostensibly the United States–Japan alliance has played a more specific and crucial role – namely, it has allowed Japan to be secure without the necessity of becoming a traditional military power. Japan could be defended while remaining a "civilian power" and this meant that Japan could rebuild and re-enter the region without triggering dangerous security dilemmas with neighboring states (Ikenberry, 2011, p. 30).

However, it should be stressed that the United States has strategically played on the fear of neighboring countries' perceptions of Japan in order to maintain the bilateral alliance system. This United States strategy is partly reflective of the so-called "cork in the bottle" theory, a phrase invented by General Henrry Stackpole, Commander of US Marines in Okinawa. The "cork in the bottle" theory was coined to prevent a resurgence of Japanese militarism and check Japan's power projection capabilities. This analogous argument asserts that if there were no "cork" (i.e., US forces in Japan) in the "bottle," the contents of the "bottle" (i.e., Japanese militarism) would spill out into Asia again. In other words, the US forces in Japan represent the "cork in the bottle" which checks Japan's military power. The message coming out of this thesis is that the US forces are indispensable to the maintenance of US global power, and without United States bases in Japan, the United States would have difficulty maintaining its superpower status in Asia. Additionally, a withdrawal from this conception would ensure Japanese remilitarization.

The Japanese Security Policy in a Dilemma

In fact, there were initial concerns of the United States at the end of the Cold War that any regional initiatives for multilateralism could undermine the United States leadership in Asia. In November 1990, for example, Secretary of State James Baker, criticized as inappropriate the notion of regional security dialogues replacing the American hub-and-spokes system, which had been at the center of Asian security and prosperity for four decades (Cha, 2014, p. 740).

Faced with an impending identity crisis in the bilateral alliance right after the end of the Cold War, the Japanese government, expressing an interest in regional security arrangements set about the task of forging new policies for the post-Cold War security policy. A Japanese government panel discussed a new direction for Japan's 1995 Defence Outline policy, and the final report was released in August 1994 (Higuchi Report). But the attempt was adamantly opposed by the United States government. What matters was the composition of the report.

The Higuchi Report proposed four basic pillars for future Japanese defense policy: (1) development of Japan's defense capability for the purpose of multilateral security cooperation, including active participation in UN peace keeping operations; (2) stronger bilateral security cooperation with the United States; (3) maintenance and qualitative improvement of Japan's self-defense capability; and (4) development of the domestic defense industry and technological infrastructure. The organizational structure – beginning with a discussion of Japan's multilateral security cooperation – was logical to security policy at the time. Moreover, at the time right after the Gulf War experience when Japan was finally beginning to participate in UN peacekeeping operations, it made sense to begin by setting forth the concept of multilateral security in these broad-based security discussions.

This organizational structure, however, alarmed some East Asian experts in the United States In their appraisal, the decision to place multilateral security cooperation ahead of Japan- United States cooperation signaled a shift toward multilateralism at the expense of the United States -Japan bilateral alliance. To these senior influential policymakers, Japan's security policy was regarded as diverging away from the United States -Japan alliance. In September 1994, newly appointed Assistant Secretary of State, Joseph Nye, began making arrangements for a bilateral security policy review, which became known as the Nye Initiative.

The Nye Initiative, more officially known as the United States Security Strategy for the East Asia-Pacific Region, published in February 1995, is a report outlining the United States security strategy for East Asia and the Pacific, emphasizing the importance of a United States forward presence in Asia and the security alliance with Japan. It argued that the United States military presence in the region had important consequences for the stability of the region, and for the success of political, economic, and security goals of the United States Specifically, Nye advocated that the United States should maintain a total of 100,000 troops in

East Asia, emphasizing the importance of the United States Marine Corps and other military forces in Okinawa (Nye, 2001, p. 98).

The Nye initiative was a turning point for Japan–United States bilateralism. Through maintaining the United States–Japan alliance, it also aimed to check Japanese initiatives to enter into multilateral security institutions. The Nye Initiative had defined United States–Japan relations as the most important bilateral relationship in East Asia and depicted Japanese security as the linchpin of US security policy in the region. This process led both countries to the same conclusion: the Japan–United States partnership had a vital role to play in post-Cold War security. Predictably therefore, the 1996 Japan–United States Joint Declaration on Security was an affirmation of this conclusion at the highest level. To reaffirm this mutual understanding, both governments shortly thereafter published the Japan–United States Joint declaration on Security Cooperation and the 1997 Guidelines for Japan–United States Defence Cooperation. Through this arrangement, the patron–client relations between the two states were consolidated.

Conclusion

Asia has inherited traditional localized tensions such as territorial disputes, ethnic antagonism, and transnational threats such as transnational terrorism and drug trafficking, and global threats such as climate change, global warming, flood disaster, nuclear proliferation, etc. Besides, there are many domestic factors which pose threats to the very lives of people including bad governance that are apt to cause democide, ethnic cleansing, and mass murder. The acknowledgement of the challenges ahead only emphasizes the importance of effective measures to address these threats all the more urgent and necessary today. It is against this background that the regional security order should be viewed.

However, the prospect for international security in the region is dim. Political leaders in Japan and China remain apathetic if not skeptical toward the building of a regional security institution. Besides, the US security policy based on a bilateral array of alliances has dampened, and even hindered the building of a new security institution. Moreover, most Asian states choose paths of security self-reliance or bilateralism, and ASEAN's embryonic move to security community building has been taking an adversarial turn in recent years. Then is the bilateral security system in East Asia a viable option for long lasting peace? How these increasingly distinct hierarchies – security and economic – operate is also a key issue for the evolution of regional order.

The hub-and-spokes system between the United States–Japan and the United States–South Korea has been operative for almost seven decades. Such duration is a rare exception in the overall history of alliance politics because generally alliances are short-lived. According to a study by Jae Jeok Park, the average lifespan of 304 alliances formed between 1815 and 1989 (excluding ongoing alliances as of 2001) is 9.3 years (Park, 2013, p. 338). Then, once the North Korean problem is resolved the Koreans will have no interest in maintaining US forces in Asia. Besides, with the stalemate of attempts at democratic peace in the region and with the enhancing of China-centered economic hierarchy of more Asian states relying on the Chinese market, there will be no rationale for the United States to stay in Asia.

In response to an increasingly dynamic and uncertain East Asian security environment, we can see that Japan is now gradually shifting toward a trajectory of becoming a so-called "normal military power," prepared to deploy military force for national security ends (Hughes, 2014, pp. 373–374). China has grown at an astonishing rate and will seek its own manifest destiny in the region and push the United States out. When the United States pulls out from Asia, however, it will be inevitable that states in the region may strengthen an arms build-up because the international system remains a balance of power one. As the arms race accelerates, the regional military balance of rival states will collapse someday, then war will follow. With 12,000 nuclear warheads stored in the hands of nuclear states, is there any guarantee that *Hiroshima* will not be repeated? With the United States hegemony gone, will Japan remain a benign power?

Apparently, the security environment in East Asia will be taking an adversarial turn. International security is protected not only by agreement on fixed principles for mutual relations, but also by institutions and trust that such principles will be observed. Principles and declarations of intention on their own are no guarantee of peace and stability. We need institutions that are capable of action to ensure that these principles are observed, to bring violations to light, and to actively pursue the organization of cooperation (Steinmeier, 2015, p. 33). Consequently, regimes that craft and defend multilateral rules for the common good are essential for the preservation of broad-based security that benefit all countries and peoples.

The security environment in East Asia is getting worse. This trend is caused by the lack of motivation on the part of political leaders of major powers including the United States, China, Russia, and Japan for security community building. To stop the worsening plight of the security environment, security community building will be all the more urgent and necessary. However, a security institution does not just come into being. Deliberate policy choices by state leaders are key to increasing the flow of political activities and the policy choice of building security. The long-term future of the Asia-Pacific area will depend heavily on the degree and nature of leadership shown by China and Japan, as well as a significant measure of United States supportive engagement in such efforts.

References

Adler, E. (1998). Seeds of peaceful change: The OSCE's security community building model. In E. Adler & M. Barnett (Eds.), *Security communities* (pp. 119–160). Cambridge: Cambridge University Press.

Ba, A. D. (2014). Asia's Regional Security Institutions. In S. M. Pekkanen, J. Ravenhill, & R. Foot (Eds.), *The Oxford handbook of the international relations of Asia* (pp. 667–689). Oxford: Oxford University Press.

Buzan, B. (1990). *People, states and fear: An agenda for international security studies in post-cold war era*. Brighton: Wheatsheaf.

Byman, D., Chalk, P., Hoffman, B., Rosenau, W., & Brannan, D (Eds.). (2001). *Trends in Outside support for insurgent movements*. Santa Monica: RAND.

Byman, D., & Van Evera, S. (1998). Why they fight: Hypotheses on the causes of contemporary deadly conflict. *Security Studies*, *7*(3), 1–50.

Cha, V. D. (2009/2010). Powerplay: Origins of the U.S. alliance system in Asia. *International Security*, *34*(3), 158–196.

Cha, V. D. (2014). American alliances and Asia's regional architecture. In S. M. Pekkanen, J. Ravenhill, & R. Foot (Eds.), *The Oxford handbook of the international relations of Asia* (pp. 737–757). Oxford: Oxford University Press.

Ciorciari, J. D. (2015). A Chinese model for patron-client relations? The Sino-Cambodian partnership. *International Relations of the Asia-Pacific*, *15*(2), 245–278.

Holsti, K. J. (1996). *The state, war, and the state of war*. Cambridge: Cambridge University Press.

Hughes, C. W. (2014). Japan's foreign security relations and policies. In S. M. Pekkanen, J. Ravenhill, & R. Foot (Eds.), *The Oxford handbook of the international relations of Asia* (pp. 371–390). Oxford: Oxford University Press.

Ikenberry, G. J. (2011, January). East Asia and liberal international order: Hegemony, balance, and consent in the shaping of East Asian regional order. Paper presented at the International Conference on Regional Integration and Institutionalization. Aoyamagakuin University, Tokyo.

Kaldor, M. (2006). *New and old wars: Organized violence in a global era*. Cambridge: Polity Press.

Karns, M. P., & Mingst, K. (Eds.). (2010). *International organizations: The politics and process of global governance*. Colorado: Lynne Rienner Publishers.

Katzenstein, P. (2005). *A world of regions: Asia and Europe in the American imperium*. Ithaca, NY: Cornell University Press.

Kikkawa, G. (1994). *Yoroppa Anzenhoshou Kyouryokukaigi (CSCE) (The Conference on Security and Cooperation in Europe)*. Tokyo: Sanreishobou.

Kikkawa, G. (2009). Japan and Cambodia. In J. Llewellyn, D. Walton, & G. Kikkawa (Eds.), *A Pacifist State in a hostile region: Japan and Post War Conflict in Southeast Asia* (pp. 157–178). New York, NY: Nova Science Publishers.

Mack, A., & Kerr, P. (1995). The evolving security discourse in the Asia-Pacific. *The Washington Quarterly*, *18*(1), 123–140.

Midford, P. (2000). Japan's leadership role in East Asian security multilateralism. *The Pacific Review*, *13*(3), 367–397.

Nye, J. S. Jr. (1992–1993, Winter). Coping with Japan. *Foreign Policy*, *89*, 96–115.

Nye, J. S. Jr. (2001). The 'Nye Report': Six years later. *International Relations of the Asia-Pacific*, *1*(1), 95–103.

Pan, C., & Kavalski, E. (2018). Theorizing China's rise in and beyond international relations. *International Relations of the Asia-Pacific*, *18*(3), 289–311.

Paris, R., & Sisk, T. (Ed.). (2009). *The dilemmas of state building: Confronting the contradictions of postwar peace operations*. London: Routledge.

Park, J. J. (2013). The Persistence of the U.S.-led alliances in the Asia-Pacific: An order insurance explanation. *International Relations of the Asia-Pacific*, *13*(3), 337–368.

Pinker, S. (2011). *The better angels of our nature*. New York, NY: Viking.

Rotberg, R. (Ed.). (2004). *When states fail: Causes and consequences*. Princeton, NJ: Princeton University Press.

Rummel, R. (1994). *Death by government*. New Jersey: Transaction Publishers.

Steinmeier, F.-W. (2015). Not a concert of powers, but an ensemble of peace: What we can learn from Helsinki for European security in the 21st Century. In *OSCE Yearbook 2015* (pp. 23–34). Hamburg: Institute for Peace Research and Security Policy at the University of Hamburg.

Stockholm International Peace Research Institute (SIPRI). (2014). *SIPRI Yearbook 2014: Armaments, disarmaments and international security*. Oxford: Oxford University Press.

Stockholm International Peace Research Institute (SIPRI). (2018). *SIPRI Yearbook 2018: Armaments, disarmaments and international security*. Oxford: Oxford University Press.

Williams, P. (2008). *Security studies: An introduction*. London: Routledge.

Xuetang, G. (2006). The energy security in Central Eurasia: The geopolitical implications to China's energy strategy. *China and Eurasia Forum Quarterly*, *4*(4), 117–137.

Yeo, A. (2018). Overlapping regionalism in East Asia: Determinants and potential effects. *International Relations of the Asia-Pacific*, *18*(2), 161–191.

Conclusion – Impact of Democratization on Civil Conflicts

N. Ganesan

The manner in which peace has been described conceptually and the broad-based acceptance of the distinction between positive peace and negative peace has implications for the impact of democratization on peace. Since peace is now understood to mean conflict transformation rather than the absence of conflict, ways to bring about such transformations have added utility. And it is in this regard that democracy and democratization can provide the greatest contributions to the achievement of peace. The ability of democratic norms to channel competitive political activities into mutually acceptable norms of civilized contestation holds the key to conflict transformation. Importantly, the accompanying rule of law that is attendant on democracies and the protection of fundamental liberties of all citizens also ensures that the tyranny of the majority does not obtain. In this regard, there are safeguards that protect and ensure the liberties and dignified treatment of the losers of the competitive electoral process as well. To the extent that democracy is both a process and a product it has both continuous and terminal utility. The continuous utility is in the management of conflict that in turn allows for peaceful settlements. And such settlements over time spawn a culture that is conducive to the active management of conflicts.

Where democracy has been actively practiced, it is incumbent upon elites and institutions to ensure that procedural norms associated with free and fair contestation are not subverted. And this can be an ongoing challenge even to established democracies that are sometimes challenged by changes that affect the fabric of society. The recent large-scale migration of peoples from countries that are ridden with conflict in the Middle East and Africa are examples of situations that have tested the liberal limits of the most democratic Western societies. It is not uncommon for the citizens of a country to respond negatively when they sense a threat to their comfort zones and way of life. Drastic changes can be unsettling and fear of the unknown is a common response and one that sometimes foments suspicion and even violence.

This edited volume is specifically concerned with the transformative value of democratization on societies that were in a state of civil war. Hence, while we are aware of the benefits of democracy on states that have practiced it for long,

International Perspectives on Democratization and Peace, 189–199

doi:10.1108/978-1-80043-067-920200011

what are the possibilities with states where it is introduced in order to transform conflicts? And beyond simply conjecturing on what the likely outcomes might be, the book looks at seven specific case studies spread across three continents to discern how the situation has unfolded. As mentioned at the outset, the process itself has been aided by the third wave of democracy in the 1990s following the end of the Cold War and its structural impact on the world and on civil conflicts. The United Nations push for peace in conflict ridden societies under Boutros Boutros Ghali provided another incentive for the international community to mediate such conflicts. All the cases examined in this book benefitted from both these developments although the end outcomes have not always been similar or consistent. Nonetheless, the number of cases chosen and their collective treatment in assessing the impact of democratization has yielded a number of general and specific observations. And the following sections are an attempt to identify some of these common and specific outcomes that have obtained.

General Comparative Observations

The first and perhaps most obvious observation deriving from the case studies is that all the countries studied had not successfully transitioned into the post-independence period to become integrated and well-functioning states. In other words, territorial consolidation as a cohesive state was not forthcoming as expected under international law. While there is general agreement that early on the process of state formation even in Western societies involved violence in order to subdue regions and peoples for a cohesive identity to evolve, such use of force by the state were to all intents and purposes regarded as having been completed by the end of World War II which is usually regarded as the marker line for modern history and politics. Such violence may have had both instrumental and exemplary value. The former was often used by states in order to subjugate unwilling areas and peoples while the latter served a much more symbolic function of serving as a warning to similar areas and peoples of the fate that would befall them in the event of non-compliance. Historically, all states have employed such violence in order to establish political supremacy and regimes established rules of the game that became accepted over time such that the likelihood of violence tended to recede (Boudreau, 2013, pp. 22–23) Additionally, such subjugation was an important means of assuring that only the state could claim the legitimate use of force. This claim is fundamental to the later preservation of law and order and the important proviso of establishing the rule of law.

Without exception, all the case studies examined in this book indicate that the state was unable to exercise its power and enforcement functions in geographical locales where its power was challenged. After all, if it was able to, the situation would not have deteriorated into a state of civil war. This inability of the state is starkly demonstrated in the case of the provinces bordering Thailand in the case of Cambodia which were controlled by the Khmer Rouge, the highland areas inhabited by the ethnic minorities in the case of Myanmar, the northern Jaffna peninsula in the case of Sri Lanka and remote and mountainous areas in Guatemala and Colombia. The Colombian case was complicated by the existence of paramilitary groups, criminal syndicates and drug traffickers that worsened the situation. The African case studies of Angola and Mozambique similarly reflected the inability of the state to enforce its will and the political contestation among armed groups for power. In fact, the author of the chapter on Angola cynically notes how political violence was often the constitutive element of power and its contestation in the African continent. Consequently, it may be argued that structural and center-periphery tensions within the countries studied tended to embed and exaggerate the civil conflicts. And conversely, if such a situation obtained it also meant that these states were unable to subdue such challenges and therefore could not claim the monopoly to the use of legitimate force.

There is also evidence that in most of the case studies countries that were geographically proximate to countries in a state of civil war were involved in the conflict as well. In some cases, such involvement was explicit like in the case of Thailand in supporting the Karen National Union and the Shan State Army-South as part of a broader buffer policy derived from historical anxieties and animosities. Similarly, there is the case of Indian involvement in the Sri Lankan conflict and interestingly aligned with different parties at different stages in the conflict. The revolutionary nature of the conflicts in Mozambique and the porosity of the borders of the country with those of its neighbors led to similar outcomes with the involvement of Southern Rhodesia, Malawi, and Tanzania in the conflict. Similarly, the conflict in Angola attracted intervention from South Africa. In this regard, it is arguable that many of the civil wars examined in this book had a spillover effect on neighboring countries. In the case of India and South Africa, these were regional hegemons that sought to contain proximate regional conflicts in order to calm the immediate external environment but also as a way to exercise what they regarded as rightful interventions in light of their superior standing in the region.

State Security Versus Regime Security

In the book *Asian Security Practice: Material and Ideational Influences,* Muthiah Alagappa had noted how in Asia there is a regular conflation of interests between state and regime security (Alagappa, 1998). In other words, elites from a particular political party often regard their personal and party interests as identical with those of state interests. Important in this assumption is the fact that there is no conceptual distinction between the state as an entity that is separate from an incumbent regime. And when this important distinction is not observed elites in political power employ state institutions in order to further their own corporate interests. This twinning is injurious to state formation and legitimacy since the state is then taken hostage and its resources appropriated to further specific partisan interests. Such a situation hardly provides impetus for inclusiveness for those marginalized by the process. And the process only serves to alienate peripheral communities and prevent their inclusion within a democratic framework. In fact, even the advent of democracy in order to transform the conflict has inadvertently led to the empowerment of groups with access to state power and resources as in the case of Guatemala, Angola, and Mozambique (to be discussed in the final section).

The conceptual distinction between the state and the regime in power is central to encouraging inclusion and important in reassuring the domestic population that state power is independent from political parties and may be exercised only by elected officials who in turn form the government. It is also a central feature of democratic governance in terms of fair and meaningful contestation. Non-Western countries like the ones examined in this book appear to display a flagrant disregard for such norms that are central to notions of inclusion and fairness that will in turn stimulate conflict transformation. Fortunately, though the case of Colombia appears to indicate that if there is sufficient political will to transform the conflict then such transformation can indeed obtain. And in fact such transformation also occurred in the case of Cambodia early on until the national unity government became disbanded with a renewed bout of civil conflict afterwards. Hence, unless parties competing for political power are able to act in good faith and not subvert the process to further their own sectoral interests, political reconciliation and conflict transformation appear doomed to failure, or at least an unfair settlement that is often a harbinger for renewed conflict as in the case of Mozambique. Additionally, Fontes Ramos notes how the situation in turn spawned an attitude of "growing disengagement" from the political process and general disillusionment with elections and democracy as a way of reconciling differences and resolving the conflict.

International Structural Norms and Their Impact on Peace

There is very clear evidence that international structural norms and especially those associated with colonization and the ideological attributes of the Cold War had an impact on the case studies examined. And the impact of colonization on civil conflicts as well as democratization has indeed been strong and long lasting. The chapter by Robert Jacobs in the first section of the book demonstrates the devastating impact of colonization on the Pacific Islands that were literally made uninhabitable as a result of nuclear weapons testing there. The callous disregard for the lives of the islanders by the United States and France is truly shocking. And in many of the case studies examined in this book, colonization provided the context for independence struggles and also affected the calibration of post-independence governments and the outlook of their elites.

In the case of Vietnam, it was the war of liberation against France in the First Indochina War that led to the Geneva Accords in July 1954 that then divided the country into two halves. The first of these, North Vietnam, was controlled by the communists while South Vietnam hosted a military authoritarian regime that was supported by the United States. This situation then dove-tailed neatly into the Cold War with China supporting the Indochinese Communist Party and its charismatic leader Ho Chi Minh in the fight against the U.S. And the communist insurgents' victory led to the reunification of the country in 1975 before it became embroiled in the Sino-Soviet conflict over Cambodia. And it was France as the previous colonial master of the French Indochinese Union that spans current day Vietnam, Laos and Cambodia that initiated the first round of talks on Vietnam in 1973 that then led to the Paris Peace Accords. Similarly, France was involved in the Cambodian peace talks that eventually led to the Paris Peace Agreements in 1991.

In the case of Myanmar that was colonized by the United Kingdom, the failure of the colonizers to weld the country into a unitary whole and the ethno-linguistic differences between the highlanders and the lowlanders was the harbinger of a fractured country after independence in 1948. British policies that lifted border controls to the Indian sub-continent and the privileging of Indians afterward led to ethno-religious tensions as well. The reification of ethnicity and the domestic political drift toward the Bamar majority and Buddhism then sealed the country's drift toward insurgency and civil war. It also laid the groundwork for the military coup of 1962 and the country's subsequent isolation. And the privileging of Indians was also one of the historical reasons for the Singhalese Buddhists' resentment and subsequent violence against the Tamil minority. In both countries the majority ethno-religious group felt discriminated against by colonial authorities and sought some form of redress to deal with what was perceived as past injustices against them in the post-independence period.

Spanish colonization of Latin America also had a strong impact on the land distribution system in Latin America and the appropriation of land and exploitation of labor that then fueled left leaning insurgencies. Both in the case of Colombia and Guatemala, these were issues that fed the insurgency before they became caught up in the Cold War dynamics. And the same can be said of the Portuguese African colonies of Angola and Mozambique that had independence suddenly thrust upon them with little preparation for political consolidation and democratization. Again the chaotic situation drew the interest of regional hegemons and Cold War adversaries, especially in Angola. In this regard, it can be argued that historical developments associated with colonization clearly had an impact on the structuration of governments, the policies they pursued and the external interest that they attracted during the Cold War.

Perhaps the only case study that appears to have been unaffected by the trappings of the Cold War is Myanmar. And the reason for that is simply because after Ne Win staged the coup that overthrew parliamentary rule in 1962 the country opted for a foreign policy that privileged passive neutrality obtained through isolationism. This policy effectively cut Myanmar off from the rest of the world until almost the turn of the century. Serious engagement with the international community and in particular Western countries obtained mostly after the inauguration of the Thein Sein administration in 2010 and resulting policy initiatives that introduced more liberal reforms that included a fairer treatment of the political opposition and Aung San Suu Kyi who led it. Apart from this statistical outlier, all the other countries examined in this edited volume indicate the strong impact that lead countries in the Cold War had on the civil conflicts.

This strong impact of the Cold War is understandable given the dynamics that were associated with it. And such dynamics included the deep ideological and military competition between the United States and the Soviet Union that also spilled over to their allies and alliance structures. Additionally, the zero sum nature of foreign policy output between the two superpowers ensured that the competitively informed policy output filtered into the rest of the world. Hence, deriving from structural dynamics between these superpowers was the percolating effect of similar structures and conflicts at the sub-structural regional levels. Other than Myanmar, the Sri Lankan case was also generally unaffected by the Cold War since India was the country that was most involved in the situation. Again, this was in the post-Cold War period and India is the regional hegemon in South Asia and that is the reason for its involvement in the attempted brokerage of the situation. Additionally, the Liberation Tigers of Tamil Eelam's assassination of Indian Prime Minister Rajiv Gandhi also significantly raised the stakes in the situation and led in turn to direct Indian involvement.

In the case of the Asian case studies, this competition is reflected in Cambodia between the Chinese support for the Khmer Rouge and the determination of the international community to wean Chinese support away from the group in order to establish the transformation of the conflict that was required for peace to obtain. And many of the lead players in the arrangements that ensued were allied with the United States during the Cold War. They included France that hosted the early peace talks, Japan that was deeply involved in the settlement and rebuilding efforts that is a strong ally of the United States in Northeast Asia and members of the Association of Southeast Asian Nations that were also allied with the United States during the Cold War. Then, there was the added dynamic of regional rivalry in the Asia-Pacific theater between the Soviet Union on the one hand and China on the other that became intensified following the Vietnamese Treaty of Friendship and Cooperation with the Soviet Union that was signed in 1978. China regarded this development as a stab in the back by Vietnam, a country that it had supported for 30 years in its war against the French up to 1954 and then against the United States up to 1975. And it was for this reason that China attacked Vietnam from the north in February 1979 for a month-long punitive expedition following the Soviet-supported Vietnamese occupation of Cambodia that lasted for a decade until 1989. At the broader structural level, it was the collapse of communism in Eastern Europe and the eventual implosion of the Soviet Union that made the Cambodian situation ripe for international settlement (Amer, 2007).

Compared to the Asian cases that were more affected by regional dynamics, the case studies from Latin America and Africa point to a clear involvement of the superpowers in the civil wars. In the case of Colombia, Margarita Cuervo points to how the Cuban revolution and the Sino-Soviet rift and split affected the ideological foundations of the insurgent groups since many of the grievances were based on landlessness and exploitation. Similarly, she references how a Colombian unit that fought alongside the United States in the Korean War led in turn to the adoption of American-styled military strategies to deal with the insurgency. Additionally, it laid the groundwork for continued American involvement in Colombia especially when the country became deeply enmeshed in the international drug trade.

The impact of the Cold War is even starker in the case of Guatemala where the United Fruit Company utilized its grievances against state-initiated land reforms that affected its land banks. Subsequently the Company used this development as an excuse to persuade the Central Intelligence Agency and the United States to overthrow the Arbenz government in 1954 on the basis of a communist threat in the country. Afterwards, the United States became deeply involved in the training of the local military and its fight against the insurgencies. And the settlement of the civil war is also described as being directly related to the end of the Cold War when regional countries Colombia, Mexico, Panama, and Venezuela that formed the Grupo Contadora became involved in trying to transform the conflict towards some form of peaceful settlement.

The pervasive impact of the Cold War is also clear in the case of Angola from Africa. The People's Movement for the Liberation of Angola (MPLA) that led the newly independent country within a Marxist-Leninist framework quickly invited external intervention in the form of US support for the National Union for Total Independence of Angola (UNITA) rebel group. South Africa also supported UNITA and the leftist government responded by inviting Cuban troops to stave off the external interventions. These developments clearly fall well within the ideological and competitive polarization of international relations during the Cold War and importantly also directly involved key players in it. Similarly, it was the United States that put together the 1988 New York Agreement that then led to the withdrawal of South Africa and Cuban forces from the country and the decoupling of the civil war from external actors. The situation in Mozambique while similar to that of Angola in terms of a leftist government coming to power and state-led development that ultimately failed however led to intervention from regional neighbors as mentioned at the outset of the book. Hence, while domestic political developments after independence mirrored Cold War dynamics in terms of the calibration of the government and its policies, the country was not subjected to the kind of direct intervention by Cold War adversaries. Rather as a result of Mozambique's support for insurgent groups it attracted intervention from South Africa and Rhodesia in particular. Again, this is the kind of pattern that was observed in the case of Sri Lanka where India as the regional hegemon intervened in the situation. South Africa was not only the regional hegemon in this instance but also strongly disapproved Mozambique's support for the African National Congress that sought shelter there across the border.

Does Democratization Yield a Peace Dividend?

Before trying to assess whether the onset of democratization yielded peaceful outcomes in the seven case studies examined in this book, a number of observations pertinent to the judgment is required. And many of these are actually embedded in perquisites associated with democracy and democratization. After all if the necessary conditions or characteristic features associated with the regime type were unavailable then it would not yield a fair assessment. In other words, there is no sense in making a judgment call whether democratization helped transform civil conflicts if the process itself was not in place. And the necessary attributes of the process as identified at the outset include free and fair electoral contestation and the inclusion of a country's adult population in the electoral process. Additionally, it was also emphasized how fundamental liberties associated with democracy should be observed. Beyond these requirements in terms of political parties being able to aggregate voter support and the ability of citizens to choose their leaders at will, a few other requirements were also identified. And these pertain to the structuration of the state itself. Structural features of democracy would naturally include territorial consolidation and the state being the only entity with claims to the legitimate use of force. The first of these considerations is often absent in countries in a state of civil war and the latter may only obtain ex-post facto. Hence, the task of making the playing field level and removing the threat or use of force is normally assigned to international agencies like the United Nations that would in turn provide a peacekeeping force during the interim period. And this condition certainly obtained in many of the cases dealt with in this book.

In the case studies from Asia, all three countries did not have territorial consolidation although the severity of the situation was uneven. So for example, Cambodia was in an active state of civil war and Hun Sen's Cambodian People's Party did not have control over the entire country. And when United Nations Transitional Authority in Cambodia (UNTAC) sought to transform the conflict the Khmer Rouge refused to go into cantonment and disarm. This situation effectively meant that the entire country was not united prior to the onset of democratization. Yet, the process itself did bring about stability and reduced actual fighting led to the establishment of a national reconciliation government. In this regard, the intervention did transform the conflict and the Khmer Rouge threat dissipated over time. The strong international presence and push for fairness in the process yielded gains at the ground level. However, as noted earlier, the government tended towards authoritarianism over time. And this is the reason why Makiko Takemoto wondered whether the onset of Western norms in a country previously unfamiliar with them was part of the reason for the longer term failure of democratization in the country. Cambodia's gravitation toward China was offered as an additional reason since unlike the Western countries and Japan, China does not make political demands for trade and investments. After all China is not a democracy and it would be self-defeating to expect other countries aligned with it to emulate what is perceived as a Western model.

In Myanmar's case unlike Cambodia, there was little by way of external intervention. The military junta in power opted to democratize the country and put in place liberal reforms that were then rewarded with the lifting of a wide-ranging international sanctions regime that previously obtained. In this regard, democratization was encouraged with external support and the West and Japan also became involved in the peace process and supported it as well. The Thein Sein government managed to persuade 8 out of the 16 ethnic armed groups to sign on to a Nationwide Ceasefire Agreement and the process has continued with more groups signing on. And the level of fighting has generally dissipated in many areas but continues to obtain in the northern states and more recently in Rakhine state to the west. Like in the case of Cambodia the state is not territorially consolidated and the government certainly cannot claim the only legitimate use of force. The fact that the country's 2008 Constitution empowers the military and grants it discretionary power over the civilian government also means that normal democratic values where there is civilian supremacy does not obtain. Hence, we are again dealing with a situation that does not conform to what is normally expected of functioning democracies.

The Sri Lankan case, just like those of Cambodia and Myanmar also involved a state that did not fully control its territory and did not have monopoly on the use of force. What is different and perhaps unique in this case is that an elected government chose to bring the conflict to a conclusion on the basis of political violence rather than conflict transformation. In this regard, the Sri Lankan case stands out from the others and international efforts to broker peace were unsuccessful. So this case is counter-intuitive to the extent that democratic norms did not lead to conflict transformation and peace. And it is unclear whether the post-conflict situation has yielded a favorable outcome for the minority Tamil ethnic group with international concerns over war crimes and the large number of unaccounted and missing persons.

While assessing the impact of democratization on the Asian case studies, it is also useful to return to the central argument in Gen Kikkawa's chapter. His basic argument is that there is a trust deficit among the major countries in East Asia and this is part of the reason why democratization has suffered in Asia. And part of the reason for this deficit is attributed to the continuation of the US hub and spokes strategy for security arrangements in the region. Kikkawa argues that consequently, while South Korea and Japan as allies of the United States have adopted democracy other large countries like China have not. His more important argument is that one of the side effects of the continued US strategy is the absence of regional political will and ambition to craft a workable region-wide security system based on shared mutual values. And in the absence of such values to undergird security structures, the region cannot hope to aspire to and achieve the regional equivalent of a trans-Atlantic styled security community. If this assessment is accurate then the Asian region will suffer from nationalistic disputes that do not provide for mutual gain and ensuing structural arrangements. Consequently, competitive norms premised on realist considerations rather than liberal views premised on complementary norms will obtain.

The Colombian case in Latin America provides the most positive evidence of the transformation of the civil conflict through democratization. Not only has the long stretch of political violence with Fuerzas Armadas Revolucionarias de Colombia (FARC) come to an end but the President very skillfully bypassed a negative outcome from a national plebiscite to further the peace process. His dedication to the process and determination to end the conflict is truly laudable and demonstrates the importance of political will and agency in bringing about conflict transformation. Although the process itself was long and drawn out even under democratic governments and the country suffers from problems of governance and political polarization, the process has eventually been successfully managed. While some technical difficulties continue to obtain the conflict has for the most part subsided and the insurgents are being slowly integrated into mainstream society. It is hoped that over time governance issues will be successfully resolved and the rule of law will obtain at the national level.

The peace process in Guatemala can also be regarded as reasonably successful. It was a conflict that was deeply embedded in the Cold War and whose successful conclusion took a long time just like in the case of Colombia. There were also notable international interventions to further the process forward, especially by Norway and the regional countries in the Grupo Contadora. The country has a truly tall order of institutional and electoral reforms going forward. Carlos Sanabria laments the fact that the political party system which is critical to the functioning of a democracy is not well established and that the reform process itself in an ongoing and fragile one. Nonetheless the conflict appears to have been successfully transformed and there are attempts towards political reconciliation.

The two African case studies have a number of structural similarities. The first of these is that they were both Portuguese colonies and the process of attempting peaceful transformation of the civil conflict was tied together with post-independence developments. Both countries had independence suddenly thrust upon them by Portugal in 1975 and had to deal with the situation. Again, fortunately both countries benefitted from international interventions and stabilization of the conflict although the Angolan situation was far more complex given the country's deep involvement in the Cold War as a contested site for proxy warfare. And just like the Latin American cases the end of the Cold War provided the structural opportunity to transform the conflict with the New York Agreement in 1988. The United Nations assisted the transition process through the presence of a peacekeeping contingent to oversee a smooth transition process and return of power to local groups and through elections. Raul Tati however argues that the transition period was too short-lived and that incumbency created an enormous advantage for one of the major parties and to the detriment of the other, leading in turn to an unfair outcome. Consequently, although peace has been brought to the country in terms of ending large-scale violence, it is viewed as a peace that is framed in terms of partisan interests and not one representing the national fabric. In this regard, the Angolan situation is only a qualified success in terms of conflict transformation.

The situation in Mozambique is also described as one favoring a specific post-independence party that consolidated its own political power and unleashed a reform process that led to widespread social dislocation and resettlement. And again the peace was brokered after the end of the Cold War and United Nations peacekeepers were deployed during the period of political transition. And while democratization brought about an end to the civil war or negative peace, the settlement like in the case of Angola is viewed as favoring a specific political party. While the peace has generally held there remains the real danger of a return to violence since the marginalized party does retain strong support in certain regions of the country. Hence, the situation is an ongoing one and makes a judgment call much harder to make. Nonetheless the author concedes that conflict transformation has occurred to the extent that leading personalities have been willing to meet and resolve their differences peacefully and this development augurs the possibility for more peaceful changes to take root.

Having gone through all the case studies and compared them a few final observations regarding the impact of democratization on peace can be made. The first of these is that it is not easy to impose democratic norms on a country where peace does not obtain. Important conditions like territorial control, rule of law, and fundamental liberties must obtain in the first instance before conflict transformation can be attempted. And it is for this reason that the United Nations has been tasked with providing a safe and stable environment during political transition in order to enable the onset of democratization. A related question would be how long should such a force stay on to ensure that democratic processes continue to obtain in the post-conflict period following conflict transformation. This is a difficult question to answer since the ground conditions in different countries may require different gestation periods. But the general rule of thumb appears to be a three years stabilization period. It is laudable that the United Nations under Boutros Boutros Ghali seized the historic opportunity after the end of the Cold War to bring about this transformation in countries that were in a state of civil war.

Equally remarkable is the commitment of individual countries like Norway to attempt political mediation in many of these cases. The Scandinavian countries and Switzerland have traditionally offered their good services to broker internal and international disputes and have gained recognition for their abilities to bring hostile factions to the negotiating table and securing lasting agreements that have transformed conflicts. And it is for this reason that they wield an enormous amount of soft power as trustworthy mediators and interlocutors. The world could certainly learn a few lessons from such countries since peace has a redounding effect on an entire region. Finally, it should be remembered that political will plays an important role in conflict transformation. Elites play a definitive role in deciding whether a conflict should be transformed and settled politically. Hence the classic dictum in politics that states do not make policies, statesmen do.

References

Alagappa, M. (1998). *Asian security and practice: Material and ideational influences*. Stanford, CA: Stanford University Press.

Amer, R. (2007). The resolution of the Cambodian conflict – Assessing the explanatory power of Zartman's 'Ripeness Theory'. *Journal of Peace Research*, *44*(6), 720–742.

Boudreau, V. (2013). Interpreting state violence in Asian settings. In N. Ganesan & Kim, Sung Chull (Eds.), *State violence in East Asia* (pp. 19–46). Lexington, KY: University Press of Kentucky.

Index

Note: page numbers followed by "*n*" indicate footnotes.

Printed and bound by CPI Group (UK) Ltd, Croydon, CR0 4YY

13/09/2026

14961064-0001